MAGIC, WITCHCRAFT, AND CURING

John Middleton
received his D.Phil. from Oxford in 1953. He has taught
anthropology at Capetown, Northwestern, and New York uni-
versities, and at present he is professor of African anthropology
at the School of Anthropology and African Studies, University
of London.

He has done field research in Uganda, Zanzibar, and Nigeria.
He is the author of *Black Africa* and *Lugbara of Uganda*, and,
with David Tait, he edited *Tribes without Rulers*. Dr. Middleton
also edited four other volumes of the Texas Press Sourcebooks
in Anthropology series: *Comparative Political Systems*, with
Ronald Cohen; *Myth and Cosmos*; *Gods and Rituals*; and
From Child to Adult.

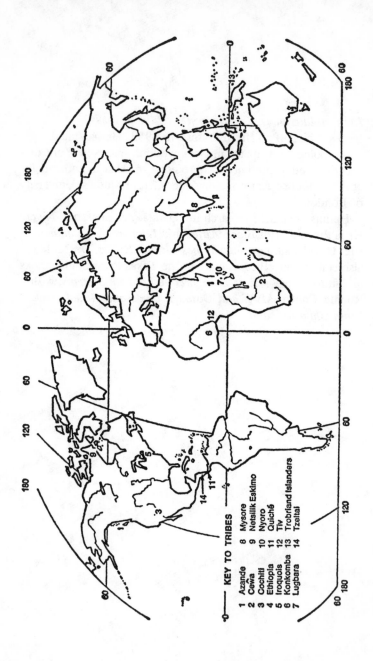

KEY TO TRIBES

1	Azande	8	Mysore
2	Cewa	9	Netsilik Eskimo
3	Cochiti	10	Nyoro
4	Ethiopia	11	Quiché
5	Iroquois	12	Tiv
6	Konkomba	13	Trobriand Islanders
7	Lugbara	14	Tzeltal

Texas Press Sourcebooks in Anthropology
were originally published by the Natural History Press, a division of Doubleday and Company, Inc. Responsibility for the series now resides with the University of Texas Press, Box 7819, Austin, Texas 78712. Whereas the series has been a joint effort between the American Museum of Natural History and the Natural History Press, future volumes in the series will be selected through the auspices of the editorial offices of the University of Texas Press.

The purpose of the series will remain unchanged in its effort to make available inexpensive, up-to-date, and authoritative volumes for the student and the general reader in the field of anthropology.

Magic, Witchcraft, and Curing

Edited by John Middleton

University of Texas Press

Austin

Library of Congress Cataloging in Publication Data

Middleton, John, 1921– comp.
  Magic, witchcraft, and curing.

  (Texas Press sourcebooks in anthropology; 7)
  Reprint of the ed. published for the American Museum of Natural History
by the Natural History Press, Garden City, N.Y., in series: American Museum
sourcebooks in anthropology.
  Bibliography: p.
  Includes index.
  1. Magic—Addresses, essays, lectures.   2. Witchcraft—Addresses, essays,
lectures. I. Title. II. Series. III. Series: American Museum
sourcebooks in anthropology.
  [GN475.M47 1976]   133.4   75-44038
  ISBN 0-292-75031-5

Published by arrangement with Doubleday & Company, Inc.
Previously published by the Natural History Press in cooperation
with Doubleday & Company, Inc.

CONTENTS

THE DEBATE AS to the borderline between "religion" and "magic" is an old one in anthropology and was a matter of much concern to writers such as Tylor, Frazer and Durkheim. More recently anthropologists, realizing that if a boundary were discoverable it would differ from one culture to the next, have tended simply to write of the "magico-religious" and to leave it at that. None the less, in general the distinction is fairly clear. We may say that the realm of magic is that in which human beings believe that they may directly affect nature and each other, for good or for ill, by their own efforts (even though the precise mechanism may not be understood by them), as distinct from appealing to divine powers by sacrifice or prayer. Witchcraft and sorcery are, therefore, close to magic, as are processes of oracular consultation, divination and many forms of curing.

Religious beliefs and practices, in the widest sense of the "magico-religious," may be said to have two purposes, sociologically speaking. They are instrumental and they are expressive. By instrumental is meant that people use them to achieve particular ends; by expressive, that they use them to state and to symbolize certain social and cosmological relationships. Magical beliefs and practices are particularly significant in being mainly instrumental, with little expressive content; by contrast, the mythological and cosmological notions described in *Myth and Cosmos*, one of the companion volumes to this one, are almost entirely expressive and symbolic.

There is a vast literature of the "primitive" and the exotic dealing with witchcraft, sorcery and magic. Most of it is non-anthropological—in the sense of its not being related to other aspects of culture—and most of it is scientifically worthless. It is only in recent years that anthropologists have made serious studies of these matters. They have seen magic and witch beliefs not as stages in the evolutionary development of religion, as did Tylor and Frazer, nor as survivals of earlier cults, as did Margaret Murray, nor as sensational accounts of savagery. They have regarded them as important aspects of all social life, in all societies. Although preceded by ethnographic works such as those by Fortune on Dobu and Malinowski on the Trobriand Islanders, the most significant works in this field were Evans-Pritchard's classic *Witchcraft, Oracles and Magic among the Azande* (1937) and Kluckhohn's *Navajo Witchcraft* (1944). They showed that beliefs in magic and in witchcraft are integral parts of cultural life, and can therefore be understood only in their total social context. They have a coherent logic of their own, given certain premises as to the mystical powers of certain human beings (even though "scientifically" these premises may not be correct). These beliefs provide explanations for coincidence and disaster, they enable individuals to project their hopes, fears and disappointments onto other human beings, and by thus personalizing the forces of what we might call "fate" or "chance" enable those afflicted by them to deal with them by direct social action against the assumed evildoers. All later research on these topics has depended largely on these pioneer works.

The plan of this volume of readings is simple: I have gathered ethnographic accounts of magical beliefs and behavior so as to cover most of the usual aspects described by anthropologists— magic, witchcraft and sorcery, divination, and curing. All the writers whose work is included have placed their analyses firmly in their social context. They are describing, not exotic bugaboos, but beliefs actually held by actual people who accept them and take note of them in their everyday lives.

JOHN MIDDLETON

MAGIC, WITCHCRAFT, AND CURING

1 THE MORPHOLOGY AND FUNCTION OF MAGIC: A COMPARATIVE STUDY OF TROBRIAND AND ZANDE RITUAL AND SPELLS[1]

E. E. Evans-Pritchard

THE USE OF THE COMPARATIVE METHOD

A WORKING hypothesis should never be allowed to become a settled conviction until it has been tested and re-tested, but every first-hand investigation requires some theoretical view to start with. In the present attempt I shall have especially in view the entire range of magic in two societies.

Very little work has yet been accomplished by specialists in the field towards presenting a full descriptive and analytical account of magic. One cannot therefore make wide comparisons which would yield general principles based on an intensive study of many primitive communities. Moreover, the work which has been accomplished has been done mainly in Melanesia and the social incidence of magic in Melanesia appears to differ considerably from the social incidence of magic in Africa. This is due in general to the difference in form between the two types of society and in particular to the bias given by a strict association of magic with a definite social grouping which profoundly affects the structure and the functional occasions of the magic. I shall attempt to demonstrate in this paper that the principles of magic deduced

Reprinted from *The American Anthropologist* 31, 1929: 619–41, by permission of the author and the American Anthropological Association.

[1] This paper contains preliminary results of an expedition to Central Africa, undertaken by the writer under the auspices of the Sudan government, in continuation of the work done by Professor and Mrs. Seligman in the years 1909–10, 1911–12, and 1921–22. The work was assisted by grants from the Royal Society and the Laura Spelman Rockefeller fund. The communities studied were mainly those of the Azande in the Bahr-el-Ghazal province of the Anglo-Egyptian Sudan.

from Melanesian data and formulated as general laws for all societies have, in view of a study of African peoples, to be reformulated and possibly modified.

I shall show how this is so by a comparison between the magic of a Melanesian society described by Professor Malinowski and the magic of an African society investigated by myself. The Melanesian community is that of the Trobriand islands, a coral archipelago lying to the northeast of New Guinea. The African tribe is a section of the Azande nation which lives in the Bahr-el-Ghazal province of the Anglo-Egyptian Sudan. I shall build up my argument mainly on the data furnished by the Trobrianders and the Azande but shall draw upon any other societies of whose magic there is a good account to check my results.

In order to understand the argument it is necessary to know the sociological distribution and balance of these two societies and their main food-procuring activities. The Trobrianders live in villages which act together in communal undertakings such as agricultural labor, trading expeditions, warfare, and public ceremonial. The villages are also largely political units, though the chief may rule over the wider area of a district. Many of these chiefs are little more than village headmen, others have great prestige in virtue of belonging to certain "families" of the four totemic clans. None wield great executive power. The four totemic clans are scattered but the "families" or sub-clans are localized. The Trobrianders are patrilocal and matrilineal, the girl going to live in her husband's village, but membership of the clan group and inheritance of wealth and rank are passed to a man's sister's son instead of to his own natural offspring. Girls are married from their father's home whilst boys as a rule return to their mother's village before marriage. The main economic activity of the Trobriander is the cultivation of his gardens. Fishing plays a great part in maintaining his food supply and is of far greater importance than hunting owing to the absence of mammalian fauna in these coral islands (Seligman 1910: ch. 49; Malinowski 1922: *passim*).

The social organization of the Azande is as different from that of the Trobrianders as are the islands of the South Seas from the vast inland tracts of Central Africa. The Azande have no village life but live in homesteads widely separated from each other. In consequence they have fewer communal undertakings. Politically they are organized into tribes which stretch over an enormous area and are governed by one chief. The tribes are divided into a number of ill-defined sections each under the leadership of a chief's deputy. The chiefs all belong to one ruling class and exercise great power. There are a large number of totemic clans which are scattered all over the country and possess little social solidarity. The Azande are patrilocal and patrilineal. Girls live in the homesteads of their husbands and inheritance of wealth and rank pass from a man to his sons and brothers. Gardening forms the main work of a Zande. Hunting and the collection of edible termites are important activities, fishing contributing little to the food supply.

If we study any such institution as magic, religion, law, or economic life, we shall find that it takes on the mould of the society in which it has its place and function. Where the morphology of society differs as between the Trobrianders and the Azande we shall expect to find that the sociological rôle of magic amongst these two peoples differs accordingly.

FUNCTION OF MAGIC

Professor Malinowski was the first writer to demonstrate clearly from a detailed study of one society wherein lies the function of magic.[2] He showed how magic filled a gap left by lack of knowledge in man's pragmatic pursuits, e.g., wind magic, and how it provided an alternative means of expression for thwarted human desires, e.g., black magic. His general conclusions as to the function of magic in society are fully borne out by a study of Zande data.

For example, the Zande uses magic to protect himself, his children, his agricultural and hunting activities from the malign power of witchcraft. He uses productive magic to multiply his crops, to ensure success in netting game, in encouraging the termites to embark on their nuptial swarmings, in smelting and forging iron, in increasing the number of his subjects. He uses magic to give him confidence in love-making or in singing, to protect his property from theft and his wife from illicit intercourse.

[2] Malinowski 1925. References will be to this paper when not stated otherwise. For the detailed facts on which Professor Malinowski based his views see Malinowski 1922 (chapters on Magic), 1926a, 1926b and 1929.

He consults the magic of the oracles to give him confidence before circumcision, before marriage, before building a new homestead. Magic plays its part in all the main biological and social
occasions of a Zande's life. I could multiply examples, and an
analysis of the social context of each would endorse Professor
Malinowski's conclusions as to the psychological and sociological
rôle of magic.

But suppose that a Trobriand Argonaut were to make an unusually long and perilous voyage, were to paddle his dug-out
canoe two thousand miles up the placid and dreary waters of the
Nile, were to make his way to Zandeland, were to learn the tongue
of the Azande and enter into their customs, how would he find
that their magic conforms to or differs from the principles of his
own society?

He would find that Zande "white" magic, whether protective
or productive in character, like his own is never looked upon as
one of the forces of nature which can be utilized by man, but is
regarded as a cherished cultural possession which derives its
powers from man's abstinence and from his knowledge of tradition. He would find that the Azande, like his own people, believe
magic to have come into the world with man and not to have been
acquired by subsequent discovery in the world of nature. The
Zande would reject as strongly as himself the idea of magic as a
universal impersonal power as expressed in the concepts *mana*
in Polynesia and *wakan* and *orenda* in North America.[3] Also
neither the Trobriander nor the Zande consider magic to be a
gift from the spirits of the dead.

The sex and food taboos which precede all acts of magic would
conform to the tradition of the Trobriand visitor. Nor would he
find anything in the rites of magic which would appear to him to
be inconceivable or unreal. But where the Trobriander would be
confused would be in noticing that whilst in structure Zande
magic is similar to his own, it stresses some of its component
parts which he regards as of less importance than others, whereas
some of the parts upon which he lays the greatest stress in his

[3] I do not wish to state that these forces are conceived of as impersonal
by the natives themselves, but that they have been described as such by
ethnographers and theoretical writers, such as Marett, Preuss, Hubert and
Mauss, Durkheim and others.

island home are performed by the Zande with a shocking freedom and carelessness. In both societies all important acts of magic consist of the rite, the spell, the condition of the performer, and the tradition of the magic, but the emphasis placed on each by the two peoples is different.

THE SPELL

To peoples such as the Trobrianders and the Maori the spell is a rigid unalterable formula which is transmitted intact from generation to generation, and the slightest deviation from its traditional form would invalidate the magic.[4] The spell is "occult, handed over in magical filiation, known only to the practitioner." Knowledge of the magic is knowledge of the spell, the ritual centers round it, it is always the core of the magical performance (Malinowski 1922: 68). Now to the Zande the spell is nearly always essential to the act of magic in all forms of "white" magic, but it is not stressed in the same way as in the Trobriand islands or in New Zealand. Indeed, the qualities of the spell in Zande magic are the direct opposite of those which we have been told characterize Trobriand magic. It is a saying rather than a formula, it is familiar, it is handed over without strict reference to genealogical ties, the knowledge of it is not confined to the practitioner.

I will give an example of owned Zande magic from my collection of texts. It is a typical hunting spell, which is pronounced over a pot in which the magical ingredients are being cooked in oil. The practitioner stirs the pot and says:

bingia (name of magic)	nga are	mu you	mi I	ye come	ka to
ra cook	ru you	ware thus	mu you	ti fall	na with
ana animals	fo for	ri me	mi I	imi kill	mbaga bushbuck
ana animals	dunduko all		mi I	ara cook	ru you ti for
ana animals		mi I	imi kill	ana animals	gbe much

"You are *bingia* magic, I come to cook you thus. You bring me animals. I kill bushbuck—all animals. I cook you on my behalf. I kill animals much."

4 For Maori magic, see Firth 1929.

This spell is not a set formula learnt by heart and repeated without variation by all who use the same magic, nor one which is handed down intact from generation to generation. It is a saying adapted to the purpose of the magic and uttered in the common form and phraseology of all Zande spells but it will vary in its word formation. The practitioner will change words on different occasions and different men will insert different details.

To make this variation in the spells quite clear I will give one more example, which embodies two texts given to me by the same informant on different occasions. There is an oil-bearing plant, a species of sesame, called *kpagu,* which yields a regular yearly crop to the Azande. The material used in this magic is a tall grass with a feather-like form of its branching stems, called *bingba,* and is known to everyone. It is a common grass which springs up on arable land and is used for thatching the roofs of the huts. Now a man who wishes to increase the yield of his *kpagu* will pluck some of these grass stems and hurling them like a dart will transfix the broad leaves of the oil-plant. The spell accompanying this action was given me in the first instance as follows:

kpagu	nga	mu	du	le	mu
(name of plant)	are	you	is	here	you

zunga	a zu	wa	kina	bingba
be	very fruitful	as	truly	(name of grass)

ni	dunga	he
with	many	it

"You are *kpagu* here, you be exceeding fruitful, indeed as *bingba,* with much fruit."

On a second occasion my informant gave me the spell for the same magic as follows:

bingba	nga	mu	sele
(name of grass)	are	you	oil

ida	ida	wa	kina	bingba
consent	very much	as	truly	(name of grass)

gi	kpagu	mu	zungu	gbe	ka	
my	(name of plant)	you	be	fruitful	much	not

mo	kanga	ya
you	refuse	not

"*Bingba* are you, oil plant take very well, just like *bingba.* My *kpagu* be exceeding fruitful, do not refuse."

It will at once be seen by a comparison between these two spells that there is more difference than similarity in the wording. The sense is the same but we find that the words are so little part of a formula that in the first spell the plant is addressed, whereas in the second spell both the plant and its magic are called upon by name.

It is true that the example I have given is of an unowned type of magic and a type of magic which has no part in communal undertakings. As will be seen later, it is consequent upon my argument that the more strictly owned is magic and the more the occasion on which it is practised is of common interest, the more it will tend to become formulated, the less it will vary from traditional form. But I will return to a consideration of this point later.

Here it is possible to make a useful distinction between the "saying" spell and the "formula" spell. The psychological background of all magic demands that utterance shall accompany the rite if its function is to be performed but it does not determine the form of the utterance. The form of the spell is dependent upon social causes not to be found in a study of the magic itself save in relation to the whole society and culture in which it is practised.

THE MATERIAL ELEMENT IN MAGIC

But if the spell in Trobriand culture is the essential part of magic, what takes its place in Zande culture? In the morphology of Zande magic it is the material element in the magic which is occult and which is known only to the practitioner. Usually this consists of strange woods and rare roots. Indeed the Zande word for magic is *ngwa*, which generally means wood and only in special contexts refers to magic. There is an interesting linguistic comparison in the Trobriand islands, for there, on the contrary, the native uses the same word for spell and magic, generally *megwa*, the material element in the ritual being of minor importance.

That it is to the material component in the ritual and not to the spell that the Azande attach main importance can be shown from many of my field-work experiences, but it is more satisfactory to illustrate their opinion from their own stories. Many of these stories, about the Zande culture-hero Ture, centre around magical powers once possessed but now lost. In one of these stories a

man, called Yangayma, possessed magical feathers which enabled
him to fly after performing a ritual dance and chanting a song-
spell:

yu	yangayma	gi	swe	ku	ba
(untranslatable)	(name of man)	these	feathers	of	father

ba	fu	yangayma
father	gave	(name of man)

"Yu Yangayma, these feathers of father, father gave Yangayma."

The culture-hero Ture stole these feathers and chanted the
song-spell, substituting his name for that of their rightful owner:
"Yu yu Ture, these feathers of father, father gave Ture." In stealing the feathers, however, Ture dropped one of them and when
Yangayma found this he put it in his hat and singing the spell as
above he gave pursuit into the air and deprived Ture of all the
stolen feathers so that the culture-hero fell to the ground and
was killed (Plas and Lagae 1921).

In another story Ture was walking with a man called Depago
who possessed magic which enabled him to enter into the ground.
When it began to rain he took some medicine from his horn where
he kept it and wiped it on an ant-hill. On the ant-hill opening
they both entered and Ture was amazed to see the fine village
and the wealth of Depago under the ground. In order to leave
the ant-hill Depago wiped some more of his magic on to the earth
and said:

Depago Depago Depago			nzinginzingi	sende
(name of man)			muddy	earth

Depago	na	yera	ngalimo
(name of man)	is	cutting	deep

sende	nzinginzingi	sende
earth	muddy	earth

"Depago, Depago, Depago, quagmire, Depago is cutting a big pit, a
quagmire."

As Ture was departing he stole some of the magical soot. He
went home and persuaded all his wives, with the exception of his
first wife Nanzagbe who knew his ways, to burn their huts and
come and live with him under the ground. He went with his wives
to an ant-hill and wiped some of the magic on the ground and

said "Deture, Deture, Deture, a quagmire, Deture is cutting a big pit, a quagmire." The ant-hill opened and they entered only to find grass and they became very hungry. Meanwhile Nanzagbe went and told Depago what had happened and he came and rescued Ture and his wives (Gore).

This story is in need of native commentary as it is not clear why Ture could not have got out of the ant-hill. Those natives whom I have questioned on this point have replied that he could not get out because he had not enough magical soot since he had foolishly wiped it all on the outside of the ant-hill.

In yet another story Ture tries to copy someone whom he has seen putting out a bush fire by placing a magical fat on his head. But in this story we are distinctly told that Ture used a different fat so that his efforts ended in failure.

I could give other instances from the folk-lore of the Zande to illustrate the manner in which the importance of the magical substance itself is stressed more than other aspects of the performance, but these three will suffice. We have seen that in the first story it was the theft of the feathers which enabled Ture to fly and that it was the loss of these feathers which caused his subsequent fall, just as it was the finding of the one dropped feather which gave Yangayma power to pursue him from the earth. In the second story it was the theft of the magical soot by which Ture entered the ant-hill and its absence which prevented him from getting out again. In the third story it was the use of a secret fat which gave power over fire and it was Ture's attempt to control fire by a different fat which led to failure.

On these occasions Ture copied the spell correctly—I do not wish to underestimate its importance in the magical performance—but it was the loss of the material of the rite which made the act of magic invalid. This is the whole point of the stories.

Now just as we found that the emphasis placed on different elements of the magic in the Trobriand islands and in Zandeland has a parallel in different linguistic symbols, *ngwa* and *megwa,* we shall find a similar parallel between the significance of the stories given above and the significance of some Trobriand myths.

Once upon a time in these South Sea islands there lived a man Mokatuboda of the Lukuba clan with his three sisters and his younger brother Toweyre'i. Mokatuboda possessed the magic of the flying canoes and the myth describes his success in a trading expedition and the envy of the other natives whose canoes had to sail on the water whilst his flew through the air. Next year they cultivated their gardens. There was a terrible drought and the rain fell only on the garden of Mokatuboda because he made an evil magic of the rain. Angry and jealous, his brothers and maternal nephews killed him, believing that they had been taught the magic (i.e., the spells) and could use it on his decease. But Mokatuboda had not taught them the real spells, neither the magic of the adze nor of the rain nor of the lashing creeper nor of the coconut oil nor of the staff. His younger brother Toweyre'i thought that he had already received all the magic but he had only part, and next year when they prepared to make a big trading expedition he discovered that by his fratricide he had deprived mankind of one of its most powerful cultural possessions, the magic of the flying canoe. The whole point of this story is that the magic was invalid because Mokatuboda had not taught all the spells to his brother (Malinowski 1922: 311 ff.).

I shall leave the spell, to return to it later, and will draw attention to another profound difference between Trobriand and Zande magic.

TRADITION

In the Trobriand islands "in the case of any important magic we invariably find the story accounting for its existence." "All important magic has its tradition and is buttressed by its myth." Do we find the same background of belief amongst the Azande?

Since all magic tends to create its own myth it would be indeed surprising if there were no tradition of a simple kind associated with Zande magic. I found that there is always a current tradition, a cycle of everyday myth encircling and generated by the magic (see also Malinowski 1922: 76–77). When I asked a Zande how he knew that his magic was of any use he told me a story from his own experience or from that of his friends or neighbors. He told me how when gathering termites by night his friend had blown his magic elephant whistle and how soon afterwards they heard the tramping and trumpeting of the elephants and next morning saw their deep spoor in the moist earth. Another told me how he had always wished to be a fine singer but had never shown any ability in the art until a famous song leader gave him medicine to eat. Another told me how his brother, and a neighboring chief also, had a swollen penis and had become impotent because of the use of a certain type of "black" magic. Always there is this halo of rumor and wonder around magic of the Azande.

We know well, for Goldenweiser (1921: 193 f.) has shown us, how in our own society magic is always associated with wonder-working, with strange coincidences too numerous to be accounted for by chance, with the rumor of uncanny personal experience, with the borrowed plumes of eastern mysticism. "There is no faith without miracles."

But this current tradition, this everyday myth is loose and short-lived whether in Melanesia, Africa, or Europe, and can be easily distinguished from the set legend and socially inherited myth by its loose form, its restricted range, and its absence of longevity.

I did not find, save in rare instances, myth of this kind associated with Zande magic. Often magic has been taken over by the Azande from some stranger people, and they will tell you how they learnt it by making blood-brotherhood with the foreigner. If you press the native to tell you how man first became acquainted with any magic he will say that Mböli, the Supreme Being, gave it to him. Thus though the myth of Mböli forms the final background of belief for all ritual, there is no specific myth for each specific type of magic.

Occasionally, however, I have found amongst the Azande a specific myth accounting for the origin of a magic, or a legend, proving its potency. Thus the clan of the Amazungu have a myth telling how they obtained their magic for healing fractures. Into the clan was born a baby quite round like a pot. The bewildered father was instructed in a dream by Mböli to incinerate the child and to use the cinders to heal broken bones. I will give another example. The corporation of medicine-men possess powerful magic known only to the members of the corporation. That their magic is genuine is proved by legends which show how in the past great medicine-men performed remarkable feats through its me-

dium. In the Golden Age of their magic the magician Rëpa, a
primitive Moses, went with his chief to wage war beyond the
great Uelle river of the Congo. On their return northwards the
army found themselves with the enemy in their rear and the wide
river to their front. In this crisis Rëpa threw some of his magic
into the water so that the waters parted, leaving a dry channel of
sand, on which they passed over to the other side. When the
enemy pursued them into the centre of the river Rëpa, like his
Hebrew prototype, closed the waters upon their fighting men.

Like Moses in the last story, his end was like the end of Elijah.

Rëpa dances exceedingly the dance of the medicine-men. He rose
on high. Then the bells say *wia wia wia wia*. He rose and rose and
rose for ever on high. He went quite out of sight so that the eyes of
men did not see him again. He dropped the bells from his hands.
The bells kept on falling and falling and falling: they fell here to
earth. They plunged and plunged to the earth right into the centre
of an ant-hill so that no one saw them.

Many were the mighty deeds performed by Rëpa and his son
Bokoparanga in virtue of their magic.

The myth of the Amazunga clan and the legends of the
medicine-men are, however, quite exceptional. Generally I have
failed to find any story accounting for the existence of magic. Just
as it was possible to make a useful distinction between the saying
and the formula in the rite of magic, so it is possible to make a
similar analysis of the tradition of magic. The psychological function of magic demands a background of belief in its tradition, but
it does not determine the form of these traditions. Whether they
exist only as loose current tradition and short-lived everyday
myths or whether they become set into the mould of a compact
myth or legend, depends upon the place they occupy in each society, and upon their relation to other parts of the culture in
which they exist.

I shall shortly return to a consideration of tradition and the
place which this conclusion occupies in my argument. Absence
of formulae and absence of specific myths are the two main characteristics which in Zandeland present a contrast with the magic
of the Trobriand isles. There are smaller differences which will
be noted in the following section.

THE RITE, THE CONDITIONS OF THE RITE, THE CONDITIONS OF THE PERFORMER

Were I to describe fully the ritual of several types of Zande magic, the reader would notice a laxity in the performance which would horrify a Melanesian. He would find confusing variations in the sequence and in the procedure of the ritual. The slightest slip in the ceremonial, a minute omission in the performance of the rite, an insignificant change in its sequence, does not, as amongst many primitive peoples, the Trobrianders and the Maori for instance, invalidate the whole act of magic.

Nothing acts more strongly in conserving tradition and compelling conformity in ritual than the publicity of the performance. Amongst the Trobrianders some rites of magic

> are ceremonial and have to be attended by the whole community, all are public in that it is known when they are going to happen and anyone can attend them (p. 31).

Amongst the Azande there is very little ceremonial in magic. There are certainly no big public ceremonies which must or may be attended by others than the family of the man concerned or his friends or by a few old men. Privacy is characteristic of Zande magic.

Lack of conservative discipline in the performance of the rites has its counterpart in the lack of uniformity in the time during which a man must observe the sex and food taboos which accompany all magic. Though agreeing in the main, different practitioners will give one different time estimates and some will observe a wider range of food restrictions than others. There is also considerable laxity in the observation of the taboos. These are often neglected, though a practitioner would always say that they had been observed as they are supposed to be.

In Zande magic the taboos and the rites are subject to variation, the spell is diffuse and unformulated, the tradition is not standardized, the performance is neither public nor ceremonial; the whole act of magic is less rigidly defined and less amenable to set form than the magic acts of Melanesia.

GROUP OWNERSHIP OF MAGIC

What then are the social causes which determine these differences between the ritual of the Trobriand islands and the ritual of the Azande of the Nile-Uelle divide? I think that they are to be found in a comparative study of the ownership of magic in the two areas. In the Trobriands

> Magic tends in all its manifestations to become specialized, exclusive and departmental, and hereditary within a family or clan (p. 45).

Amongst the Azande magic is seldom specialized within or exclusive to a family or clan, but is spread widely amongst the community without reference to kindred ties.

If you ask a Zande whence he obtained his magic he will tell you that he received it from his father for it is handed from father to son like any other wealth; or he will tell you that he or his father bought the magic, for magic, being the property of an individual, can be bought and sold; or he will tell you that one of his friends told him about the magic out of comradeship, or that knowledge of that type of magic is possessed by everybody.

Trobriand magic presents a contrast in that in its most important systems, such as garden magic, fishing magic, the ritual of weather, rain, and sun, it must be transmitted through the binding custom of kinship which compels a man to hand over his knowledge of spells with his other property to the son of his sister. It is true that some magic can be bought, but its transference is always accompanied and restricted by social qualifications. Very little magic is unowned.

In this difference between Trobriand magic owned by the family or clan, not open to sale and purchase outside these groups, and Zande magic, owned by the individual and able to be transmitted beyond the restricted domain of genealogical or clan relationship, it is possible to see a solution to the problem of formulae and standardized tradition.

The formula is surety of undisputed ownership of magic and compels filiation of the magic in the family or clan, for the long set formula is a value which can only be handed over laboriously and slowly. But amongst the Azande magic is not generally associated with any social group, being diffused widely without reference to ties of relationship. Consequently there is no need for the formula which tends to restrict the use of the magic to the group already possessing it. Moreover, the core of the magic being not the spell but the material element, it is easily transferred from one person to another. To the Trobriander the spell is the most important part of the magic, in a sense is the magic, because the formula keeps the magic in the group with which it is traditionally associated, whereas the Azande have no magical formulae, but only sayings, because magic is not generally associated with any social grouping. The formula is correlated with group ownership.

I attribute the emphasis placed upon tradition to the same social cause. The function of the myth is to project the facts of group ownership into the realms of belief, to provide a convincing sanction to the ownership. This is the rôle which it plays in the Trobriand islands, but as Zande magic is not associated exclusively with any section of the community there is no need for the myth as it would have no social function to fulfil.

If this explanation is correct, then in those exceptional cases in which Zande magic is associated with a social grouping it should also be associated with myth. This is what we do find, and I have already given examples from the clan of the Amazungu and the corporation of the medicine-men. Inversely the Trobriand "white" magic, which is not owned by any segment of society, should be found without a background of myth and is so found.

The conclusion drawn is that an utterance is an essential psychological accompaniment of all magical rites and that tradition is an essential sanction for their performance, but that these only crystallize into the set formula and standardized myth when the social mobility of the magic is restricted by its ownership being invested in the family or clan or some departmental grouping. Ownership is always a conservative and standardizing agent in society.

This thesis can be illustrated more widely than by the two areas from which my data have mainly been drawn, but I do not wish to make a compilation, for not only magical but all exceptional privileges invested in one class in society require the halo of myth. Thus amongst the Azande only those clans which are differentiated from the rest of the Zande totemic clans by a special social function have specific clan mythology. In some societies all the clans have differentiated social functions with associated myths, as, for example, the Winnebago Indians (Radin 1915–16).

It will be found also that all important magic in any society is restricted in use to a few members of the community whether these few persons derive their credentials from membership of a family, kinship, or departmental grouping or not. By important magic I refer to all magic associated with those pursuits on which the life of the community depends; magic used in communal undertakings such as agriculture, fishing, hunting, trading expeditions; magic practised on behalf of the whole community such as the magic of rain and of the sun, magic to increase the totem animal or plant; magic used to reinforce some essential function of society such as government and leadership in war.

In the Trobriand islands all really important magic performances are carried out by men who have received their knowledge of the spells from their mother's brother according to the law of this matrilineal society. If a man passes on the spells to his own son, this latter may use them but may not teach them to another. Important magic is consequently restricted to a very few men who practise in virtue of membership of family or clan. To take another example, amongst the Kiwai Papuans (Landtmann 1927) a society in which group ownership of magic appears to be unknown and where knowledge of the rites and spells is common property, important communal activities such as house-building, agricultural and fishing pursuits, and other collective acts of labor have their magic performed by one old man and one old woman who know the secret parts of the rites and whose death is a certain result of the performance.

Amongst the Azande there are only occasional communal activities in contrast to the Trobriand islanders or the Kiwai Papuans, but the stronger and more important medicines are known only to a few men.

POSSIBLE RESULTS OF SPREAD OF MAGIC

If all the more important magic is in the hands of a few individuals in any society, the logical inference to be drawn is that the wider spread the magic the less important the social function it fulfils; the more the performance of magic becomes public property, the less social utility it possesses. This inference can be checked from observation.

Amongst the Trobrianders such magic as is known to all members of the community has very little social significance. The same is true of the Azande, amongst whom much magic is common property and much can be bought so cheaply that it is not even sought after by most men.

In a society such as this, where magic is not restricted in use to members of a group, but is characterized by its social nobility, it is possible to suggest tentatively that certain features in the domain of magic are due to the absence of exclusive ownership. I think that it is possible that the great extension of the magic of oracles, divination, and ordeal amongst the Azande and in many other parts of Africa in contrast to the little importance attached to them throughout Polynesia and Melanesia, may be attributed to the absence of hereditary ownership, set formulae, and standardized tradition. For it must be remembered that, although the object of oracles is to know about future events and not to produce or influence them, nevertheless it fulfils the same psychological function as other types of magic by giving man confidence in his social and economic undertakings. We have, therefore, various types of magic fulfilling the same function. However, in the present state of my researches into Zande customs I do not wish to stress this point too much.

This same phenomenon, this reduplication of rôle in many types of Zande magic, is seen in the special associations for the practice of magic (secret societies). Insofar as I have investigated these associations I have found that the purpose of their magic is already covered by other types of magic. The spread and popularity of these societies may, I believe, be accounted for by the need to systematize and stabilize magic by affiliating its use to an association and by this means enhancing its social utility. In these societies the knowledge of the magic is restricted to the leader of the society. However, the secret societies at present found in Zandeland are of recent introduction. Generally they are of easy access, short-lived, and replaced by other associations of a like nature.

CREATION OF NEW MAGIC

Not only have all the secret societies of the Azande of the Bahr-el-Ghazal entered from across the Congo border, but many hunting and other medicines are learnt from the Baka, Mundu, Avokaiya, and Moro peoples to the East, the Pambia to the West, the Bongo and Bellanda to the North, the Mangbettu, Amade, Abarambo to the South. Medicines have also been incorporated into Zande culture from the many peoples who now call themselves Azande, but who a generation ago spoke their own language and had their own distinctive customs. The territorial spread of magic is quick and far-reaching. In at least one instance the Azande have borrowed magic from even the distant and hostile Dinka tribes. The Azande find in the magic of their neighbors a constant source of new and powerful medicine.

Nor do I think that all Zande magic is of great age. We have already noted that all Zande magic has its current tradition, its halo of rumor, mystery, and wonder, the birthplace in all societies from which springs transmitted tradition, set legend, and standardized myth, stabilized by group ownership and handed over by the customary procedure of kinship, or other social machinery. However, in saying that magic creates its own mythology the problem has been simplified. Does not belief create magic? Often a native will tell you, for example, that a certain man has powerful magic to kill leopards. If you ask your informant what magic is possessed by the hunter, he will say that he does not know, but that he must own some magic or he would not be so successful in killing leopards.

Actual achievement is demanded of the man who wishes to sell his magic. The fate of unsuccessful magicians, especially rainmakers in many parts of the world, is evidence of this demand. But the production of rain is a supposed and not an actual achievement. Amongst the Moro of the Yei river in the Southern Sudan it is only when a man becomes renowned as a hunter that he plants medicine roots at the side of his hut and becomes a practitioner (Evans-Pritchard, field notes).

It would be a barren discussion whether the myth follows the practice of the magic in all cases or whether sometimes the practice of the magic springs out of current tradition. The rite of magic and the myth always interlace and shape each other. I only wish to suggest that new magic is constantly being created, and that it is created by successful men influenced by the rumors of magic which attend their success, and that whilst magic gives men confidence in their undertakings, it also represents a record of man's actual achievement. Primitive man is not a romantic but a practical hard-headed being, even in his magic, and there is no magic to attempt the impossible.

FUNCTIONAL OCCASIONS OF MAGIC

So far I have endeavored to show by correlations how the morphology of magic amongst the Trobrianders and the Azande is determined by the social structure of the two societies. The same is true of the functional occasions of magic. This cannot be demonstrated at length, as it would then be necessary to describe fully the occasions of use and the specific function of all magic in both communities. Moreover the statement is so obvious in simpler instances that it hardly requires demonstration. The Zande has no canoe magic because he has no canoes. The Trobriander has no magic of iron-forging because he lives in a stone age.

The problem becomes more complicated when we consider the sociological aspects of magic. It is clear that the communal garden magic of the Trobrianders is absent from Zande life because the Azande do not cultivate their gardens by joint labor.

It is more difficult to see why the Trobriand chief uses magic as part of his machinery of government, whereas the Zande chief does not use this weapon of chastisement, but this difference can readily be understood when the position of the chief is known in both societies. The Trobriand chief was unable to exercise great executive power as may readily be judged from the almost entire absence of corporal punishment, whereas the mutilations and executions inflicted on their subjects by the Zande chiefs are one of the many signs of their real power. The Zande chief, therefore, had little need of magic to enforce his rule.

On the other hand, the Azande move their homesteads freely over the countryside and a chief who has angered his people may lose his subjects. Also a young chief anxious to conquer or acquire new territory by peaceful means has to rely entirely upon his popularity to attract followers. Hence we find a system of magic for attracting dependents.

Magic used in communal undertakings such as we find in the Trobriands, in garden work, in trading expeditions, in building canoes, and in other forms of economic enterprise has no counterpart in Zande life. This is because there is a lack of cohesion in Zande social life, solidarity either due to close aggregation of dwellings or good means of communication, being absent. Thus while magic amongst the Kiwai Papuans or the Trobrianders is often associated with village activities, this cannot be so amongst the Azande because there are no villages.

Also amongst the Azande we do not find the institution of magic associated, save in one instance, with the clan. This is because the clans have little solidarity. Political functions are in the hands of a class and the clans also lack the cohesion which localization would give them. For magic is an important social institution, and for it to be orientated after a group, that group must have solidarity without which it cannot exercise important social functions.

SUMMARY AND CONCLUSIONS

I set out at the commencement of this paper to show that the social incidence of magic in Melanesia differs from the social incidence of magic in Africa and that this difference affects the structure and functional occasions of the magic. I have attempted to do this by a comparison between the data of the Trobriand islands and the data of the Azande of the Nile-Uelle divide. I explained how the Trobriander and the Zande regarded magic not as a force of nature, but as a cultural heritage, not as something discovered but as something co-existent in time with man, not as a vague impersonal power but as a tangible weapon of culture, not activated by the spirits of the dead but deriving its power from the knowledge of tradition and the abstinence of living men.

I then analyzed the structure of magic in these two societies and showed how the spell amongst the Trobrianders is a standardized formula whilst amongst the Azande it is only a saying adapted to the purpose of the magic and accompanying the rite. I concluded that the psychological purpose of magic is not served unless an utterance is made in conjunction with the rite, but that the crystallization of the utterance into a standardized formula is determined by the affiliation of the magic with a group through the institution of ownership.

The analysis of magic in the two societies showed also that amongst the Trobrianders myth, like the spell, is a standardized formula, a set story transmitted intact to the succeeding generation by the social mechanism of kinship, whilst among the Azande magic generates only a loose current myth and everyday tradition, save in exceptional instances in which the magic is owned by a restricted social grouping and a stereotyped and permanent element of culture takes the place of the ephemeral mythology. For here again I concluded that the psychological purpose of magic is not served unless the ritual has a background of belief in mythology, a halo of stories about its wonder-working powers, but that the crystallization of these stories into standardized myth is determined by the affiliation of the magic with a group through the institution of ownership.

I suggested that any section of society enjoying special privileges, whether magical or otherwise, produces its own mythology, the function of the myth being to give sanction to the possession of the exclusive privileges.

I suggested that important magic, that is, magic which plays its rôle in large communal undertakings or is practised on behalf of the whole community or reinforces an essential function of society such as war or government, is always to be found in the hands of a few men. I gave some examples to support this view. Since all important magic is in the hands of a few individuals the more it becomes spread among the members of the community at large, the more it loses its importance and social utility. This gives rise to the creation of new magic, magical redundancy, and an attempt to stabilize the magic through new groups or associations.

I have described how today magic is taken over by one people from another. This is one way in which new magic comes into being, but it is also created by individuals and I have discussed the manner of its birth.

In the earlier part of my paper I attempted to show that the form of magic depends upon the structure of society as a whole, and at the end I indicated that the functional occasions of magic are also determined by the social structure. Examples were given to show how the occasion on which magic is used, the social activities with which it is correlated, and the groups after which it is orientated differ with differences of social structure.

It is one of the aims of social anthropology to interpret all differences in the form of a typical social institution by reference to difference in social structure. In this paper I have attempted to show that differences in the form of the institution of magic, in particular between two societies, can be explained by showing the variation in social structure between these societies.

By the method of correlation we attempted to show that the formalization of the components of magic rites depends on the factor of ownership. It may be asked why magic is owned by the kin or clan groups in the Trobriand isles and not amongst the Azande. The answer is that in the Trobriands these groups have important social and economic functions to carry out which we do not find associated with the same groups amongst the Azande. Now since the rôle of magic is to enable these social and economic processes to be carried out, it is naturally associated with the groups fulfilling these functions. The purpose of this paper was to show how such an association affects the form of the magic.

2 THE SORCERER AND HIS MAGIC

Claude Lévi-Strauss

SINCE THE PIONEERING work of Cannon, we understand more clearly the psycho-physiological mechanisms underlying the instances reported from many parts of the world of death by exorcism and the casting of spells (Cannon 1942). An individual who is aware that he is the object of sorcery is thoroughly convinced that he is doomed according to the most solemn traditions of his group. His friends and relatives share this certainty. From then on the community withdraws. Standing aloof from the accursed, it treats him not only as though he were already dead but as though he were a source of danger to the entire group. On every occasion and by every action, the social body suggests death to the unfortunate victim, who no longer hopes to escape what he considers to be his ineluctable fate. Shortly thereafter, sacred rites are held to dispatch him to the realm of shadows. First brutally torn from all of his family and social ties and excluded from all functions and activities through which he experienced self-awareness, then banished by the same forces from the world of the living, the victim yields to the combined effect of intense terror, the sudden total withdrawal of the multiple reference systems provided by the support of the group, and, finally, to the group's decisive reversal in proclaiming him—once a living man, with rights and obligations—dead and an object of fear, ritual, and taboo. Physical integrity cannot withstand the dissolution of the social personality.[1]

Reprinted from Claude Lévi-Strauss, *Structural Anthropology*, New York, © 1963, by permission of the author and Basic Books Inc., New York. The essay was originally published as "Le sorcier et sa magie" in *Les Temps modernes* 41, 1949.

[1] An Australian aborigine was brought to the Darwin hospital in April 1956, apparently dying of this type of sorcery. He was placed in an oxygen

How are these complex phenomena expressed on the physiological level? Cannon showed that fear, like rage, is associated with a particularly intense activity of the sympathetic nervous system. This activity is ordinarily useful, involving organic modifications which enable the individual to adapt himself to a new situation. But if the individual cannot avail himself of any instinctive or acquired response to an extraordinary situation (or to one which he conceives of as such), the activity of the sympathetic nervous system becomes intensified and disorganized; it may, sometimes within a few hours, lead to a decrease in the volume of blood and a concomitant drop in blood pressure, which result in irreparable damage to the circulatory organs. The rejection of food and drink, frequent among patients in the throes of intense anxiety, precipitates this process; dehydration acts as a stimulus to the sympathetic nervous system, and the decrease in blood volume is accentuated by the growing permeability of the capillary vessels. These hypotheses were confirmed by the study of several cases of trauma resulting from bombings, battle shock, and even surgical operations; death results, yet the autopsy reveals no lesions.

There is, therefore, no reason to doubt the efficacy of certain magical practices. But at the same time we see that the efficacy of magic implies a belief in magic. The latter has three complementary aspects: first, the sorcerer's belief in the effectiveness of his techniques; second, the patient's or victim's belief in the sorcerer's power; and, finally, the faith and expectations of the group, which constantly act as a sort of gravitational field within which the relationship between sorcerer and bewitched is located and defined.[2] Obviously, none of the three parties is capable of forming a clear picture of the sympathetic nervous system's activity or of the disturbances which Cannon called homeostatic. When the sorcerer claims to suck out of the patient's body a foreign object whose presence would explain the illness and pro-

---

tent and fed intravenously. He gradually recovered, convinced that the white man's magic was the stronger. See Arthur Morley in the *London Sunday Times*, April 22, 1956, p. 11.

[2] In this study, whose aim is more psychological than sociological, we feel justified in neglecting the finer distinctions between the several modes of magical operations and different types of sorcerers when these are not absolutely necessary.

duces a stone which he had previously hidden in his mouth, how does he justify this procedure in his own eyes? How can an innocent person accused of sorcery prove his innocence if the accusation is unanimous—since the magical situation is a consensual phenomenon? And, finally, how much credulity and how much skepticism are involved in the attitude of the group toward those in whom it recognizes extraordinary powers, to whom it accords corresponding privileges, but from whom it also requires adequate satisfaction? Let us begin by examining this last point.

It was in September, 1938. For several weeks we had been camping with a small band of Nambicuara Indians near the headwaters of the Tapajoz, in those desolate savannas of central Brazil where the natives wander during the greater part of the year, collecting seeds and wild fruits, hunting small mammals, insects, and reptiles, and whatever else might prevent them from dying of starvation. Thirty of them were camped together there, quite by chance. They were grouped in families under frail lean-tos of branches, which give scant protection from the scorching sun, nocturnal chill, rain, and wind. Like most bands, this one had both a secular chief and a sorcerer; the latter's daily activities—hunting, fishing, and handicrafts—were in no way different from those of the other men of the group. He was a robust man, about forty-five years old, and a *bon vivant*.

One evening, however, he did not return to camp at the usual time. Night fell and fires were lit; the natives were visibly worried. Countless perils lurk in the bush: torrential rivers, the somewhat improbable danger of encountering a large wild beast—jaguar or anteater—or, more readily pictured by the Nambicuara, an apparently harmless animal which is the incarnation of an evil spirit of the waters or forest. And above all, each night for the past week we had seen mysterious campfires, which sometimes approached and sometimes receded from our own. Any unknown band is always potentially hostile. After a two-hour wait, the natives were convinced that their companion had been killed in ambush and, while his two young wives and his son wept noisily in mourning for their dead husband and father, the other natives discussed the tragic consequences foreshadowed by the disappearance of their sorcerer.

Toward ten that evening, the anguished anticipation of imminent disaster, the lamentations in which the other women began to join, and the agitation of the men had created an intolerable atmosphere, and we decided to reconnoiter with several natives who had remained relatively calm. We had not gone two hundred yards when we stumbled upon a motionless figure. It was our man, crouching silently, shivering in the chilly night air, disheveled and without his belt, necklaces, and arm-bands (the Nambicuara wear nothing else). He allowed us to lead him back to the camp site without resistance, but only after long exhortations by his group and pleading by his family was he persuaded to talk. Finally, bit by bit, we extracted the details of his story. A thunderstorm, the first of the season, had burst during the afternoon, and the thunder had carried him off to a site several miles distant, which he named, and then, after stripping him completely, had brought him back to the spot where we found him. Everyone went off to sleep commenting on the event. The next day the thunder victim had recovered his joviality and, what is more, all his ornaments. This last detail did not appear to surprise anyone, and life resumed its normal course.

A few days later, however, another version of these prodigious events began to be circulated by certain natives. We must note that this band was actually composed of individuals of different origins and had been fused into a new social entity as a result of unknown circumstances. One of the groups had been decimated by an epidemic several years before and was no longer sufficiently large to lead an independent life; the other had seceded from its original tribe and found itself in the same straits. When and under what circumstances the two groups met and decided to unite their efforts, we could not discover. The secular leader of the new band came from one group and the sorcerer, or religious leader, from the other. The fusion was obviously recent, for no marriage had yet taken place between the two groups when we met them, although the children of one were usually betrothed to the children of the other; each group had retained its own dialect, and their members could communicate only through two or three bilingual natives.

This is the rumor that was spread. There was good reason to suppose that the unknown bands crossing the savanna belonged to the tribe of the seceded group of which the sorcerer was a member. The sorcerer, impinging on the functions of his colleague the political chief, had doubtless wanted to contact his former tribesmen, perhaps to ask to return to the fold, or to provoke an attack upon his new companions, or perhaps even to reassure them of the friendly intentions of the latter. In any case, the sorcerer had needed a pretext for his absence, and his kidnapping by thunder and its subsequent staging were invented toward this end. It was, of course, the natives of the other group who spread this interpretation, which they secretly believed and which filled them with apprehension. But the official version was never publicly disputed, and until we left, shortly after the incident, it remained ostensibly accepted by all (Lévi-Strauss 1955: ch. XXIX).

Although the skeptics had analyzed the sorcerer's motives with great psychological finesse and political acumen, they would have been greatly astonished had someone suggested (quite plausibly) that the incident was a hoax which cast doubt upon the sorcerer's good faith and competence. He had probably not flown on the wings of thunder to the Rio Ananaz and had only staged an act. But these things might have happened, they had certainly happened in other circumstances, and they belonged to the realm of real experience. Certainly the sorcerer maintains an intimate relationship with the forces of the supernatural. The idea that in a particular case he had used his power to conceal a secular activity belongs to the realm of conjecture and provides an opportunity for critical judgment. The important point is that these two possibilities were not mutually exclusive; no more than are, for us, the alternate interpretations of war as the dying gasp of national independence or as the result of the schemes of munitions manufacturers. The two explanations are logically incompatible, but we admit that one or the other may be true; since they are equally plausible, we easily make the transition from one to the other, depending on the occasion and the moment. Many people have both explanations in the back of their minds.

Whatever their true origin, these divergent interpretations come from individual consciousness not as the result of objective analysis but rather as complementary ideas resulting from hazy and unelaborated attitudes which have an experiential character for each of us. These experiences, however, remain intellectually diffuse and emotionally intolerable unless they incorporate one or another of the patterns present in the group's culture. The assimilation of such patterns is the only means of objectivizing subjective states, of formulating inexpressible feelings, and of integrating inarticulated experiences into a system.

These mechanisms become clearer in the light of some observations made many years ago among the Zuni of New Mexico by an admirable field-worker, M. C. Stevenson (1905). A twelve-year-old girl was stricken with a nervous seizure directly after an adolescent boy had seized her hands. The youth was accused of sorcery and dragged before the court of the Bow priesthood. For an hour he denied having any knowledge of occult power, but this defense proved futile. Because the crime of sorcery was at that time still punished by death among the Zuni, the accused changed his tactics. He improvised a tale explaining the circumstances by which he had been initiated into sorcery. He said he had received two substances from his teachers, one which drove girls insane and another which cured them. This point constituted an ingenious precaution against later developments. Having been ordered to produce his medicines, he went home under guard and came back with two roots, which he proceeded to use in a complicated ritual. He simulated a trance after taking one of the drugs, and after taking the other he pretended to return to his normal state. Then he administered the remedy to the sick girl and declared her cured. The session was adjourned until the following day, but during the night the alleged sorcerer escaped. He was soon captured, and the girl's family set itself up as a court and continued the trial. Faced with the reluctance of his new judges to accept his first story, the boy then invented a new one. He told them that all his relatives and ancestors had been witches and that he had received marvellous powers from them. He claimed that he could assume the form of a cat, fill his mouth with cactus needles, and kill his victims—two infants, three girls, and two boys—by shooting the needles into them. These feats, he claimed, were due to the magical powers of certain plumes which were used to change him and his family into shapes other than human. This last detail was a tactical error, for the judges called upon him to produce the plumes as proof of his new story. He gave various excuses which were rejected one after another, and he was forced to take his judges to his house. He began by declaring that the plumes were secreted in a wall that he could not destroy. He was commanded to go to work. After breaking down a section of the wall and carefully examining the plaster, he tried to excuse himself by declaring that the plumes had been hidden two years before and that he could not remember their exact location. Forced to search again, he tried another wall, and after another hour's work, an old plume appeared in the plaster. He grabbed it eagerly and presented it to his persecutors as the magic device of which he had spoken. He was then made to explain the details of its use. Finally, dragged into the public plaza, he had to repeat his entire story (to which he added a wealth of new detail). He finished it with a pathetic speech in which he lamented the loss of his supernatural power. Thus reassured, his listeners agreed to free him.

This narrative, which we unfortunately had to abridge and strip of all its psychological nuances, is still instructive in many respects. First of all, we see that the boy tried for witchcraft, for which he risks the death penalty, wins his acquittal not by denying but by admitting his alleged crime. Moreover, he furthers his cause by presenting successive versions, each richer in detail (and thus, in theory, more persuasive of guilt) than the preceding one. The debate does not proceed, as do debates among us, by accusations and denials, but rather by allegations and specifications. The judges do not expect the accused to challenge their theory, much less to refute the facts. Rather, they require him to validate a system of which they possess only a fragment; he must reconstruct it as a whole in an appropriate way. As the fieldworker noted in relation to a phase of the trial, "The warriors had become so absorbed by their interest in the narrative of the boy that they seemed entirely to have forgotten the cause of his appearance before them" (Stevenson 1905: 401). And when the magic plume was finally uncovered, the author remarks with great insight, "There was consternation among the warriors, who exclaimed in one voice: 'What does this mean?' Now they felt assured that the youth had spoken the truth" (Stevenson 1905: 404). Consternation, and not triumph at finding a tangible proof of the crime—for the judges had sought to bear witness to the reality of the system which had made the crime possible (by validating its objective basis through an appropriate emotional expression), rather than simply to punish a crime. By his confession, the defendant is transformed into a witness for the prosecution, with the participation (and even the complicity) of his judges. Through the defendant, witchcraft and the ideas associated with it cease to exist as a diffuse complex of poorly formulated sentiments and representations and become embodied in real experience. The defendant, who serves as a witness, gives the group the satisfaction of truth, which is infinitely greater and richer than the satisfaction of justice that would have been achieved by his execution. And finally, by his ingenious defense which makes his hearers progressively aware of the vitality offered by his corroboration of their system (especially since the choice is not between this system and another, but between the magical system and no system at all—that is, chaos), the youth, who at first was a threat to the physical security of his group, became the guardian of its spiritual coherence.

But is his defense merely ingenious? Everything leads us to believe that after groping for a subterfuge, the defendant participates with sincerity and—the word is not too strong—fervor in the drama enacted between him and his judges. He is proclaimed a sorcerer; since sorcerers do exist, he might well be one. And how would he know beforehand the signs which might reveal his calling to him? Perhaps the signs are there, present in this ordeal and in the convulsions of the little girl brought before the court. For the boy, too, the coherence of the system and the role assigned to him in preserving it are values no less essential than the personal security which he risks in the venture. Thus we see him, with a mixture of cunning and good faith, progressively construct the impersonation which is thrust upon him—chiefly by drawing on his knowledge and his memories, improvising somewhat, but above all living his role and seeking, through his manipulations and the ritual he builds from bits and pieces, the experience of a calling which is, at least theoretically, open to all. At the end of the adventure, what remains of his earlier hoaxes? To what extent has the hero become the dupe of his own impersonation? What is more, has he not truly become a sorcerer? We are told that in his final confession, "The longer the boy talked the more absorbed he became in his subject. . . . At times his face became radiant with satisfaction at his power over his listeners" (Stevenson 1905: 406). The girl recovers after he performs his curing ritual. The boy's experiences during the extraordinary ordeal become elaborated and structured. Little more is needed than for the innocent boy finally to confess to the possession of supernatural powers that are already recognized by the group.

We must consider at greater length another especially valuable document, which until now seems to have been valued solely for its linguistic interest. I refer to a fragment of the autobiography of a Kwakiutl Indian from the Vancouver region of Canada, obtained by Franz Boas (1930, pt. II).

Quesalid (for this was the name he received when he became a sorcerer) did not believe in the power of the sorcerers—or, more accurately, shamans, since this is a better term for their specific type of activity in certain regions of the world. Driven by curiosity about their tricks and by the desire to expose them, he began to associate with the shamans until one of them offered to make him a member of their group. Quesalid did not wait to be asked twice, and his narrative recounts the details of his first lessons, a curious mixture of pantomime, prestidigitation, and empirical knowledge, including the art of simulating fainting and nervous fits, the learning of sacred songs, the technique for inducing vomiting, rather precise notions of auscultation and obstetrics, and the use of "dreamers," that is, spies who listen to private conversations and secretly convey to the shaman bits of information concerning the origins and symptoms of the ills suffered by different people. Above all, he learned the *ars magna* of one of the shamanistic schools of the Northwest Coast: The shaman hides a little tuft of down in a corner of his mouth, and he throws it up, covered with blood, at the proper moment—after having bitten his tongue or made his gums bleed—and solemnly presents it to his patient and the onlookers as the pathological foreign body extracted as a result of his sucking and manipulations.

His worst suspicions confirmed, Quesalid wanted to continue

his inquiry. But he was no longer free. His apprenticeship among the shamans began to be noised about, and one day he was summoned by the family of a sick person who had dreamed of Quesalid as his healer. This first treatment (for which he received no payment, any more than he did for those which followed, since he had not completed the required four years of apprenticeship) was an outstanding success. Although Quesalid came to be known from that moment on as a "great shaman," he did not lose his critical faculties. He interpreted his success in psychological terms—it was successful "because he [the sick person] believed strongly in his dream about me" (Boas 1930, II: 13). A more complex adventure made him, in his own words, "hesitant and thinking about many things" (Boas 1930, II: 19). Here he encountered several varieties of a "false supernatural," and was led to conclude that some forms were less false than others—those, of course, in which he had a personal stake and whose system he was, at the same time, surreptitiously building up in his mind. A summary of the adventure follows.

While visiting the neighboring Koskimo Indians, Quesalid attends a curing ceremony of his illustrious colleagues of the other tribe. To his great astonishment he observes a difference in their technique. Instead of spitting out the illness in the form of a "bloody worm" (the concealed down), the Koskimo shamans merely spit a little saliva into their hands, and they dare to claim that this is "the sickness." What is the value of this method? What is the theory behind it? In order to find out "the strength of the shamans, whether it was real or whether they only pretended to be shamans" like his fellow tribesmen (Boas 1930, II: 17), Quesalid requests and obtains permission to try his method in an instance where the Koskimo method has failed. The sick woman then declares herself cured.

And here our hero vacillates for the first time. Though he had few illusions about his own technique, he has now found one which is more false, more mystifying, and more dishonest than his own. For he at least gives his clients something. He presents them with their sickness in a visible and tangible form, while his foreign colleagues show nothing at all and only claim to have captured the sickness. Moreover, Quesalid's method gets results, while the other is futile. Thus our hero grapples with a problem which perhaps has its parallel in the development of modern science. Two systems which we know to be inadequate present (with respect to each other) a differential validity, from both a logical and an empirical perspective. From which frame of reference shall we judge them? On the level of fact, where they merge, or on their own level, where they take on different values, both theoretically and empirically?

Meanwhile, the Koskimo shamans, "ashamed" and discredited before their tribesmen, are also plunged into doubt. Their colleague has produced, in the form of a material object, the illness which they had always considered as spiritual in nature and had thus never dreamed of rendering visible. They send Quesalid an emissary to invite him to a secret meeting in a cave. Quesalid goes and his foreign colleagues expound their system to him: "Every sickness is a man: boils and swellings, and itch and scabs, and pimples and coughs and consumption and scrofula; and also this, stricture of the bladder and stomach aches. . . . As soon as we get the soul of the sickness which is a man, then dies the sickness which is a man. Its body just disappears in our insides" (Boas 1930, II: 20–21). If this theory is correct, what is there to show? And why, when Quesalid operates, does "the sickness stick to his hand"? But Quesalid takes refuge behind professional rules which forbid him to teach before completing four years of apprenticeship, and refuses to speak. He maintains his silence even when the Koskimo shamans send him their allegedly virgin daughters to try to seduce him and discover his secret.

Thereupon Quesalid returns to his village at Fort Rupert. He learns that the most reputed shaman of a neighboring clan, worried about Quesalid's growing renown, has challenged all his colleagues, inviting them to compete with him in curing several patients. Quesalid comes to the contest and observes the cures of his elder. Like the Koskimo, this shaman does not show the illness. He simply incorporates an invisible object, "what he called the sickness" into his head-ring, made of bark, or into his bird-shaped ritual rattle (Boas 1930, II: 27). These objects can hang suspended in mid-air, owing to the power of the illness which "bites" the house-posts or the shaman's hand. The usual drama unfolds. Quesalid is asked to intervene in cases judged hopeless by his predecessor, and he triumphs with his technique of the bloody worm.

Here we come to the truly pathetic part of the story. The old shaman, ashamed and despairing because of the ill-repute into which he has fallen and by the collapse of his therapeutic technique, sends his daughter to Quesalid to beg him for an interview. The latter finds his colleague sitting under a tree and the old shaman begins thus: "It won't be bad what we say to each other, friend, but only I wish you to try and save my life for me, so that I may not die of shame, for I am a plaything of our people on account of what you did last night. I pray you to have mercy and tell me what stuck on the palm of your hand last night. Was it the true sickness or was it only made up? For I beg you have mercy and tell me about the way you did it so that I can imitate you. Pity me, friend" (Boas 1930, II: 31).

Silent at first, Quesalid begins by calling for explanations about the feats of the head-ring and the rattle. His colleague shows him the nail hidden in the head-ring which he can press at right angles into the post, and the way in which he tucks the head of his rattle between his finger joints to make it look as if the bird were hanging by its beak from his hand. He himself probably does nothing but lie and fake, simulating shamanism for material gain, for he admits to being "covetous for the property of the sick men." He knows that shamans cannot catch souls, "for . . . we all own a soul"; so he resorts to using tallow and pretends that "it is a soul . . . that white thing . . . sitting on my hand." The daughter then adds her entreaties to those of her father: "Do have mercy that he may live." But Quesalid remains silent. That very night, following this tragic conversation, the shaman disappears with his entire family, heartsick and feared by the community, who think that he may be tempted to take revenge. Needless fears: He returned a year later, but both he and his daughter had gone mad. Three years later, he died.

And Quesalid, rich in secrets, pursued his career, exposing the impostors and full of contempt for the profession. "Only one shaman was seen by me, who sucked at a sick man and I never found out whether he was a real shaman or only made up. Only for this reason I believe that he is a shaman; he does not allow those who are made well to pay him. I truly never once saw him laugh" (Boas 1930, II: 40–41). Thus his original attitude has changed considerably. The radical negativism of the free thinker has given way to more moderate feelings. Real shamans do exist. And what about him? At the end of the narrative we cannot tell, but it is evident that he carries on his craft conscientiously, takes pride in his achievements, and warmly defends the technique of the bloody down against all rival schools. He seems to have completely lost sight of the fallaciousness of the technique which he had so disparaged at the beginning.

We see that the psychology of the sorcerer is not simple. In order to analyze it, we shall first examine the case of the old shaman who begs his young rival to tell him the truth—whether the illness glued in the palm of his hand like a sticky red worm is real or made up—and who goes mad when he receives no answer. Before the tragedy, he was fully convinced of two things—first, that pathological conditions have a cause which may be discovered and second, that a system of interpretation in which personal inventiveness is important structures the phases of the illness, from the diagnosis to the cure. This fabulation of a reality unknown in itself—a fabulation consisting of procedures and representations—is founded on a threefold experience: first, that of the shaman himself, who, if his calling is a true one (and even if it is not, simply by virtue of his practicing it), undergoes specific states of a psychosomatic nature; second, that of the sick person, who may or may not experience an improvement of his condition; and, finally, that of the public, who also participate in the cure, experiencing an enthusiasm and an intellectual and emotional satisfaction which produce collective support, which in turn inaugurates a new cycle.

These three elements of what we might call the "shamanistic complex" cannot be separated. But they are clustered around two poles, one formed by the intimate experience of the shaman and the other by group consensus. There is no reason to doubt that sorcerers, or at least the more sincere among them, believe in their calling and that this belief is founded on the experiencing of specific states. The hardships and privations which they undergo would often be sufficient in themselves to provoke these states, even if we refuse to admit them as proof of a serious and fervent calling. But there is also linguistic evidence which, because it is indirect, is more convincing. In the Wintu dialect of California, there are five verbal classes which correspond to knowledge by sight, by bodily experience, by inference, by reasoning, and by hearsay. All five make up the category of knowledge as opposed to conjecture, which is differently expressed. Curiously enough, rela-, tionships with the supernatural world are expressed by means of the modes of knowledge—by bodily impression (that is, the most intuitive kind of experience), by inference, and by reasoning. Thus the native who becomes a shaman after a spiritual crisis conceives of his state grammatically, as a consequence to be inferred from the fact—formulated as real experience—that he has received divine guidance. From the latter he concludes deductively that he must have been on a journey to the beyond, at the end of which he found himself—again, an immediate experience— once more among his people (Lee 1941).

The experiences of the sick person represent the least important aspect of the system, except for the fact that a patient successfully treated by a shaman is in an especially good position to become a shaman in his own right, as we see today in the case of psychoanalysis. In any event, we must remember that the shaman does not completely lack empirical knowledge and experimental techniques, which may in part explain his success. Furthermore, disorders of the type currently termed psychosomatic, which constitute a large part of the illnesses prevalent in societies with a low degree of security, probably often yield to psychotherapy. At any rate, it seems probable that medicine men, like their civilized colleagues, cure at least some of the cases they treat and that without this relative success magical practices could not have been so widely diffused in time and space. But this point is not fundamental; it is subordinate to the other two. Quesalid did not become a great shaman because he cured his patients; he cured his patients because he had become a great shaman. Thus we have reached the other—that is, the collective—pole of our system.

The true reason for the defeat of Quesalid's rivals must then be sought in the attitude of the group rather than in the pattern of the rivals' successes and failures. The rivals themselves emphasize this when they confess their shame at having become the laughingstock of the group; this is a social sentiment *par excellence*. Failure is secondary, and we see in all their statements that they consider it a function of another phenomenon, which is the disappearance of the *social consensus,* re-created at their expense around another practitioner and another system of curing. Consequently, the fundamental problem revolves around the relationship between the individual and the group, or, more accurately, the relationship between a specific category of individuals and specific expectations of the group.

In treating his patient the shaman also offers his audience a performance. What is this performance? Risking a rash generalization on the basis of a few observations, we shall say that it always involves the shaman's enactment of the "call," or the initial crisis which brought him the revelation of his condition. But we must not be deceived by the word *performance.* The shaman does not limit himself to reproducing or miming certain events. He actually relives them in all their vividness, originality, and violence. And since he returns to his normal state at the end of the séance, we may say, borrowing a key term from psychoanalysis, that he *abreacts*. In psychoanalysis, abreaction refers to the decisive moment in the treatment when the patient intensively relives the initial situation from which his disturbance stems, before he ultimately overcomes it. In this sense, the shaman is a professional abreactor.

We have set forth elsewhere the theoretical hypotheses that might be formulated in order for us to accept the idea that the type of abreaction specific to each shaman—or, at any rate, to each shamanistic school—might symbolically induce an abreaction of his own disturbance in each patient (Lévi-Strauss 1949b). In any case, if the essential relationship is that between the shaman and the group, we must also state the question from another point of view—that of the relationship between normal and pathological thinking. From any non-scientific perspective (and here we can exclude no society), pathological and normal thought processes are complementary rather than opposed. In a universe which it strives to understand but whose dynamics it cannot fully control, normal thought continually seeks the meaning of things which refuse to reveal their significance. So-called pathological thought, on the other hand, overflows with emotional interpre-

tations and overtones, in order to supplement an otherwise deficient reality. For normal thinking there exists something which
cannot be empirically verified and is, therefore, "claimable." For
pathological thinking there exist experiences without object, or
something "available." We might borrow from linguistics and
say that so-called normal thought always suffers from a deficit
of meaning, whereas so-called pathological thought (in at least
some of its manifestations) disposes of a plethora of meaning.
Through collective participation in shamanistic curing, a balance
is established between these two complementary situations. Normal thought cannot fathom the problem of illness, and so the
group calls upon the neurotic to furnish a wealth of emotion here-
tofore lacking a focus.

An equilibrium is reached between what might be called supply and demand on the psychic level—but only on two conditions.
First, a structure must be elaborated and continually modified
through the interaction of group tradition and individual invention. The structure is a system of oppositions and correlations,
integrating all the elements of a total situation, in which sorcerer,
patient, and audience, as well as representations and procedures,
all play their parts. Furthermore, the public must participate in
the abreaction, to a certain extent at least, along with the patient
and the sorcerer. It is this vital experience of a universe of symbolic effusions which the patient, because he is ill, and the sorcerer, because he is neurotic—in other words, both having types
of experience which cannot otherwise be integrated—allow the
public to glimpse as "fireworks" from a safe distance. In the
absence of any experimental control, which is indeed unnecessary, it is this experience alone, and its relative richness in each
case, which makes possible a choice between several systems and
elicits adherence to a particular school or practitioner.[3]

In contrast with scientific explanation, the problem here is
not to attribute confused and disorganized states, emotions, or
representations to an objective cause, but rather to articulate
them into a whole or system. The system is valid precisely to

[3]This oversimplified equation of sorcerer and neurotic was justly criticized by Michel Leiris. I subsequently refined this concept in Lévi-Strauss
1950.

the extent that it allows the coalescence or precipitation of these diffuse states, whose discontinuity also makes them painful. To the conscious mind, this last phenomenon constitutes an original experience which cannot be grasped from without. Because of their complementary disorders, the sorcerer-patient dyad incarnates for the group, in vivid and concrete fashion, an antagonism that is inherent in all thought but that normally remains vague and imprecise. The patient is all passivity and self-alienation, just as inexpressibility is the disease of the mind. The sorcerer is activity and self-projection, just as affectivity is the source of symbolism. The cure interrelates these opposite poles, facilitating the transition from one to the other, and demonstrates, within a total experience, the coherence of the psychic universe, itself a projection of the social universe.

Thus it is necessary to extend the notion of abreaction by examining the meanings it acquires in psychotherapies other than psychoanalysis, although the latter deserves the credit for rediscovering and insisting upon its fundamental validity. It may be objected that in psychoanalysis there is only one abreaction, the patient's, rather than three. We are not so sure of this. It is true that in the shamanistic cure the sorcerer speaks and abreacts *for* the silent patient, while in psychoanalysis it is the patient who talks and abreacts *against* the listening therapist. But the therapist's abreaction, while not concomitant with the patient's, is nonetheless required, since he must be analyzed before he himself can become an analyst. It is more difficult to define the role ascribed to the group by each technique. Magic readapts the group to predefined problems through the patient, while psychoanalysis readapts the patient to the group by means of the solutions reached. But the distressing trend which, for several years, has tended to transform the psychoanalytic system from a body of scientific hypotheses that are experimentally verifiable in certain specific and limited cases into a kind of diffuse mythology interpenetrating the consciousness of the group, could rapidly bring about a parallelism. (This group consciousness is an objective phenomenon, which the psychologist expresses through a subjective tendency to extend to normal thought a system of interpretations conceived for pathological thought and to apply to facts of collective psychology a method adapted solely to the study of individual psychology.) When this happens—and perhaps it already has in certain countries—the value of the system will no longer be based upon real cures from which certain individuals can benefit, but on the sense of security that the group receives from the myth underlying the cure and from the popular system upon which the group's universe is reconstructed.

Even at the present time, the comparison between psychoanalysis and older and more widespread psychological therapies can encourage the former to re-examine its principles and methods. By continuously expanding the recruitment of its patients, who begin as clearly characterized abnormal individuals and gradually become representative of the group, psychoanalysis transforms its treatments into conversions. For only a patient can emerge cured; an unstable or maladjusted individual can only be persuaded. A considerable danger thus arises: The treatment (unbeknown to the therapist, naturally), far from leading to the resolution of a specific disturbance within its own context, is reduced to the reorganization of the patient's universe in terms of psychoanalytic interpretations. This means that we would finally arrive at precisely that situation which furnishes the point of departure as well as the theoretical validity of the magico-social system that we have analyzed.

If this analysis is correct, we must see magical behavior as the response to a situation which is revealed to the mind through emotional manifestations, but whose essence is intellectual. For only the history of the symbolic function can allow us to understand the intellectual condition of man, in which the universe is never charged with sufficient meaning and in which the mind always has more meanings available than there are objects to which to relate them. Torn between these two systems of reference—the signifying and the signified—man asks magical thinking to provide him with a new system of reference, within which the thus-far contradictory elements can be integrated. But we know that this system is built at the expense of the progress of knowledge, which would have required us to retain only one of the two previous systems and to refine it to the point where it absorbed the other. This point is still far off. We must not permit the individual, whether normal or neurotic, to repeat this collective misadventure. The study of the mentally sick individual has shown us that all persons are more or less oriented toward contradictory systems and suffer from the resulting conflict; but the fact that a certain form of integration is possible and effective practically is not enough to make it true, or to make us certain that the adaptation thus achieved does not constitute an absolute regression in relation to the previous conflict situation.

The reabsorption of a deviant specific synthesis, through its integration with the normal syntheses, into a general but arbitrary synthesis (aside from critical cases where action is required) would represent a loss on all fronts. A body of elementary hypotheses can have a certain instrumental value for the practitioner without necessarily being recognized, in theoretical analysis, as the final image of reality and without necessarily linking the patient and the therapist in a kind of mystical communion which does not have the same meaning for both parties and which only ends by reducing the treatment to a fabulation.

In the final analysis we could only expect this fabulation to be a language, whose function is to provide a socially authorized translation of phenomena whose deeper nature would become once again equally impenetrable to the group, the patient, and the healer.

3 MICHING MALLECHO,
THAT MEANS WITCHCRAFT

Laura Bohannan

THREE DAYS before I once again left Oxford for West Africa, conversation turned to the season at Stratford. 'You Americans,' said a friend, 'often have difficulty with Shakespeare; he was, after all, a very English poet, and one can easily misinterpret the universal by misunderstanding the particular.'

I protested that human nature is pretty much the same the whole world over; the general plot and motivation of the greater tragedies at least would always be clear—everywhere—though some details of custom might have to be explained and difficulties of translation might produce other slight changes. To end an argument we could not conclude, my friend gave me a copy of *Hamlet* to study in the African bush; it would, he hoped, lift my mind above its primitive surroundings and possibly I might, by prolonged meditation, achieve the grace of correct interpretation.

It was my second field trip to that African tribe, and I thought myself ready to live in one of its remote sections—an area difficult to cross even on foot. I eventually settled on the hillock of a very knowledgeable old man, the head of a homestead of some hundred and forty people, all of whom were either his close relatives or their wives and children. Like the other elders of the vicinity, the old man spent most of his time performing ceremonies seldom seen these days in the more accessible parts of the tribe. I was delighted. Soon there would be three months of enforced isolation and leisure, between the harvest just before the rising of the swamps and the clearing of new farms when the

Reprinted from *From the Third Programme* (edited by J. Morris), London, Nonesuch Press, 1956, by permission of the author.

water went down. Then, I thought, they would have even more time to perform ceremonies and explain them to me.

I was quite mistaken. Most of the ceremonies demanded the presence of elders from several homesteads. As the swamps rose, the old men found it too difficult to walk from one homestead to the next; the ceremonies gradually ceased. As the swamps rose even higher, all activities but one came to an end. The women brewed beer from maize and millet. Men, women and children sat on their hillocks and drank it.

People began to drink at dawn. By mid morning the whole homestead was singing, dancing and drumming. When it rained, people had to sit inside their huts: there they drank and sang or they drank and told stories. In any case, by noon or before, I had either to join the party or retire to my own hut and my books. 'One does not discuss serious matters when there is beer. Come, drink with us.' Since I lacked their capacity for the thick native beer, I spent more and more time with *Hamlet*.

Before the end of the second month, grace descended on me: I was quite sure that *Hamlet* had only one possible interpretation, and that one obvious universally.

Early every morning I used to call on the old man, in the hope of having some serious talk before the beer party, at his reception hut: a circle of posts supporting a thatched roof above a low mud wall to keep out wind and rain. One day I crawled through the low doorway and found most of the men of the homestead sitting huddled in their ragged cloths on stools, low plank beds and reclining chairs, warming themselves against the chill of the rain around a smoky fire. In the centre were three pots of beer. The party had started.

The old man greeted me cordially. 'Sit down and drink.' I accepted a large calabash full of beer, poured some into a small drinking gourd and tossed it down. Then I poured some more into the same gourd for the man second in seniority to my host before I handed my calabash over to a young man for further distribution. Important people shouldn't ladle beer themselves.

'It is better like this,' the old man looked at me approvingly and plucked at the thatch that had caught in my hair. 'You should sit and drink with us more often. Your servants tell me that when you are not with us, you sit inside your hut looking at a paper.'

The old man was acquainted with four kinds of 'papers': tax receipts, bride price receipts, court fee receipts and letters. The messenger who brought him letters from the chief used them mainly as a badge of office, for he always knew what was in them and *told* the old man. Personal letters for the few who had relatives in the government or mission stations were kept until someone went to a large market where there was a letter writer and reader. Since my arrival, letters were brought to me for the reading. A few men also brought me bride price receipts, privately, with requests to change the figures to a higher sum. I found moral arguments were of no avail since in-laws are fair game, and the technical hazards of forgery difficult to explain to an illiterate people. I did not wish them to think me silly enough to look at any such papers for days on end, and I hastily explained that my 'paper' was one of the 'things of long ago' of my country.

'Ah,' said the old man. 'Tell us.'

I protested that I was not a story teller. Story telling is a skilled art among them; their standards are high, the audiences critical and vocal in their criticism. I protested in vain. This morning they wanted to hear a story while they drank. They threatened to tell me no more stories until I told them one of mine. Finally, the old man promised that no one would criticize my style, 'for we know you are struggling with our language.' 'But,' put in one of the elders, 'you must explain what we do not understand, as we do, when we tell you our stories.' Suddenly realizing that here was my chance to prove *Hamlet* universally intelligible, I agreed.

The old man handed me some more beer to help me on with my story telling. Men filled their long wooden pipes and knocked coals from the fire to place in the pipe bowl; then, puffing contentedly, they sat back to listen. I began in the proper style, 'Not yesterday, not yesterday, but long ago, a thing occurred. One night three men were keeping watch outside the homestead of the great chief, when suddenly they saw the former chief approach them.'

'Why was he no longer their chief?'

'He was dead,' I explained. 'That is why they were troubled and afraid when they saw him.'

'Impossible,' began one of the elders, handing his pipe on to his neighbour, who interrupted. 'Of course it wasn't the dead chief; it was an omen sent by a witch. Go on.'

Slightly shaken, I continued. 'One of these three was a man who knew things'—the closest translation for scholar, but unfortunately it also meant witch. The second elder looked triumphantly at the first. 'So he spoke to the dead chief saying, "Tell us what we must do so you may rest in your grave," but the dead chief did not answer. He vanished, and they could see him no more. Then the man who knew things—his name was Horatio—said this event was the affair of the dead chief's son, Hamlet.'

There was a general shaking of heads round the circle. 'Had the dead chief no living brothers? Or was this son the chief?'

'No,' I replied. 'That is, he had one living brother who became the chief when the elder brother died.'

The old men muttered: such omens were matters for chiefs and elders, not for youngsters; no good could come of going behind a chief's back; obviously this Horatio was not a man who knew things.

'Yes, he was,' I insisted, shooing a chicken away from my beer. 'In our country the son is next to the father. The dead chief's younger brother had become the great chief. He had also married his elder brother's widow only about a month after the funeral.'

'He did well,' the old man beamed and announced to the others, 'I told you that if we knew more about Europeans, we would find they really were very like us. In our country also,' he added to me, 'the younger brother marries the elder brother's widow and becomes the father of his children. Now, if your uncle, who married your widowed mother, is your father's full brother, then he will be a real father to you. Did Hamlet's father and uncle have one mother?'

His question scarcely penetrated my mind; I was too upset and thrown too far off balance by having one of the most important elements of *Hamlet* knocked straight out of the picture. Rather uncertainly I said that I thought they had the same mother, but I wasn't sure; the story didn't say. The old man told me severely that these genealogical details made all the difference; when I got home I must ask the elders about it. He shouted out the door to one of his younger wives to bring his bag.

Determined to save what I could of the mother motif, I took a deep breath and began again. 'The son Hamlet was very sad because his mother had married again so quickly. There was no need for her to do so and it is our custom for a widow not to go to her next husband until she has mourned for two years.'

'Two years is too long,' objected the wife who had appeared with the old man's battered goatskin bag. 'Who will hoe your farms for you while you have no husband?'

'Hamlet,' I retorted without thinking, 'was old enough to hoe his mother's farms himself. There was no need for her to remarry.' No one looked convinced. I gave up. 'His mother and the great chief told Hamlet not to be sad, for the great chief himself would be a father to Hamlet. Furthermore, Hamlet would be the next chief: therefore he must stay there to learn the things of a chief. Hamlet agreed to remain, and all the rest went off to drink beer.'

While I paused, perplexed at how to render Hamlet's disgusted soliloquy to an audience convinced that Claudius and Gertrude had behaved in the best possible manner, one of the young men asked me who had married the other wives of the dead chief.

'He had no other wives,' I told him.

'But a chief must have many wives! How else can he brew beer and prepare food for all his guests?'

I said firmly that in our country even chiefs had only one wife, that they had servants to do their work and that they paid these servants from tax money.

It was better, they returned, for a chief to have many wives and sons who would help him hoe his farms and feed his people; then everyone loved the chief who gave much and took nothing; taxes were a bad thing.

I agreed with the last comment, but for the rest fell back on their favourite way of fobbing off my questions: 'That is the way it is done, so that is how we do it.'

I decided to skip the soliloquy. Even if Claudius was here thought quite right to marry his brother's widow, there remained the poison motif and I knew they would disapprove of fratricide. More hopefully I resumed, 'That night Hamlet kept watch with the three who had seen his dead father. The dead chief again appeared, and although the others were afraid Hamlet followed his dead father off to one side. When they were alone, Hamlet's dead father spoke. . . .'

'Omens can't talk,' the old man was emphatic.

'Hamlet's dead father wasn't an omen; seeing him might have been an omen, but he was not.' My audience looked as confused as I sounded. 'It *was* Hamlet's dead father. It was a thing we call a "ghost".' I had to use the English word, for unlike many of the neighbouring tribes, these people didn't believe in the survival after death of any individuating part of the personality.

'What is a "ghost"? An omen?'

'No, a "ghost" is someone who is dead but who walks around and can talk and people can hear him and see him but not touch him.'

They objected. 'One can touch zombies.'

'No, no! It was not a dead body the witches had animated to sacrifice and eat. No one else made Hamlet's dead father walk. He did it himself.'

'Dead men can't walk,' protested my audience as one man.

I was quite willing to compromise. 'A "ghost" is the dead man's shadow.'

But again they objected. 'Dead men cast no shadows.'

'They do in my country,' I snapped.

The old man quelled the babble of disbelief that arose immediately and told me with that insincere but courteous agreement one extends to the fancies of the young, ignorant and superstitious, 'No doubt in your country the dead can also walk without being zombies.' From the depths of his bag he produced a withered fragment of kola nut, bit off one end to show it wasn't poisoned, and handed me the rest as a peace offering.

'Anyhow,' I resumed, 'Hamlet's dead father said that his own brother, the one who became chief, had poisoned him. He wanted Hamlet to avenge him. Hamlet believed this in his heart, for he did not like his father's brother.' I took another swallow of beer. 'In the country of the great chief, living in the same homestead, for it was a very large one, was an important elder who was often with the chief to advise and help him. His name was Polonius, Hamlet was courting his daughter, but her father and her brother . . .' (I cast hastily about for some tribal analogy) '. . . warned her not to let Hamlet visit her when she was alone on her farm, for he would be a great chief and so could not marry her.'

'Why not?' asked the wife, who had settled down on the edge of the old man's chair. He frowned at her for asking stupid questions and growled his answer, 'They lived in the same homestead.'

'That was not the reason,' I informed them. 'Polonius was a stranger who lived in the homestead because he helped the chief, not because he was a relative.'

'Then why couldn't Hamlet marry her?'

'He could have,' I explained, 'but Polonius didn't think he would. After all, Hamlet was a man of great importance who ought to marry a chief's daughter, for in his country a man could have only one wife. Polonius was afraid that if Hamlet made love to his daughter, then no one else would give a high bride price for her.'

'That might be true,' remarked one of the shrewder elders, 'but a chief's son would give his mistress's father enough presents to more than make up the difference, and patronage. Polonius sounds like a fool to me.'

'Many people think he was,' I agreed. 'Meanwhile, Polonius sent his son Laertes off to Paris to learn the things of that country, for it was the homestead of a very great chief indeed. Because he was afraid that Laertes might waste a lot of money on beer and women and gambling, or get into trouble by fighting, he sent one of his servants to Paris secretly, to spy out what Laertes was doing. One day Hamlet came upon Polonius's daughter Ophelia. He behaved so oddly that he frightened her. Indeed'— I was fumbling for words to express the dubious quality of Hamlet's madness—'the chief and many others had also noticed that when Hamlet talked one could understand the words but not what they meant. Many people thought that he had become mad.' My audience suddenly became much more attentive. 'The great chief wanted to know what was wrong with Hamlet, so he sent for two of Hamlet's—age mates' (school friends would have taken long explanation) 'to talk to Hamlet and find out what troubled his heart. Hamlet, seeing that they had been bribed by the chief to betray him, told them nothing. Polonius however insisted that

Hamlet was mad simply because he had been forbidden to see Ophelia whom he loved.'

'Why,' inquired a bewildered voice, 'should anyone bewitch Hamlet on that account?'

'Bewitch him?'

'Yes, only witchcraft can make anyone mad, unless, of course, one sees the beings that lurk in the forest.'

I stopped being a story teller, pulled out my notebook and demanded to be told more about these two causes of madness. Even while they spoke and I jotted notes, I tried to calculate the effect of this new factor on the plot. Hamlet had not been exposed to the beings that lurk in the forests. Only his relatives in the male line could bewitch him. Barring relatives not mentioned by Shakespeare, it had to be Claudius who was attempting to harm him. And, of course, it was.

For the moment I staved off questions by saying that the great chief also refused to believe that Hamlet was mad for the love of Ophelia and nothing else. 'He was sure that something much more important was troubling Hamlet's heart.'

'Now Hamlet's age mates,' I continued, 'had brought with them a famous story teller. Hamlet decided to have this man tell the chief and all his homestead a story about a man who had poisoned his brother because he desired his brother's wife and wished to be chief himself. Hamlet was sure the great chief could not hear the story without making a sign if he was indeed guilty, and then he would discover whether his dead father had told him the truth.'

The old man interrupted, with deep cunning, 'Why should a father lie to his son?' he asked.

I hedged: 'Hamlet wasn't sure that it really was his dead father.' It was impossible to say anything, in that language, about devil-inspired visions.

'You mean,' he said, 'it actually was an *omen,* and he knew witches sometimes send false ones. Hamlet was a fool not to go to one skilled in reading omens and divining the truth in the first place. A man-who-sees-the-truth could have told him how his father died, if he really had been poisoned, and if there was witchcraft in it; then Hamlet could have called the elders to settle the matter.'

The shrewd elder ventured to disagree. 'Because his father's brother was a great chief, one-who-sees-the-truth might therefore have been afraid to tell it. I think it was for that reason that a friend of Hamlet's father—a witch and an elder—sent an omen so his friend's son would know. Was the omen true?'

'Yes,' I said, abandoning ghosts and the devil; a witch-sent omen it would have to be. 'It was true, for when the story teller was telling his tale before all the homestead, the great chief rose in fear. Afraid that Hamlet indeed knew his secret he planned to have him killed.'

The stage set of the next bit presented some difficulties of translation. I began cautiously. 'The great chief told Hamlet's mother to find out from her son what he knew. But because a woman's children are always first in her heart, he had the important elder Polonius hide behind a cloth that hung against the wall of Hamlet's mother's sleeping hut. He started to scold his mother for what she had done.'

There was a shocked murmur from everyone; a man should never scold his mother.

'She called out in fear, and Polonius moved behind the cloth. Shouting, "A rat!", Hamlet took his matchet and slashed through the cloth.' I paused for dramatic effect. 'He had killed Polonius!'

The old men looked at each other in supreme disgust. 'That Polonius truly was a fool and a man who knew nothing! What *child* would not know enough to shout, "It's me!"' With a pang I remembered: these people are ardent hunters, always armed with bow, arrow and matchet; at the first rustle in the grass, an arrow is aimed and ready; the hunter shouts 'Game!' If no human voice immediately answers, the arrow speeds on its way. Like a good hunter Hamlet had shouted, 'A rat!'

I rushed in to save Polonius's reputation. 'Polonius did speak. Hamlet heard him. But he thought it was the chief and wished to kill him to avenge his father. He had meant to kill him earlier that evening. . . .' I broke down, unable to describe to these pagans who had no belief in individual afterlife the difference between dying at one's prayers and dying 'unhousel'd, disappointed, unaneled'.

This time I had shocked my audience seriously. 'For a man to raise his hand against his father's brother and the one who has become his father—that is a terrible thing.' 'The elders ought to let such a man be bewitched.'

I nibbled at my kola nut in some perplexity, then pointed out that after all the man had killed Hamlet's father.

'No,' pronounced the old man, speaking less to me than to the young men sitting behind the elders. 'If your father's brother has killed your father, you must appeal to your father's age mates; *they* may avenge him. No man may use violence against his senior relatives.' Another thought struck him. 'But if his father's brother had indeed been wicked enough to bewitch Hamlet and make him mad . . . that would be a good story indeed, for it would be his own fault that Hamlet, being mad, no longer had any sense and thus was ready to kill his father's brother.'

There was a murmur of applause. *Hamlet* was again a good story to them, but it no longer seemed quite the same story to me. As I thought over the coming complications of plot and motive, I lost courage and decided to skim over dangerous ground quickly.

'The great chief,' I went on, 'was not sorry that Hamlet had killed Polonius. It gave him a reason to send Hamlet away, with his two treacherous age mates, with letters to a chief of a far country, saying that Hamlet should be killed. But Hamlet changed the writing on their papers, so that the chief killed his age mates instead.' I encountered a reproachful glare from one of the men whom I had told undetectable forgery was not merely immoral but beyond human skill. I looked the other way.

'Before Hamlet could return, Laertes came back for his father's funeral. The great chief told him Hamlet had killed Polonius. Laertes swore to kill Hamlet because of this, and because his sister Ophelia, hearing her father had been killed by the man she loved, went mad and drowned in the river.'

'Have you already forgotten what we told you?' The old man was reproachful. 'One cannot take vengeance on a madman; Hamlet killed Polonius in his madness. As for the girl, she not only went mad, she was drowned. Only witches can make people drown. Water itself can't hurt anything. It is merely something one drinks and bathes in.'

I began to get cross. 'If you don't like the story, I'll stop.'

The old man made soothing noises and himself poured me

some more beer. 'You tell the story well, and we are listening. But it is clear that the elders of your country have never told you what the story really means. No, don't interrupt! We believe you when you say your marriage customs are different, or your clothes and weapons. But people are the same everywhere; therefore, there are always witches and it is we, the elders, who know how witches work. We told you it was the great chief who wished to kill Hamlet, and now your own words have proved us right. Who were Ophelia's male relatives?'

'There were only her father and her brother.' *Hamlet* was clearly out of my hands.

'There must have been many more; this also you must ask of your elders when you get back to your country. From what you tell us, since Polonius was dead, it must have been Laertes who killed Ophelia, though I do not see the reason for it.'

We had emptied one pot of beer, and the old men argued the point with slightly tipsy interest. Finally one of them demanded of me, 'What did the servant of Polonius say on his return?'

With difficulty I recollected Reynaldo and his mission. 'I don't think he did return before Polonius was killed.'

'Listen,' said the elder, 'and I will tell you how it was and how your story will go, then you may tell me if I am right. Polonius knew his son would get into trouble, and so he did. He had many fines to pay for fighting, and debts from gambling. But he had only two ways of getting money quickly. One was to marry off his sister at once; but it is difficult to find a man who will marry a woman desired by the son of a chief. For if the chief's heir commits adultery with your wife, what can you do? Only a fool calls a case against a man who will someday be his judge. Therefore Laertes had to take the second way: he killed his sister by witchcraft, drowning her so he could secretly sell her body to the witches.'

I raised an objection. 'They found her body and they buried it. Indeed Laertes jumped into the grave to see his sister once more—so, you see, the body was truly there. Hamlet, who had just come back, jumped in after him.'

'What did I tell you?' The elder appealed to the others. 'Laertes was up to no good with his sister's body. Hamlet prevented him, because the chief's heir, like a chief, does not wish any other man to grow rich and powerful. He would be angry, because he would have killed his sister without benefit to himself. In our country he would try to kill Hamlet for that reason. Is this not what happened?'

'More or less,' I admitted. 'When the great chief found Hamlet was still alive, he encouraged Laertes to try to kill Hamlet and arranged a fight with matchets between them. In the fight both the young men were wounded to death. Hamlet's mother drank the poisoned beer that the chief meant for Hamlet in case he won the fight. When he saw his mother die of poison, Hamlet, dying, managed to kill his father's brother with his matchet.'

'You see, I was right!' exclaimed the elder.

'That was a very good story,' added the old man, 'and you told it with very few mistakes. There was just one more error, at the very end. The poison Hamlet's mother drank was obviously meant for the survivor of the fight, whichever it was. If Laertes had won, the great chief would have poisoned him, for no one would know that he arranged Hamlet's death; then, too, he need not fear Laertes's witchcraft: it takes a strong heart to kill one's only sister by witchcraft.

'Sometime,' concluded the old man, gathering his ragged toga about him, 'you must tell us some more stories of your country. We, who are elders, will instruct you in their true meaning, so that when you return to your own land your elders will see that you have not been sitting in the bush, but among those who know things and who have taught you wisdom.'

4 THE CONCEPT OF "BEWITCHING" IN LUGBARA

John Middleton

IN THIS PAPER I consider some Lugbara notions about witches, ghosts, and other agents who bring sickness to human beings. I do not discuss the relationship of these notions, and the behaviour associated with them, to the social structure. The two aspects, ideological and structural, are intimately connected, but it is possible to discuss them separately: on the one hand, to present the ideology as a system consistent within itself and, on the other, to show the way in which it is part of the total social system.[1] Here I attempt only the former.

The Lugbara live along the Nile–Congo divide, which forms a section of the political boundary between north-west Uganda and the north-east Belgian Congo. They number almost exactly a quarter of a million. They and the neighbouring Madi are the most easterly groups of a belt of related Sudanic-speaking peoples stretching from French Equatorial Africa through the south-west Sudan and northern Congo to Uganda. They are primarily agriculturists, living on the very fertile, open and almost treeless uplands of the Nile–Congo watershed. The population is very dense, being well over 200 to the square mile in many parts. Settlements are separated from each other by the many permanent streams or by small patches of bush. There are a few mountains

Reprinted from *Africa* 25(3), 1955: 252–60, by permission of the International African Institute.

[1] Field-work among the Lugbara was carried out between 1949 and 1952 with assistance from the Worshipful Company of Goldsmiths of the City of London and the British Colonial Social Science Research Council. A grant was also received, for the writing up of material, from the Wenner-Gren Foundation for Anthropological Research, New York. I make grateful acknowledgment to these bodies.

rising from the plains, and in most parts of the country one can see for many miles across thick settlement and cultivation. There is no centralized political authority. The largest independent groups in the indigenous organization consist of some 5,000 people only. These are territorial units, each based on a core supplied by a dominant agnatic clan; clans are segmented into lineages. The head of a cluster of cognatically related families—which I call the family cluster—is the *'ba wara,* or elder. Such a family cluster is the group of which a man considers himself a member in everyday affairs, and is the unit concerned in most political situations. It is based on a minimal lineage, the smallest named lineage segment and usually from three to five generations in depth. There is no higher indigenous authority than the elder.

It is not necessary to describe the Lugbara concepts of the soul, breath, shadow, spirit, spectre, and so on. Men and women who die having begotten or borne children are ancestors (*a'bi*). Sooner or later shrines are built for them by their descendants and they become ghosts (*ori*), the shrines being known as ghost-houses (*orijo*) or merely by the same term, *ori.* They live in the ground under the huts and also in the sky, and come into direct communication with their descendants by accepting offerings of meat, blood, and beer put for them in their shrines. They are aware of what their descendants do and think, or at least they are able to be so if they wish. There are many categories of ancestor (men, women, childless men, children, and so on) but I shall not describe them here; there are also many types of shrine. Lugbara see blood-relationship between ancestors and descendants as subsisting through both men and women, although it is agnatic descent which is the more significant, descent through women being forgotten after three or four generations.

The number of generations from the tribal hero-ancestors to the present living generation of elders is usually reckoned as between eight and thirteen. The first two or three ancestors are the founders of the larger groups and rarely affect the living by bringing sickness to them. It is the more recent ancestors who enter directly into their descendants' everyday lives, by bringing sickness. They do so in two ways: either they are invoked by their living descendants or they cause sickness on their own account without being invoked.

The head of a family cluster, an elder (*'ba wara*), has sacrificial rights in most of the ghost shrines of the group: he must perform certain rites and sacrifices. In particular he has a special shrine, in which are two very distant ghosts, which only he can visit and at which only he can sacrifice. These are not called *orijo* but by a number of terms which vary in different parts of Lugbara. I call them 'external' shrines, since they are always outside the homestead, whereas *orijo* are within the compounds. An elder has the power to invoke the ghosts to bring sickness to any of his dependants if they or their families or kin behave in a way which he thinks to be improper or dangerous to the well-being of the group. Dependants comprise his close agnatic kin, in particular those living in the family cluster of which he is the head, their wives, his wives, his sisters' children, and his daughters' children, who are all related by 'blood', as Lugbara see it. The last two categories are doubtfully included by many Lugbara, since, although they are related, they are not usually under the domestic authority of the elder and are not within the effective range of the founding ancestor's shrine, the external shrine, when sacrifices are made at it. Although a man may invoke his ghosts against a person living elsewhere (e.g. a sister's son), this is regarded as an insult to the head of the victim's own family cluster, who has general domestic and ritual authority over him. Besides these kin a man may invoke the ghosts against other kin who may be living in his family cluster (e.g. a wife's brother), or so it is said by some people, though others disagree; I know of no such case actually happening. Lugbara say that any man who has ghost shrines in his homestead (that is, whose father is dead), even if he is only a child, can invoke the ghosts against his kin, but it is usually an elder who is thought to do so. Women are said to invoke ghosts against their younger siblings, but this is rare. Most cases of invocation I know or have heard about were directed against a son who did not obey his father (the most common situation), against a wife married into the group who did not obey her husband and so brought strife among those who gave bridewealth for her, and against a woman married out of the group whose husband had defaulted on his bridewealth payments. Such a woman and her children are the only members of her husband's group who can be reached in this way by her father. Affinal obligations forbid any open hostility on the part of the husband towards her father, with whom quarrels are formally forbidden.

The invocation is made by the elder (or whoever is concerned) at his ghost shrines. Lugbara say 'he wails to the ghosts', *eri auwu oritia*, or 'he "bewitches" his son to the ghosts', *eri oritia mva erini ro olesi ra,* a phrase which I discuss below. He sits near the shrines and thinks the words in his mind so that the ghosts in their shrines, or more particularly one of them who takes his thoughts to heart, will be aware of the facts of the case. The particular ghost is left to judge of its seriousness and to see that the guilty person suffers sickness in due course. The elder should *think* the words: if he *says* them, if he 'whispers into the shrine', then the guilty person is likely to die. An elder will not threaten the victim with angry words. The duty of an elder is 'to be silent, to speak with few words'. Silence in the face of offence, or merely the words 'you will see me later' from an elder or kinsman of the same family cluster, are ominous and tantamount to a threat to invoke the ghosts. If the guilty person suspects this, he may make immediate reparation to the offended elder and so avert the threatened sickness; or he will wait until he is struck down and then consult oracles to make sure that invocation of the ghosts by the offended elder is in fact the cause. It then becomes known and publicly acknowledged that the elder has used his powers in this way. Sickness is removed by the elder calling the victim and the men of his kin-group to the shrines (the actual congregation varies in different situations, but details are irrelevant here); beer and, if the oracles have decreed it, a goat or other animal are offered to the ghosts. The elder explains the circumstances and blesses the victim with his spittle, using sacred leaves as a brush, to show that he has no anger left in him. All the senior men of the group do the same, to show that the breach in community well-being has been healed. No matter who was the invoker, the rite is carried out by the group's elder, since it is only he who can represent the group to the ghosts.

This process is considered to be ethically good and essential to the well-being of the community. Its purpose is 'to make the place clean, that the home may be well', *angu edezu, 'buru ma ovu alaru.* A man will not deny that he has invoked ancestral help if he has had good cause to do so. But he will usually hide the fact until the victim takes his case to the oracles; then he will admit his part and offer his justification. If the victim dies, then the elder's position is difficult since it means that he has misused his powers. I return to this point later.

The term given to the invocation of ghosts is *ole rozu* or *rozu olesi* (*-si* is the instrumental suffix). The threatening of the victim is *trizu,* 'to curse'; the process becomes *ole rozu* when the ghosts actually become involved, when they 'hear the words'. *Ole* is said by Lugbara to be the feeling aroused by watching a man eat good rich food, with succulent vegetables, without asking one to join in the meal. It is the feeling aroused by seeing another man dancing alone at a dance to show off his agility, at seeing another man surrounded by girls while one is alone, and so on. *Ro* is a verb (*-zu* is the infinitive suffix) used only in this and in one other context, which I shall now describe, and means something like 'bring sickness by mystical means' or 'bewitch'.

The same term, *ole rozu,* is used in connexion with the activity of witches, *oleu.*[2] Lugbara say that a witch brings sickness to a person towards whom he feels the sentiment of *ole,* either because he has been refused food by him or because he resents his worldly success, or because he has quarrelled with him for other reasons. He 'walks at night' and enters his victim's hut silently 'like a rat creeping over the wall'. Often he may take the form of an animal, especially of a leopard, wild cat, snake, jackal, owl, or screech monkey, or any other night animal or indeed any animal seen suspiciously near a hut or seen by the victim in a dream. Lugbara say that a dream is the vision seen by one's soul (*orindi*) which sees the souls of other people while their bodies remain in their huts in sleep. When a witch enters a hut in the form of an animal, this is his *orindi;* his everyday body is still in his hut. In some parts of Lugbara there is a very terrible form of witch who vomits blood on his victim's doorstep; in the morning the victim touches it and becomes sick. Or a witch may become visible as a light on the top of a hut, or as a light moving rapidly across fields, and it is a characteristic of all witches that they have a glowing light at their wrists and anus. They are said to be the same type of witch as those of the neighbouring and related Logo and

---

[2] Witches do not exist in actuality, but are only figures of belief. Here I discuss them as Lugbara do.

Keliko, to the west of Lugbara in the Congo, called *kule* or *kole,* who walk about upside down.

There are day witches, also called *oleu,* who walk about in the daytime spitting on children's heads: the children become sick and fade away. These men are always strangers to the area who behave as they do for some whim of their own. But any stranger is suspected of being a spitter of witchcraft: 'why else does he come here away from his own country?'

Oleu is used to refer to evil-eye men: *ole* can mean the evil eye or the power to harm people by the evil eye. You can tell an evil-eye man by his red or squinting eyes, or some other unusual facial feature, and by his grumpy greedy disposition. Since you can tell them by external signs you take care to behave carefully to them, always giving them beer or tobacco when they obviously want some. They are therefore not so greatly feared as are witches, for you cannot easily tell a witch and never know who may be one. It would seem that evil-eye men are those people whose physical appearance or personality corresponds in some way to the stereotype of a witch.

Another type of witch is the man who is envious of his neighbour's cattle. He uses various means to bewitch the cattle so that they weaken and die. The means include the use of cattle ropes stolen from the kraal. There is nothing that can be done: once the cattle are affected the witch is satisfied and has begun to bewitch those of others. Later he returns to console with kind words, but he is gleeful in his heart; he is unlikely to bewitch the same cattle twice. This process is also called *rozu olesi,* but in some ways it is similar to the work of sorcerers, who use medicines and poisons; they are distinguished in terminology from witches, and I do not propose to discuss them in this paper.

A man who sits alone and, above all, eats alone is always thought of as being a witch. Therefore witches usually pretend to be chatty and friendly to everyone. Lugbara say that if a man is always seen walking about greeting people in their homes then he is likely to be a witch: a witch would rarely sit alone at home all day because then people would think he was brooding over his wrongs and would know him to be a witch, so he simulates friendship as a bluff. Either of these extremes of behaviour is suspect. It is thought to be especially true that witches eat alone:

their motive (the sentiment of *ole*) is always primarily associated with food, with generosity in sharing food and beer, and envy in other situations is not so significant. I was often taken to be a witch since I conformed to both these extremes of behaviour, and was in addition a stranger, that is, without known kinship ties and therefore likely to have been expelled from a kin-group elsewhere for witchcraft.

Witches do not get their power from the possession of a witchcraft substance in their bodies. A witch is a witch because 'his heart is bad; it is his work to bewitch people', *eri ma asi onzi; e'yo erini 'ba rozu*. Details of the way he actually brings sickness or death are not understood. People say 'those are the words of witches. How should we other people know them?' The power to be a witch is not generally thought to be hereditary, but a son may follow his father's example and be taught by him. Since certain types of personality are thought to conform to that of a witch, and Lugbara recognize that a child may take after his father in personality, the son of a suspected witch is usually avoided for this reason. A witch can bewitch people both within and outside his own kin-group, but generally suspicions of witchcraft are directed against unrelated neighbours, or at least against those who are not closely related. The people who are feared as witches are especially old men and, in particular, lineage elders. As in the case of ghost invocation, silence or the words 'you will see me' or 'we shall see each other' are tantamount to a threat of bewitching if from an unrelated old man.

There are many ways of describing the behaviour of a witch in Lugbara. He is *oleu,* witch; *'ba oleberi,* a person with *ole; 'ba oleuru,* a witchlike person; *'ba 'ba ropiri,* a person who bewitches people; *'ba acipi eniberi,* a person who walks at night; and there are others. To 'bewitch' is *rozu, ole rozu,* or *rozu olesi,* the terms I have mentioned earlier in connexion with ghost invocation. If Lugbara are asked the meaning of *ole,* no conceptual reference being given, they will almost always say something like *'ole* is like this: a father cries to the ghosts that his son is bad and they hear his words and bring sickness to that man's son'. Occasionally they associate *ole* with the activity of witches or evil-eye men, but this is not so common.

The concept may be better understood if it is seen in its relationship to God. The Lugbara concept of God is of a God with two aspects. There is first *Adroa 'ba o'bapiri,* God the creator of men, also called *Adroa 'bua,* God in the sky. In the beginning of the world he created a man, a woman, and cattle, and it is he who takes away men in death. He is a transcendent deity who has final power over men, ancestors, and all other worldly beings. But he is far away and does not affect men in their everyday lives, except that he is liable to take them in death at any time. His will cannot be altered or influenced by sacrifice. Then there is the earthly aspect of God, called *Adro. Adro,* with his wives and children, lives in rivers; he appears in whirlwinds and can be heard crying in grass fires, especially those on the small hilltops so common in this country. But rivers are the principal places where he can be found. He is terrible and greatly feared. He takes people away and eats them, and sometimes it is he who is thought to take people in death. He can cause sickness to people who wander too near rivers at dusk and see or tread on him or his wives or children; he is especially associated with streams at dusk and in darkness. He takes possession of adolescent girls to give them the power of divination. He is described as being white or transparent and also as having only one leg and one arm, his head and his whole body being split downwards so that he is only half a man in form and terrible to see. I do not wish to discuss these concepts further here, except to emphasize that *Adro* is thought of as an inversion or opposite of *Adroa* in the sky. In fact Lugbara often distinguish between them as *Adroa onyiru* and *Adro onzi,* 'good' God and 'bad' God; 'good' and 'bad' are only very approximate translations.

Death is always thought of as being due to the intervention of God. An elder who *speaks* words into a shrine (that is, does not think them silently) and so brings death to one of his dependants is blamed not so much for having caused the death himself as for having given God the chance of thinking about carrying off that person in death. He would have done so at some time and in some other way, but the elder provided an opportunity. Not all opportunities for God to carry away a man in death are attributed to human agents, including witches. For example, if a man is killed by a buffalo Lugbara see no reason to suspect witchcraft: it was God who put the buffalo there and made him angry at that moment. A sudden unexpected sickness is usually due to the action of poison; but if it leads to death people say, 'if God didn't want him to die, why should a man offer him poison and why should he accept it?'

In the case of sickness of a type usually thought to have come from a ghost,[3] whether as a result of ghost invocation or other processes associated with the ghosts, the patient or his representative consults the oracles. If they confirm the cause of sickness, a promise is made that, if the sickness goes, the victim or his ritual guardian will make the appropriate sacrifice. If the oracle indicates a certain animal, that animal is led around the compound in which the shrines are, in order to 'show it'. It is then placed by the gate to urinate; if it does so quickly the man will get well; if not, then 'God refuses', thus showing that he has decided to take the man away in death and so it is futile to do more. The leading round the compound and the beast's urinating mean that it is dedicated to be sacrificed when the sick man is better. It is not sacrificed until then, because one never knows whether God will intervene and cause the man to die, in which case it is futile to cut the beast. God's will cannot be altered. But all these sicknesses brought by the ghosts are 'known' by the oracles, whose power is said to come from God.

Not all causes of sickness can be known by oracles. Some are self-evident and such cases are not put to them (e.g. venereal disease). Neither are sicknesses such as cerebro-spinal meningitis and other epidemics which regularly visit Lugbara. They are known to be caused by God through wind-spirits, and offerings are made at special shrines. Sickness of a type that is known usually to come from witches may be put to the oracles to make sure of its nature, but oracles cannot know witches individually as they can ghosts. They can only confirm that the sickness is so caused. Another significant difference between these sicknesses and those that are known by oracles is that the former cannot be cured by sacrifice or promise of sacrifice. Treatment for them is given by the *ojou* (doctor or diviner) and is given to effect the cure, not after the patient has recovered. *Ojou* also divine and

---

[3] Certain sicknesses, especially growing thin, are thought to be so caused, and other sicknesses have other specific causes. I cannot enlarge upon this point here.

cure sickness caused by poison and medicine given by sorcerers.[4]

Ojou means a doctor (from *ojoo*, a bulb with magical medical qualities) or a diviner who divines with a calabash. They are usually women, in High Lugbara at any rate. The power (*tali* or *ondua*) is given to a woman by *Adro* (the earthly aspect of God) through his possession of her when an adolescent girl. She runs into the bush and wanders about for several days without eating, often showing physical signs of possession. The power is inherited in the female line; by no means all women who have the power use it, but all have a shrine to *Adro* under the eaves of their huts. Diviners can divine the name of a witch or a sorcerer and in cases of sorcery can cure the sickness by magical and therapeutic means. The significance of diviners in this context is in their difference from oracles. Oracles are mechanical and get their power from God in the sky: the power is in the oracle and not in the operator. They can know ghosts and ghostly sickness. They are operated in public in the open air. Only men can operate an oracle, and any senior man can do so, although some are more proficient than others. Diviners are not mechanical in this sense, although they are mediums; their power is put into their hearts by *Adro*. They can also know the ancestors, but are rarely consulted in cases of ghostly sickness. On the other hand, they are always consulted in cases of witchcraft and sorcery and in other cases when the disease is not recognized or the victim cannot think of a possible agent who would ask the ghosts to bring sickness. They are also the only means by which sickness caused by witchcraft or sorcery can be cured. They are consulted in private and, when they divine, usually do so in the semi-darkness of a hut, although they may act as doctors in the open.

The two aspects of *ole rozu* together form a single concept or process in Lugbara thought. It contains both good and evil. What is normal is 'good', what is abnormal is 'bad'. The dichotomy is closely related to the distinction made by Lugbara between what is social and what is anti-social, a difference expressed in some

[4] I cannot discuss Lugbara sorcerers in this paper. They are of various types, all using medicines or poisons. This is the criterion: sorcerers use material medicines, witches do not. Lugbara distinguish between them in terminology, but say that sorcerers, like witches, are motivated by the feeling of *ole*.

contexts in terms of inversion, the possession of inverted attributes (see Middleton 1954).

A witch has the characteristics of an abnormal person. His face is grey and drawn, 'like a corpse', he may have red eyes or a squint, he may vomit blood, he walks at night, and is associated with night creatures (all of which are also thought of as being suitable ingredients for the poisons used by sorcerers, and all of which constitute *o'du,* evil omens, if they do not happen to be witches at work). His daily behaviour is either that of a solitary individual brooding over his wrongs or that of an over-jovial person friendly with everyone. Lugbara say that you cannot feel friendly towards everyone in your heart because it is the nature of man to feel anger, envy, greed, and so on, and also because you know there are many people who feel these emotions towards you and hate you in their hearts. Similar witches in other tribes present inverted attributes, such as walking on their hands. Witches are thought of in connexion with diviners, who are feared and considered to be uncanny and rather evil people. They are women, and connected with *Adro,* who is 'bad', an inversion of the 'good' God in the heavens who created men and women living in an orderly relationship. *Adro,* who is literally only half-human in form, is connected with the dark (as are the activities of diviners) and lives in the streams and patches of bush, the feared places which lie between the densely occupied human settlements. Even some of the physical characteristics of *Adro* are similar to those of a witch. The Lugbara stereotype of a witch is both a socially abnormal person and a personification of characteristics which people consider to be individualistic and anti-social and fear both in others and in themselves.[5] Lugbara consider that witchlike sentiments are in some way 'natural' to a human being; to be an acceptable member of society a man must canalize them into socially accepted patterns. The relationship between a witch and his victim is an individual one, not concerned with relationships based on kinship or status. The people called *atibo,* typically war captives or lone individuals who have come from

[5] Unfortunately it would take too long to show what are the sentiments thought to be socially desirable in a good member of society. They include behaviour that is 'slow', a lack of envy or greed or ambition, and others that are the opposite of sentiments said to motivate witches.

elsewhere and become clients to rich men, have no kin and are given kinship ties with their hosts when they become clients; they are almost always considered to be possible witches because of this fact and there are many sayings which refer to the connexion between *atibo* and witchcraft. Thus when outside society they may have 'natural' witchlike sentiments, which they control when they become members of society. It is significant that a victim makes no reparation to a witch, with whom it is thought, perhaps, that no social ties could be created or repaired in this way.

In contrast, the legally permitted and socially approved invocation of ghosts by old men, who are allowed and expected to do so as part of their role of leaders and protectors of society, is associated with all that is normal. Ghost invocation is restricted to punishment of a man's own kin and so is related directly to the formal order of society, whereas witchcraft is not so restricted and can reach anyone, whether related to the witch or not and whether of the witch's own territorial group or not. Ghostly sickness is seen by oracles, things made by God and operated in public by men. Ancestors and ghosts are 'good' as parts of a world created by God. Sacrifice to them is 'good': when a beast for sacrifice is led around the compound and urinates, people say that God accepts it (although the sacrifice is very definitely not to God but to the ghosts). A sacrifice must take place in sunny weather: if it rains or even grows dark during the rite, the sacrifice is futile and can have no effect. When an elder makes sacrifice, he first walks up and down the compound holding sacred grasses and telling the ghosts and assembled congregation the facts of the case. This is called *a'di* and is a vital part of the ritual. The concept of a social order, of peaceful relationships between men, is prominent in all *a'di,* and at the end the assembled men are always bidden to eat their share of the meat to show that there is no *ole* in their hearts, which would destroy the efficacy of the rite. Authority within the kin-group which is significant in everyday affairs, the family cluster, is held by the elder of the group. There is no higher authority. Although it is the sentiment of *ole* that is the motivation in both ghost invocation and witchcraft, the behaviour of a witch is anti-social because he usurps the authority of an elder. A man who is insulted should not take the law into his own hands but should delegate punishment of the offender to the offender's own elder, who can bring sickness upon him in the socially approved manner. The elder's feeling of *ole* is aroused by an action which causes a breach in normal social relations, which can be restored by a public rite of sacrifice; the witch's feeling of *ole* is selfish and individualistic, and is not related to a breach of formal relations of a kinship or status nature.

In a short article it is not possible to consider this process of *ole rozu* in its full social setting. Ghost invocation and witchcraft provide important sanctions for social behaviour; the significance of these sanctions cannot be appreciated without a consideration of other mystical means of causing sickness—ancestral vengeance, cursing, breaking of tabus, use of medicines and sorcery poisons, adverse public opinion, and so on—and also a study of the use of socially approved force. Here I have attempted only to show something of the nature of the Lugbara concept of *ole rozu* in an ideological setting without attempting to place it in any wider context.

5 NAGUAL, WITCH, AND
SORCERER IN A QUICHÉ VILLAGE

Benson Saler

O NE OF THE oldest war horses in the Middle Americanist's sta-
ble is a semantically skittish creature named Nagual. This
curious beast has a respectably ancient pedigree in the literature
on Middle America, references to it being encountered in early
Spanish historical and ecclesiastical writings (for bibliographies
see Brinton 1894 and Foster 1944). In the nineteenth century
"nagualism" excited—and to a significant extent was the product of
—the imaginations of Brasseur de Bourbourg (1859) and Brinton.
The latter, indeed, opined (Brinton 1894: 69) that "nagualism"

> was not merely the belief in a personal guardian spirit, as some
> have asserted; not merely a survival of fragments of the ancient
> heathenism, more or less diluted by Christian teachings, as others
> have maintained; but that above and beyond these, it was a power-
> ful secret organization, extending over a wide area, including
> members of different languages and varying culture, bound together
> by mystic rites, by necromantic powers and occult doctrines; but,
> more than all, by one intense emotion—hatred of the whites—and
> by one unalterable purpose—that of their destruction, and with them
> the annihilation of the government and religion which they had
> introduced.

Brinton's colorful conjectures with reference to "nagualism,"
along with certain other (if more pedestrian) notions on the subject, have been exploded by the scholarship of George Foster,
who demonstrates with ample documentation that "in Mexico
and Guatemala the word *nagualism* has been used as a convenient
container into which could be dumped a variety of magical beliefs

Reprinted from *Ethnology* 3 (3), 1964: 305–28, by permission of the author
and the editor, *Ethnology*.

and practices which among themselves show considerable variation and no necessary relationship" and that *"As a trait or complex, there is no such thing as nagualism"* (Foster 1944: 103;
italics his). Accepting an Aztec derivation for the word *nagual,*
Foster (1944: 89) is of the opinion that this term was originally
applied to the "transforming witch":

> The word appears to have spread to other south Mexican and
> Guatemalan languages, probably as the result of Aztec migrations
> that carried branches of this group as far as Nicaragua. The original
> application of the word to the transforming witch did not always re-
> main, for in this region it encountered another basic American
> concept, that of the guardian animal spirit or personal totem, to
> which it came to be applied.

Inasmuch as the words *tonal* and *nagual* are both Aztec in
origin, Foster (1944: 103) suggests that

> the logical procedure would be to use the former in the sense of fate
> or fortune, and the derived idea of the companion animal; *nagual,*
> in its original sense of the transforming witch, would be applied to
> those individuals believed capable of metamorphosis.

This suggestion has been accepted in principle by Kaplan (1956)
and Holland (1961), though with some necessary ethnographic
qualifications. Wagley (1949: 65n), however, has seen fit to reject it explicitly for the Mam of Santiago Chimaltenango, and a
number of other authors have in effect rejected it implicitly in
their ethnographic reports.

That the word *nagual* is assigned various meanings in the ethnographic literature is in large measure a direct consequence of
the fact that the diverse Indian groups which were the objects
of investigation themselves employ the term in different ways.
Thus, for example, while Lewis (1951: 279) tells us that among
the Nahuatl of Tepoztlán "The *Nagual* is a person who has the
power to change into an animal, such as a dog or pig," Nash
(1958: 71) writes of the Quiché of Cantel: "All know why four
crosses mark the entrances and exits of the municipio—that with
this symbol a *nawal* or guardian spirit keeps evil from entering the
village."

In broad and general terms, the kinds of meanings most frequently associated with *nagual* in the ethnographic literature can

be classed under two headings: the "companion" or "guardian" spirit and the "transforming witch." Some contemporary Middle American Indian populations may entertain beliefs about one or both of these constructs, whereas the belief systems of other groups do not incorporate notions about either. Some populations, while holding beliefs about "companion spirits" and/or "transforming witches," do not employ the term *nagual;* other Indian groups, however, do use that word. Furthermore, some populations make terminological distinctions between the "companion spirit" and the "transforming witch" while others, such as the Tzeltal of Amatenango (Nash 1960: 121–22), may not.

Basic to many beliefs in "companion" or "guardian" spirits in Middle America is the notion that the vital force and destiny of a human being are linked to some organic or inorganic object or natural phenomenon—the individual human being's *alter ego.* Should the *alter ego* suffer harm, it is widely believed, the individual whose destiny is linked to it is likely to suffer harm in corresponding degree. Among some populations the *alter ego* is known as a person's *nagual;* among other groups, however, terms other than *nagual* are applied to it in the local vocabularies. While the *alter ego* may sometimes be a natural phenomenon, such as wind or a comet (Wagley 1949: 65), it is most commonly reported to be an animal. Contingent on associated local beliefs, *nagual* in this sense, or some equivalent term in a given local vocabulary, has been variously translated as "guardian spirit" (Parsons 1936: 80; Wagley 1949: 65; Nash 1958: 71), "spirit-counterpart" (Siegel 1941: 70), "birth-spirit" or "birth-guardian" (Parsons 1936: 80), "soul-bearer" (La Farge and Byers 1931: 134), "companion spirit" (La Farge and Byers 1931: 134; La Farge 1947: 151–53), and "destiny animal" (Bunzel 1952: 274). Subject to local variation, there are diverse methods for determining a person's *alter ego,* insofar as it is believed possible to do so: the perception of some animal, object, or natural phenomenon under conditions or circumstances that are construed as unusual (Wagley 1949: 65–66; Bunzel 1952: 274); identifying the tracks of an animal in ashes or sand (Parsons 1936: 80); calendrical associations (Mendelson 1957: 398); and observation of the coincidental harm that befalls some object or animal and a given human being at roughly the same time (Wagley 1949: 66; Bunzel 1952: 274–75).

Basic to contemporary beliefs in "transforming witches" in Middle America is the presumption that certain human beings have the power to change themselves into various forms—usually infra-human animals. A common corollary belief holds that individuals who activate their powers of metamorphosis normally do so in order to accomplish sinister ends. Examination of only a small number of sources indicates that belief in transforming witches, whatever the local terms applied to them may be, is widespread in Mexico and Guatemala. It is found among such diverse peoples as the Nahuatl of Tepoztlán (Lewis 1951: 279–80), the Zapotec of Mitla (Parsons 1936: 80, 226–27), the Tzeltal of Amatenango (Nash 1960: 121–26), the Maya of Chan Kom (Redfield and Villa 1934: 178–79), the Mam of Todos Santos (Oakes 1951: 170–77), the Kanhobal of Santa Eulalia (La Farge 1947: 151–55), and the Tzutuhil of Santiago Atitlan (Mendelson 1957: 405).

The possibilities of ethnological misunderstanding arising from the fact that different populations which make use of the term *nagual* do so in different ways are exacerbated by the practice of some ethnographers in employing the term generically even where, properly speaking, the native vocabularies themselves may lack it. Villa (1947: 580), for example, utilizes *nagual* as a convenient synonym for the *lab* of the Oxchuc Tzeltal: ". . . certain spirits known as *lab* in the vernacular or *nagual* to the outsiders. . . ."

Because of the variety of applications of *nagual* in the ethnographic literature, any simple, parsimonious definition of the term would be problematical at best. Foster (1944: 103), in an effort to obviate further confusion in the literature, soundly advises that:

> The investigator should . . . always make clear what particular practices and beliefs are being described, and he should specify whether the words *nagual* and *tonal* are included in the native vocabulary, or whether he is applying them in the generic sense.

In my own field work[1] among the Quiché of Santiago El Palmar, I encountered conceptions approximating the ideas of both

[1] Field work in Guatemala, 1958–59, was supported by an Organization of American States Fellowship and a research grant from the Department of Anthropology of the University of Pennsylvania.

"companion spirit" and "transforming witch" given above. The Palmar Quiché make terminological and categorical distinctions among the companion spirit, witch, and sorcerer, and these distinctions are tacitly expressive of certain pervasive postulates in their world view. It is to the exposition of their conceptualizations of *nagual*, witch, and sorcerer that the remainder of this paper is addressed.

SANTIAGO EL PALMAR

The village or pueblo of Santiago El Palmar is the administrative center of the municipio of El Palmar, Department of Quezaltenango. Situated at an altitude of 2,788 feet above sea level, Santiago El Palmar is located in the coffee-producing piedmont of southwestern Guatemala. According to the official government census of 1950, the village contained 977 Indians and 113 Ladinos, while the population of the municipio as a whole was said to number 6,350 Indians and 2,159 Ladinos. Surrounding the relatively densely settled village are comparatively scattered dwellings in a sylvan setting (*los montes*) and farms (*las fincas*) mainly given over to the cultivation of coffee and bananas. The larger coffee farms, none of which is owned by Indians, contain fixed settlements of resident Indian and Ladino workers stemming from diverse areas of Guatemala. A substantial number of pueblo Indians, permanent village folk and inveterate agriculturists, find part-time or seasonal employment on the larger *fincas*. Even though many of the village Indians own and/or rent land which they work, a goodly number of the less prosperous among them deem it important to hire themselves out as wage laborers "in order," as several of them put it, "to earn our pennies."

The great majority of village Indians are Quiché who either trace their ancestry to nineteenth and twentieth century migrants from Momostenango, Department of Totonicapán, or are themselves migrants from that highland Quiché center (Saler 1962b). Momostenango is famous throughout Guatemala for the blankets its people weave. Momostecos, in addition, engage in widespread trade. But Momostenango has poor and limited land resources, and its inhabitants must import most of the corn and beans they consume (Tax 1947: 5). El Palmar was originally settled by

Momostecos who came to the piedmont in search of agricultural land.

With the development of intensive coffee cultivation in El Palmar in the latter part of the nineteenth century, and the further expansion of non-Indian land holdings in the twentieth, the Indians resident there have for the most part been losers in a power struggle over land. Concern over land has undoubtedly influenced culture change in Santiago El Palmar. Significant aspects of Indian acculturation in the last several decades partially represent Indian attempts to shield themselves from further manipulation by non-Indians. Thus many Indians express themselves in favor of education largely because "If a man can read and write, then he can have documents and people cannot deceive him." Similarly, political parties, foisted upon the Indians by Ladinos, are now regarded by growing numbers of Indians as instruments through which Indian goals and interests might be protected and served (Saler 1960). Devereux and Loeb (1943) have aptly termed acculturative responses of this sort "antagonistic acculturation."

As yet, however, the Indians are still egregiously subordinate in the municipio's power structure, as they themselves well know from a variety of negatively cathected experiences. That the traditional Indian way of life—including, of course, traditional Indian knowledge as manifested in habitual modes of action—has not sufficed to protect them from exploitation by Ladinos was at least intuitively grasped by most of my informants. Coupled with this awareness was a complex of ambivalent attitudes toward Ladinos; while Ladinos are generally disliked (and to some extent feared), the Indians at the same time accorded them a kind of backhanded admiration in keeping with their superordination in the power structure. Interestingly enough, Indian conceptions and attitudes relating to the ineffectuality of certain traditional means of action as a protection against manipulation, and their oblique respect for naked power, are subtly reflected in their religious beliefs, especially with reference to sorcery and witchcraft.

NAGUAL

The Quiché of Santiago El Palmar employ the term *nagual* in varying ways. The range of application of the term, insofar as I was able to trace it, may be subsumed under five categories.

(1) Several informants, when questioned as to the meaning of the term, reported that "some people" believe that there is an affinity between a human being and a single, living animal, which is the person's *nagual*. Integral to the assumed affinity between a person and his *nagual* is the belief that the character traits of the animal are likely to find an echo in those of the human being whose destiny is linked to it. Should, for instance, an individual's *nagual* be a *balam* (*tigre* in Spanish), the person is likely to be "brave," "outspoken," physically "strong" and adroit, and possibly even a bit "savage." It was also said that if a person's *nagual* were injured or killed, the person himself might suffer harm, but informants were vague as to the particulars and probabilities. No informant, however, went so far as to insist that the relationship between an individual and his *nagual* is such that harm to the latter must inevitably be mirrored in harm to the former.

Although several informants thus approximated in their reports the definitions of *nagual* as companion animal spirit encountered in the ethnographic literature, none appeared to subscribe seriously to this conceptualization. They maintained that *nagual* in this sense is a *creencia,* a belief that some people entertain and others do not. Yet while none of my informants seemed to give emphatic credence to the notion of a companion animal spirit, neither were they prepared to reject it entirely, to place it beyond the pale of the possible.

(2) Many informants associated the word *nagual* with the signs of the zodiac. Soon after a baby is born its parents, or some other relative, or, more rarely, non-kin friends of the parents, may search out the baby's birthday in an almanac or request someone to do it for them if they are illiterate. (A number of Indians own almanacs; those who do not can consult one in a neighbor's house or in the municipal building.) The almanac, thus utilized, reveals under which of the twelve signs of the zodiac the baby was born. The zodiacal sign is said to be the baby's *nagual* and to have some predictive value as to the character the baby may manifest as it develops. If the *nagual* is a bull (Taurus), the baby may grow into a person who is physically strong and resolute; if it is a balance (Libra), the baby may develop into a fickle person, etc. But while the zodiacal *nagual* is thus imbued with some value as a predictive device, it is far from being regarded as a pre-eminent and inevitable causal factor in the de-

velopment of personality dispositions. The Palmareños take cognizance of other determinants of personality, and they do not ascribe even major causality to the zodiacal *nagual*. As is the case with horoscopes elsewhere, correlations of an *ex post facto* nature are sometimes made, reinforcing the identification between prediction and actuality.

(3) Several informants referred the term *nagual* to that day of the 260 days in the Maya-Quiché calendar round on which a person was born. While recording a man's army experiences, for instance, his mother interrupted the narrative and said that her son was able to endure the rigors of army life "because his *nagual* is four horses" (*cuatro caballos*). That is, she went on to explain, her son had been born on the day *4 kiej*. Translating *kiej* as "horse," she maintained that her son had great strength—the strength, metaphorically speaking, of four horses. A calendar shaman with whom I discussed this particular case, however, found the woman's interpretation of *4 kiej* to be uninformed and unsophisticated. A person's *nagual*, the shaman asserted, is the day name of the day on which the person was born—not the day number. In the case under discussion, the man's *nagual* is *kiej*, but not *4 kiej*. *Kiej*, the shaman went on to point out, can be translated variously as "horse," "camel," or "deer," but this is not to say that the man's *nagual* is a real horse, camel, or deer. The day-name *nagual* signifies something; it is a symbol which must be interpreted in accordance with the canons of calendrical divination. *Kiej* is a day name especially associated with shamans; to be born on a day with this name suggests that one may become a shaman. But the day number of the day on which one was born must also be considered. The numbers, from one to thirteen, are held to represent a continuum, the lower numbers being "weak" and the higher ones "strong." For divinatory purposes, the weaker (i.e., the lower) the day number, the less probable are the implications in the day name; conversely, the stronger (i.e., the higher) the day number, the more probable is the interpretation of the day name. The calendar shaman interpreted *4 kiej* as follows: *kiej* suggests that the person might become a shaman, but *4* is a weak number, and consequently there is no great probability that the individual will actually become a shaman. With reference to the differing interpretations of *4 kiej* by the shaman

and the woman, the distinction made by Radin (1927, 1953) between "the thinker" and "the man of action" is possibly relevant.[2]

(4) An old woman, with whom I was discussing the saints,
spontaneously referred to St. James the Apostle, the patron saint
of El Palmar, as "the *nagual* of El Palmar." I questioned several
other people regarding this usage, and they all maintained that it
was acceptable, but I never heard anyone else employ the term
in this way.

(5) An Indian medium who is said to suffer possession by
the Earth Essence, "El Mundo" or "Santo Mundo," is known as
an *aj-nagual mesa,* which title I translate as "one who pertains
(*aj*) to the spiritual essence (*nagual*) of the Table (*mesa*)." The
medium allegedly becomes possessed while sitting at a consecrated wooden table (see Saler 1962a for further details), which
immediately suggests that El Mundo, the Earth Essence, is the
nagual of the table. In point of fact, however, *nagual mesa* is
best appreciated within a wider context. The calendar shaman
(*ajk'ij,* "one who pertains to the days") also employs the term
mesa, but in his case it does not mean a specific, consecrated
wooden table. For the shaman, the *mesa* of the World is any
place on which people burn copal to El Mundo, the Master of the
World and the spiritual essence of the material earth from which
man draws his food. And the *mesa* of a shaman is a special
power, symbolized by the possession of a wooden cross, which
distinguishes a minority of shamans "who have received the
mesa" from the majority who have not. The potsherd altars which
surround the village are the consecrated "burning places" or "tables" of El Mundo, and a shaman, when divining, will often
invoke the altars by name, in effect invoking their spiritual es-
sences to come to his aid. Since each altar is a material manifesta-
tion of the Holy World, El Mundo is the spiritual essence of each
altar. The shaman's conception of El Mundo as the spiritual essence of the material earth, and particularly of certain consecrated landmarks thereof, is paralleled by the contention of the
aj-nagual mesa that he receives the Earth Essence at the locus of a
consecrated wooden table.

As is apparent from the above, no single, simple lexical defi-

[2] I shall discuss Radin's distinction at some length in a monograph on
Palmar Quiché calendar shamanism now in preparation.

nition of *nagual* can approximate the total psychological reality of the term for all the Quiché of Santiago El Palmar. The term is employed in varying ways by different individuals, depending on context. Even an apparently idiosyncratic usage—the reference to St. James the Apostle as "the *nagual* of El Palmar"—was judged acceptable by my informants, presumably because it fell within the semantic range of tolerance with which the Palmareños have invested the term.

All the varying meanings, however, attest to certain pervasive themes and associated attitudes in the Quiché world view. In the first place, the Indians hold that there are a variety of extra-human forces at work in the cosmos which affect the unfolding life histories of human beings. Every man is under the influence of his special fate, and one may sometimes gain a predictive understanding of such influences from the zodiacal *nagual* or the Maya-Quiché day *nagual*. But human life is not exclusively shaped by extra-human forces. Man is not passive and without responsibility. Human and extra-human agencies interact in structuring the course of one's life. Some of the extra-human forces which influence human life are favorably disposed, or can sometimes be persuaded to be favorably disposed, toward individual persons. Thus the Earth Essence which possesses the *aj-nagual mesa,* according to those who believe in such possession, is held to possess the medium in order to help the latter's clients. The emphasis is on aid and assistance to the individual *qua* individual. But the woman who called St. James the Apostle "the *nagual* of El Palmar" seems to me to have generalized on this theme, extending it to the level of the societal. Just as the Earth Essence may favor and succor an individual, so, too, a patron saint may be supposed to favor and succor the community at large.

Though there are extra-human forces in the cosmos which may directly or indirectly influence human life, man lacks a perfect knowledge of them. It is a cardinal tenet in the Palmar Quiché world view that the universe and its principles of action are imperfectly understood. Knowledge is limited. *Hay algo más allá;* there is something beyond. Though one may doubt a mystery, a prudent person realizes the limits of his own understanding and does not doubt completely. It is probably only a "superstition" that you will suffer harm if some living animal whose destiny is allegedly linked to yours should suffer harm, but who can say so with certainty?

THE TRANSFORMING WITCH

Industriousness is a highly valued virtue in the normative system of the Palmar Quiché. A man should work to be materially secure (*por necesidad,* as several informants phrased it), to obtain for himself and his family such rewards as he can above the level of mere subsistence, and to receive the approbation of God and his fellow men. A person whose behavior is interpreted by others as manifesting a lack of proper respect for industry is likely to become an object of malicious gossip, and he may even be accused of possessing evil and preternatural powers. A hard worker, on the other hand, is likely to be admired, especially if he prospers materially and does not antagonize other people; a prudent person should neither boast of his accomplishments nor flaunt his wealth lest he excite the "envy" of others and thus become a candidate for black magic.

A person's industriousness or putative lack thereof, though by no means the only criterion by which others judge him, tends to be generalized by the Indians to betoken the presence or absence of other virtues. To accuse a person of being lazy, as in gossip, is to imply that he is remiss in his familial obligations, and such an accusation can be expanded to encompass charges of antisocial behavior of concern to the community. One such charge is that the individual in question may be a transforming witch.

The transforming witch, or *win,* is the polar opposite of the good man. He is at the same time a stereotype of loathsome evil and an example of the possible consequences of an indolent disposition. A *win* is a lazy and avaricious human being who magically metamorphosizes himself into an animal or bird at night and stealthily enters the houses of his sleeping neighbors to rob them of money and goods. In human form a transforming witch may be either an Indian or a Ladino, but he is characteristically conceived of as male rather than female. In animal form he may take sexual advantage of sleeping women—a heinous indignity since it combines bestiality and rape. He is also a malicious nuisance who interferes with the sleep of people fatigued from hard and virtuous labor by deliberately making noises near their homes at night.

A lazy and avaricious Indian or Ladino who desires to become a *win* is said to sleep for nine nights in the cemetery, where he prays to the Devil. On the ninth night the latter appears and engages the man in combat with machetes or swords. If the Devil succeeds in inflicting the first wound, the man will die within seven days. If, on the other hand, the man first wounds the Devil, the latter will confer on him the power to become a *win*. Thereafter he returns frequently to the cemetery to transform himself into his nonhuman form, to commune with the Devil, and to feast on the bones of the dead.

It is clear that a person becomes a *win* through his own deliberate initiative. My informants attributed the desire to achieve witchhood to laziness coupled with cupidity. On further questioning, they expressed mystification as to why the person was so indolent and grasping in the first place. They agreed that a *win* begins as a human being with some excessively grave character defect, but they were at a loss to explain from whence such a defect comes. When I asked if it might be predestined, perhaps through the agency of *nagual,* they treated the suggestion as something they themselves had not previously considered but would now ponder.

There are certain signs by which a person of discernment can recognize a *win*. In the form of an animal or bird, the transforming witch behaves in a manner alien to genuine members of the species, and any animal or bird encountered at night that acts in an unexpected manner can be suspected of being a *win*. It is also a suspicious circumstance if any animal or bird met at night appears unusually ugly for its species and/or has blazing red eyes. In human form, the transforming witch is reported to have bloodshot eyes, large and protruding canine teeth, sometimes a cross of lines or "letters that no one can read" on the skin of his upper torso, and, in addition, a propensity for sleeping rather than working during the daytime.

If one encounters a *win* in his nonhuman form, that which he assumes on his nefarious missions, his power to harm can allegedly be negated by reciting the "Our Father" nine times, especially if it is then repeated another nine times backwards (which no one I asked could do). In his nonhuman form a *win* cannot be killed with a gun, knife, or machete, but he can be beaten to death with a stick, kicked to death, or strangled with bare hands or a rope. Informants stated that it would be imprudent to kill a witch in his human form: "If I kill a person, the police will arrest me and put me in jail, but if I kill a dog or buzzard, it is not a murder."

I collected 54 drawings of transforming witches made by boys between the ages of seven and fifteen. Twenty of them depicted the *win* as birds, nine as dogs, five as human beings, and three as pigs; there were also one cat, one rooster, and fifteen creatures that I was unable to identify.

Every Indian whom I questioned on the subject claimed to believe in the existence of the *win,* regardless of differences in levels of acculturation. This unanimity is noteworthy in view of the fact that there was a certain amount of disagreement in Santiago El Palmar with respect to a number of other beliefs. Even the elder of one of the two small Protestant sects in the pueblo, a man who has enjoyed firsthand contacts with missionaries from the United States for several decades, appeared convinced of the reality of the *win.* "Your countrymen," he informed me, had told him repeatedly that witches do not exist, but in this the good missionaries were mistaken. Not only are there witches, but when he left the Catholic faith, gave up the practice of calendrical shamanism, and became a Protestant, transforming witches persecuted him by flying over his house for a number of nights to prevent him from sleeping. The local Secretary of the Revolutionary Party, a Seventh Day Adventist and a champion of agrarian reform, also believed in transforming witches; though he has never seen them, he has heard them at night. An Indian who teaches school on one of the coffee *fincas* reported that, when he was outside of his house one night, he was attacked by buzzards who swooped down on him and extinguished the flame of his candle; he was of the opinion that the buzzards were witches sent against him by his father-in-law, a shaman whom he accused of being a sorcerer and with whom he had had a long and acrimonious dispute over land.

Transforming witches may figure in an individual's self-evaluation. A person who fears them—or, better still, is attacked by them—can derive a measure of conscious comfort therefrom inasmuch as witches normally threaten or attack only virtuous persons. Thus to fear that one is the object of the malignant attentions of the *win* is in effect to reassure oneself as to one's own moral state. A case in point is the Protestant elder referred to above. He was one of the first Indians in the village to become a Protestant. In relating to me the events leading to his conversion, he spoke of his doubts about rejecting the old religion and embracing the new. He recognized that a sincere conversion would inevitably cut him off from many of the customs of his (Catholic) face-to-face group. Inasmuch as the referential dimensions of morality in his society are partially grounded in the traditional religion, the very thought of rejecting this religion precipitated anxiety. Once he had taken the step, indeed, he was subjected to the contempt and open threats of other Indians in the village. Anxieties stemming from these sources were reduced by a fervent identification with the new religion, reinforced by dreams in which God approved of his actions and demonstrated the falseness of the old religion, and by the "persecution" he suffered from witches, which he himself interpreted as additional proof that he trod the path of righteousness. Having already received the approbation of God, he found a further corroboration of his virtue from infernal powers.

The transforming witch, like many another image of evil discussed in the ethnographic literature, can be interpreted as a cultural formulation involved in processes of ego defense. With regard to the mechanism of projection, for instance, the *win* image can play a role in protecting an individual from the conscious awareness of his own proclivities to aggressive behavior and lack of industry. By attributing one's own antisocial tendencies to the transforming witch, hostility can be directed from the self to that object. The *win* is in a sense an ideal target for hostility. Because he transforms himself into a bird or animal, he in effect vitiates the human condition. Hence hostility to the witch is hostility toward something no longer fully human and thus does not directly challenge the cultural ideal of treating human beings with sympathy.

The *win* can also be considered with reference to the mechanism of displacement. Nash (1958: 78), writing about the Quiché of Cantel, gave it as his impression that "aggression is never very far from the surface. . . ." I formed the same impression with regard to the Quiché of Santiago El Palmar. Among the Palmareños, as among the Cantelenses, aggression is vented in a number of ways, some of the characteristic modalities being gossip, drunkenness, and litigation before the local justice of the peace over trivia. In addition, there are sometimes heated public quarrels among women occasioned by alleged adultery, failure to return borrowed objects, and real or imagined slights. These arguments infrequently degenerate into physical assaults. Interestingly enough, public quarrels and physical fights almost never occur among men unless they are drunk and therefore, in the Indian view, not responsible for their behavior. (In psychodynamic perspective, the greater public circumspection of men as contrasted to women may be related to the characteristic depiction of the witch as masculine rather than feminine.) While Indians of both sexes accurately characterize women in their society as being more overtly hostile than men, the cultural ideal is to contain one's hostility whatever one's sex. This ideal, however, is only imperfectly realized. In compensation for efforts to suppress overt hostility, aggressive tendencies find partial expression in being redirected from the objects and situations that stimulate them and displaced to an object of loathing, the *win.*

LOCALIZATION OF TRANSFORMING WITCHES

Where are transforming witches in their human form to be found? My informants showed a significant amount of individual variability in answering this question. Taken as a group, however, they exhibited a general disposition to localize witches along a diminishing continuum from out-group to in-group. To come to some understanding of these facts, it will be necessary first to consider the spatial dimension involved. Four geographically identifiable population entities are recognized by the Indians of Santiago El Palmar as of primary economic importance in their lives: (1) the pueblo, (2) the *montes,* and (3) the coffee *fincas* which together comprise the municipio of El Palmar, and (4) the Pacific coastal plain where many village Indians rent land

and go to raise corn. The highlands and their inhabitants are of less immediate economic importance to them.

The Pueblo

The village is a bicultural community; the Indians resident there live in face-to-face association with resident Ladinos. For our purposes, we shall refer to the Indians of the pueblo as the Indian community. Primarily of Momosteco descent, they characterize their group as being of the "race" (*raza*) of Momostenango. As such, the group is heir to a set of "customs" (*costumbres*) which its members regard as the legacy "of the race of Momostenango" and the distinctive cultural attributes of that "race." The *costumbres* operate as boundary-maintaining mechanisms, demarcating those who are entitled by descent to share them from those who are not. The few Indians resident in the village who do not trace their ancestry to Momostenango are also Quiché in speech and do not constitute a residential or economic isolate. Even though they may have married individuals of Momosteco descent, and may have taken over many of the local customs, they do not regard themselves as members "of the race of Momostenango," nor are they so regarded by those of Momosteco descent. The Indians account those Ladinos who are permanent residents of the village as belonging to "our pueblo," though they do not share "our customs," nor belong to "our race," nor speak "our language." (While very few Ladinos can speak more than a few words in Quiché, most Indians can carry on sustained conversations in Spanish.)

The Montes

The *montes* are areas in the municipio with relatively few inhabitants per unit of land and usually an abundance of vegetation, wild or cultivated. When a pueblo Indian refers to a place as "pure *monte*," and emphasizes the word "pure," he implies that the place in question is a veritable wilderness insofar as human habitation is concerned. In the main, the *montes* contain scattered families living on their own land. They may have neighbors within sight of their homes but usually not as close as a villager's neighbors. The inhabitants of the adjacent *montes* are mostly Indians who trace their ancestry to Momostenango. They use the facilities of the village, and a very few own properties there, but they dwell in comparatively rural surroundings.

To a greater or lesser degree, the village Indians share the following stereotypes of the *montes* population: Though predominantly Indian and of "our race," the *montes* people are less sophisticated than the Indians of the pueblo. They tend to be cruder, less sanitary, and more traditionally Indian in their family life than are we; they have less "civilization." Although many of us have relatives in the *montes,* and these are like us in many ways and share our customs, they are nonetheless not quite the same as us. It is hard for a girl of the pueblo when she marries a man of the *montes;* her mother-in-law treats her as a servant, and she must work without corn-grinding machines and other things that we have. The women in the *montes* care less how they dress because their neighbors do not live close to them. Most families in the *montes* do not have to worry about what people will think of them because no one knows what goes on in their houses. If a man in the *montes* beats his wife all the time, who will hear her scream? Because they live by themselves, the people in the *montes* are not as sociable as we. Everyone knows if we do something bad, but in the *montes* all kinds of things can happen and no one knows.

The Fincas

Although many pueblo Indians find employment on the coffee farms, most would not want to live on them as resident workers. Life on the *fincas* is negatively evaluated by the pueblo Indians in such stereotypes as the following: Life on the *fincas* is very sad. The people on the coffee farms do not own their own houses and land; everything is owned by the *patrón*. If the *patrón* does not like a field hand, the poor man is told to go; he has no house, no food, no money. It is better to have your own little house. On a coffee farm, a person's neighbors are not often his relatives or people from the same place. In one house lives a Momosteco, in another a person from Todos Santos, in another somebody from some place else. These people are always jealous of each other, always quarreling. The women have little work to do, so they gossip about their neighbors. All of this gossip is bad, and there is much envy, much sorcery. It is better to live in the pueblo, where the people are of the same race and do not hate each other.

The Coast

The pueblo Indians consider the Pacific coastal plain the worst of the four population groupings under consideration, and they associate it with negative stereotypes: The coast is a very good place for agriculture, and the people who live there are very rich, but they are also very outspoken. They do not much care for each other. If an Indian man of San Sebastián (Department of Retalhuleu) wants a girl but she does not want him, he makes magic to seduce her. That is their way; when they want something, they want it. The Ladinos of the coast are very rude. They are not like the Ladinos of (highland) Quezaltenango, where there are many lawyers. The Ladinos and Indians of the coast are always looking for money. If a poor person from El Palmar goes to the coast, they ask him, "Do you have any money?" If he says "No," they tell him not to bother them. There is much evil magic on the coast and many witches. The climate there is very bad; when we go there to make our *milpas,* we always come home sick. The people on the coast are accustomed to the climate, but we are not. The climate in El Palmar is better; it is not as hot. And the people of El Palmar are more friendly.

In terms of these stereotypes, the *fincas* and Pacific coast are decidedly unpleasant places, places where many evil people can be found. The *montes,* though not precisely evil, are relatively isolated and "uncivilized," and dark things can happen there. This is not to say that any of the regions is entirely evil; "in whatever place, there are good people, and there are bad people." For the most part, my informants did not voice blanket condemnations, but they did manifest a general agreement as to the relative ranking of each place in terms of sinister associations.

These stereotypes are paralleled in the assignment of localities to transforming witches. Seventeen adult informants were asked where witches in human form are found. Their replies are summarized in Table 1.

As indicated in Table 1, all seventeen informants maintained that there were "many" transforming witches in the Pacific coast. The coastal plain lies beyond the borders of the municipio of El

TABLE 1

Localization of Transforming Witches

Informant	Sex	Coast	*Fincas*	*Montes*	Pueblo
A	F	many	many	many	many
B	F	many	many	many	many
C	F	many	many	many	many
D	F	many	many	none	none
E	F	many	a few	none	none
F	M	many	many	many	many
G	M	many	a few	many	a few
H	M	many	a few	a few	a few
I	M	many	a few	a few	a few
J	M	many	a few	a few	none
K	M	many	a few	a few	none
L	M	many	a few	a few	none
M	M	many	a few	none	none
N	M	many	a few	none	none
O	M	many	none	none	none
P	M	many	none	none	none
Q	M	many	none	none	none

Palmar, and the Palmar Quiché perceive the coastal population as the out-group farthest removed from their own in-group, not only spatially but also in terms of the prevailing behavioral stereotypes. But what of the pueblo itself? This is the population grouping for which we might expect the informants to manifest the most intense solidarity feelings. Yet, while ten informants denied that there are witches among their neighbors of the pueblo, three asserted that there are "a few," and four stated that there are "many." How do we account for these differences? My analysis of the relevant data, though as yet incomplete, suggests a number of factors that should be taken into account. For heuristic purposes, I offer the following considerations:

(1) I do not pretend that my seventeen informants necessarily constitute a representative sample of the Quiché of Santiago El Palmar.

(2) I entertain the hypothesis that among my seventeen informants, differences in the localization of the transforming witch provide a crude index for measuring interpersonal differences in hostility directed toward the four population groupings. In other

words, the greater the number of witches declared to exist in a given population, the greater the hostility toward that population.

(3) I suspect that individuals who maintain that there are "many" witches in their own pueblo group have a greater need, largely in terms of self-justification, to perceive witches in their village than those individuals who assert that there are "few" or "no" witches in the pueblo.

(4) I am inclined to believe that those individuals who declared that there are witches in the pueblo have made a less satisfactory social adjustment to their face-to-face community than those who denied the presence of witches in the village. As partial support for this belief, I will limit myself to citing one very suggestive bit of evidence: There appears to be a high correlation between membership in large, patronymic kin groups and unwillingness to assert that there are many witches in the pueblo. The large, patronymic kin groups are quite important in the organization of interpersonal relationships in Santiago El Palmar, and individuals who are not connected to such groups are usually impoverished in their social intercourse. This fact seems relevant to an hypothesis advanced by Newcomb (1959: 199) concerning "the conditions under which hostile impulses develop into persistent attitudes":

> the likelihood that a persistently hostile attitude will develop varies with the degree to which the perceived interpersonal relationship remains autistic, its privacy maintained by some sort of barriers to communication.

THE SORCERER

The sorcerer (*ajitz*, "one who pertains to evil") is a person, characteristically depicted as a male Indian, who attempts to harm other individuals through magic. In other places, I was told, sorcerers are likely to be practitioners whose services are hired by others on a client basis, but local sorcerers, insofar as informants believed that such exist, were said to act primarily for themselves and to have few or no clients.

Unlike the transforming witch, the sorcerer's evil abilities do not derive from a covenant made with the Devil. A sorcerer is reputed to be a master of magical formulas and rites which he has learned from another sorcerer or from "books of magic" (occasionally described to me as "books of the Jews"). In point of fact, however, it is very doubtful that there is any formal instruction in sorcery, let alone manuals on the subject. Certain beliefs about the methodology of sorcery are widely held, and anyone who desires to try his hand at black magic has a number of common-knowledge instrumentalities upon which to draw. During the course of my field work, for instance, a young man from the *montes,* with the help of male friends, opened the grave of a Ladina in the cemetery, removed a few bones, and reburied them on land belonging to an Indian woman, with the objective, most informants said, of rendering the Indian woman witless to the point where she would sell her land cheaply. Unfortunately for the alleged sorcerer, however, he was seen in the act, apprehended by the Ladino police, and quickly removed to Quezaltenango, the departmental capital. The young man had been observed drinking before the event in question, and there was considerable discussion in the village after his arrest as to whether he was actually a sorcerer or merely a drunk who had been carried away momentarily by rum and cupidity. The fact that he had utilized a sorcery technique, I was told, did not necessarily mean that he was a "legitimate sorcerer."

A genuine as contrasted to a spurious sorcerer, apparently, is one who seriously and soberly performs a magical act against another human being. The commonest of such acts are doll burial, the exhumation and reburial of human remains, the burial of other objects (e.g., photographs, nail clippings, hair, or a piece of the clothing of the individual against whom the action is directed), prayers recited over copal fires or burning, black candles, and incantations delivered in the cemetery. In all cases, the act is believed to be potentially most effective if performed at night.

While a sorcerer may likewise be a transforming witch, informants did not think such an association was necessary or even likely. The two categories of evildoers are terminologically and conceptually distinct; "apart the *ajitz,* apart the *win.*" Interestingly enough, all the informants who maintained that there were "many" transforming witches in the village also asserted that there were at least some pueblo residents who might occasionally attempt sorcery, and all but one of the ten informants who declared that there were no witches in the village also said that there were no individuals in the village who would seriously attempt sorcery. Even those who thought that some of their neighbors might incline toward sorcery, however, were for the most part skeptical as to whether their magical actions would be successful.

COMPARISON OF THE WITCH AND THE SORCERER

Some of the relevant data for comparing the witch and the sorcerer are presented below in tabular form.

	Witch	*Sorcerer*
Motivations for initiating evil actions (in decreasing order of probability)	Material gain; revenge; envy; accommodating another evil being; sexual gratification. Coupled with the above is a sadistic satisfaction in the suffering of the virtuous.	Revenge; material gain; envy; sexual gratification; accommodating a client. Derivation of sadistic gratification from the suffering of the virtuous is not necessarily true of all sorcerers.
Objects against which evil action is likely to be taken (in decreasing order of probability)	Anyone (excluding members of the witch's families of orientation and procreation) who is virtuous and has something worth stealing; anyone (normally excluding members of the witch's family of procreation but including members of his family of orientation) who has offended the witch; anyone (probably excluding members of the witch's families of orientation and procreation) against whom a sorcerer or other evil being has enlisted the witch's aid; sleeping women (excluding those with whom a sexual relationship would be incestuous).	Someone (excluding members of his family of procreation but including members of his family of orientation) who has offended the sorcerer; someone (excluding members of his family of procreation but including members of his family of orientation) of whom he wishes to take material advantage; someone (excluding members of his family of procreation and his parents but including his siblings) who is wealthier, more industrious, more handsome, or in other ways more lucky and successful than himself; women who have rebuffed his sexual advances. The above refer to evil actions performed by the sorcerer on his own behalf.

	Witch	*Sorcerer*
Types of evil action likely to be attempted (in decreasing order of probability)	Nocturnal thievery; nocturnal annoying of victim (as by making noises near his house to keep him awake); nocturnal rape.	Murder by magic; rendering the victim (or some close kinsman of his) sick; rendering the victim witless or favorably disposed; very low probability of any attempt to harm the victim's crops or livestock.
Public vs. private nature of the attempted evil action	The witch, though he singles out specific victims, is perpetually and relentlessly at war with the society of the virtuous.	The sorcerer is normally at odds with a private person rather than the society at large.
Source of special capacity to accomplish evil	Power derived from a compact with the Devil.	Knowledge of special rites and formulas learned from other sorcerers, books, or common gossip.
Probability of accomplishing evil intentions	High.	Low.

The reader will note that the most probable offense of a witch is theft, whereas that most likely to be attempted by a sorcerer is magical homicide. Yet the witch is considered far more reprehensible and loathsome than the sorcerer. If we were to assume that the offender is judged exclusively by the character of his offense, we might conclude that the Palmar Quiché consider theft a greater offense than murder. This, however, is not the case, for all informants agreed that murder is more serious and reprehensible than theft. How then do we account for the differential evaluation of the witch and sorcerer? Why is the witch considered the more evil? Several factors seem to me of especial moment in formulating an adequate answer.

In the first place, the witch is a dramatic construct in the Palmar Quiché world view. He represents, among other things, an extreme in unsocialized egocentricity and a symbolic warning that antisocial proclivities, if allowed full rein, may result in a loathsome debasement of the human condition. He is, I believe, a cultural expression of the view that immoral man may, through perversity, even become non-man. Significantly, however, man cannot achieve the infra-human state solely by his own volition; he requires the help of an infernal power. In order to obtain such help, however, he must take the first positive action himself. Furthermore, he must defeat the Devil in combat, thus proving to satanic satisfaction that his human strength, resolve, and evil character are deserving of transmogrification to the infra-human state. The witch has obtained superhuman help, whereas the sorcerer has not. The witch is so evil and loathsome because, among other things, he transmogrifies the human condition. The sorcerer, though evil, still remains a man.

A second factor of consequence, I believe, revolves around the public-private distinction. The sorcerer singles out specific victims, as does the witch, but his canons of selection are likely to have a different focus. The sorcerer is usually motivated by personal feelings directed against specific individuals, some of whom may even, by local standards, be adjudged deserving of punishment because of their own immoral or imprudent actions. The intended victim is, in any case, his or his client's private enemy. The witch, on the other hand, is animated by a perverse delight in harming or harassing any person of virtue and is thus at war with society at large. From a social point of view his transgression is manifestly the greater.

The witch and the sorcerer may also be compared with respect to the likelihood of their accomplishing their respective sinister intentions. A witch is quite likely to succeed unless his potential victims counteract him by defensive maneuvers, e.g., hiding valuables that he might covet or reciting the paternoster. A person who attempts sorcery, however, is very likely to fail regardless of whether or not his intended victim takes defensive measures. The sorcerers of San Sebastián (Department of Retalhuleu) are said to be powerful, and those of Samayac (Department of Suchitepéquez)—that same "Zamayac" which Brasseur (1859: 823) and Brinton (1894: 36–37) cited as an ancient center of "nagualism" —are alleged to be very powerful indeed, but the Palmar Quiché do not accredit their own sorcerers or would-be sorcerers with much potency. Formerly, a number of informants related, Palmar sorcerers "knew much" and were powerful, but contemporary would-be sorcerers are deficient in the knowledge of powerful rites and spells and are therefore little to be feared. The witch, however, is feared because he depends not on traditional knowledge, which may become ineffectual with the passage of time, but on power granted him by the Devil.

KNOWLEDGE AND POWER

The cultural differences among Guatemalan Indian communities have been much noted by observers. They cannot be attributed to lack of contacts with Indians and Ladinos resident in other communities since these are usually fairly appreciable. Furthermore, the cultural exclusiveness of Indian communities, which most often takes the form of idiosyncratic variations on common themes, has been maintained in the face of a certain amount of diffusion. As Tax (1941: 31) has put it:

> The average Indian could no doubt write large fragments of the ethnography of half-a-dozen towns other than his own. Although occasionally scornful of the customs of other communities, he more frequently does not evaluate them. "That is their custom; it is all right for them," appears to be the most general attitude. To the Indians cultural differences between themselves and outsiders are as much to be expected as differences in kinds of trees. It would be inaccurate to say that the close contact and resultant knowledge on the part of one group of Indians of differences of culture among others have not resulted in some diffusion. Many cases of borrowing of crops and the techniques for growing them have been noted; when it is a matter of dollars and cents, the Indians do not ordinarily evidence conservatism; indeed, the free competition of individuals, each looking for a profitable enterprise, would discourage such conservatism. There also appears to be a fairly free interchange of folklore remedies and the like. But it is a curious kind of interchange, one that recognizes the local nature of culture.

In attempting to explain why such cultural distinctions have continued to exist, Tax (1941: 33) has drawn our attention to several factors, including "the impersonal character of social relations of all kinds, both within the community and between people of different communities." This, Tax (1941: 34–35) goes on to suggest, may also be considered a reason why the Indians "can continue indifferent to cultural diversities, even as such indifference makes possible the impersonal plane on which the social relations are maintained." Our understanding of the situation has been greatly enriched in recent years by the model and socio-historical analysis of "closed corporate peasant communities" provided by Eric Wolf (1955, 1957). Many of the Indian communities in the western highlands of Guatemala—and Tax was primarily concerned with these—fit or come close to fitting Wolf's model.

The closed corporate peasant community, as Wolf (1955: 456) describes it, "represents a bounded social system with clear-cut limits, in relations to both outsiders and insiders." There is strong communal sentiment against selling land to outsiders, and the community tends to be poor. "Hard work and poverty as well as behavior symbolic of these, such as going barefoot or wearing 'Indian' clothes . . . are extolled, and laziness and greed and behavior associated with these vices are denounced" (Wolf 1955: 459). Wolf (1955: 458) points out that

> The need to keep social relationships in equilibrium in order to maintain the steady state of the corporate community is internalized in the individual as strong conscious efforts to adhere to the traditional roles, roles which were successful in maintaining the steady state in the past. Hence there appears a strong tendency on the social psychological level to stress "uninterrupted routine practice of traditional patterns". . . . Such a psychological emphasis would tend to act against overt expressions of individual autonomy, and set up in individuals strong fears against being thrown out of equilibrium. . . .

Significantly, the closed corporate peasant community is typically located on "marginal land." "Needs within the larger society which might compel the absorption and exploitation of this land are weak or absent, and the existing level of technology and transportation may make such absorption difficult" (Wolf 1955: 457).

Does the Indian community of Santiago El Palmar fit Wolf's model? Some 40 or 50 years ago, insofar as the recollections of elderly informants provided me with relevant information, the community appears closely to have approximated the configuration described by Wolf. But since that time, as I have pointed out in some detail elsewhere (Saler 1960: 211–62), a number of the structural and situational elements defining the closed corporate peasant community have either disappeared or become significantly modified. Among the factors responsible for the erosion of the community's corporate character have been the expansion of non-Indian coffee *fincas* in the municipio—indicative of a reduction in the "marginality" of the municipio's land—and the increasing dependence of the Indians on the world market for coffee. Wages earned on the coffee farms are very important to the contemporary Indians. So, too, is the money a number of them obtain by selling coffee raised on their own land. When the world price of coffee drops, as it did during the period of my field work in 1958–59, the Indians receive less in both wages and sales. During my stay in Santiago El Palmar, the depressed price of coffee was reflected in a number of ways, two of the salient reactions being a decrease in expenditures for traditional ceremonials and a marked enhancement of anxiety.

Anxiety is an especially poignant factor among the Palmar Quiché in view of the competition between them and non-Indians over land. Not only do the Indians feel threatened by the expansionism of the coffee farmers (*finqueros*), but competition is all the more keen because of "progressive soil exhaustion, the ruination of previously fertile land by lava and ash as a result of the volcanic eruption of 1902, and an increase in the municipio's population" (Saler 1962b: 339). Many Indians now rent land on the Pacific coastal plain in order to grow what corn they need for themselves, but they would prefer not to have to do so.

The Indians are very well aware of the competition that exists between them and non-Indians. My informants frequently pointed out tracts of land now belonging to one *finca* or another and recounted their versions of how these tracts had become alienated from Indian ownership. I was told—and in part could see for myself—how Indians were manipulated by Ladinos.

As the municipio's land became less marginal in relation to the national economy, the traditional Indian way of life became less adaptive. New conditions engendered new threats to Indian security, and traditional modalities of behavior were not always sufficient to bear the load. While many of the traditional *costumbres* linger on today, though sometimes in markedly attenuated form, the Indians are becoming increasingly restive and less inclined to honor the customs of their fathers. There is a palpable but oblique retrenchment from traditional Indian knowledge which involves in part a quasi-romantic projection. It is said, for instance, that the sorcerers of old "knew much" and were powerful in consequence—traditional knowledge was once worth something—but their counterparts today "don't know much." It is not the traditional knowledge which is defective, asserted my informants, but rather the contemporary heirs of that knowledge. Their reasoning, however, impressed me as being as defensive as it was subtle.

Most of my informants did not voice a blanket condemnation of the old knowledge. To do so would not accord with the Indian predilection for prudence—for the same reason that informants would not dismiss as impossible or nonsensical the idea of *nagual* as companion animal spirit. Moreover, to dismiss out of hand the old knowledge and the traditional customs would represent too severe a rupture with historical consciousness in relation to their self-image. The Indians regard themselves as members of the special "race of Momostenango." Various situational factors impose limits on the rate of their acculturation (Saler 1960), and so, as it were, they are to a certain extent and for the time being stuck with being members of this "race." Furthermore, it is a cardinal premise in their metaphysics that one does not escape one's ontological status except under special and extreme circumstances. Hence, in their thinking, they must be what they are. But being a member of "the race of Momostenango" does not mean that one must do all of the things that the members of that "race" used to do. It means only that one identifies oneself as being heir to a particularized tradition. To ridicule that tradition in its entirety would therefore be both unnecessary and psychologically deleterious in that it would further place in jeopardy an already low self-image. Many Indians find partial relief by declaring that it is not the tradition that is deficient so much as it is the modern heirs of that tradition. At the same time, however, most do not advocate a return to the old traditions. They hold this to be impossible because much of the traditional knowledge has become debased or lost, because Indians today are held to be too corrupt, and because it would mean an even greater inferiority and vulnerability *vis-à-vis* the Ladinos.

While traditional knowledge is romanticized and, in masked

form, depreciated, power is respected. The Indians perceive
themselves to be relatively powerless and dependent in their inter-
actions with the agents and symbols of Ladino power. Characteristically enough, a number of Indians hope that their lot in life
will be bettered by a new national government—a government of
Ladinos, of course—which will be sympathetic to their interests
and promote agrarian reform.

Ultimate dependency on the national government is by no
means a recent development. Years ago, when the Indian community came closer to approximating Wolf's model of a closed
corporate peasant community than it does today, internal community affairs were to a great extent colored by the existence of
an oligarchy of elders known as *principales*. The *principales* were
not creative innovators so much as they were traditionalists who
sought to direct, in a traditional manner, those community affairs which revolved around the civil-religious hierarchy. While
the *principales* were men of great prestige within the Indian community, they were creatures of little power when a conflict of
interests arose between them and the Ladino authorities. They
apparently recognized this fact and sought to minimize friction
by identifying and ingratiating themselves with the Ladino powers
whom they could appeal to but could not control. They called
themselves *gobiernistas,* supporters of the national government.
As a contemporary Indian recalled it,

> The *principales* were always *gobiernistas*. It was not important what
> government. Whatever government, the *principales* supported it.
> When Cabrera was President, the *principales* said, "Long live
> Cabrera!" When Ubico was President, the *principales* said, "Long
> live Ubico!" When there was a revolution, the *principales* said,
> "Long live the Revolution!"

Silvert (1954: 2) has observed that, among rural Guatemalan
Indian populations in general, "their outwardly directed political
activity was managed by others." We could, I think, trace Indian
inferiority in Guatemalan power rankings back to the traumata
of the Conquest.

The Palmar Quiché impressed me as having realistically appreciated the facts of the socio-political situation. At the same
time that they regret their inferiority, and dislike Ladinos, they
are impressed by the greater power of the latter. Their realistic

understanding of the socio-political situation strikes me as having a distant analogy in their fantasy construct, the transforming witch. Just as they think that it will be necessary for an agency separate from and more powerful than the local community to intervene if there is to be a profound alteration in community life, so too, in the case of the witch, must an agency distinct from and more powerful than the individual intercede if the individual is to alter his ontological status. In this sense, I would interpret the witch as expressing indirectly, on the level of fantasy, the powerlessness and dependency the Indians experience on the level of socio-political reality.

CONCLUSION

My primary aim in this paper has been to describe Palmar Quiché beliefs about *nagual,* witch, and sorcerer and to relate those beliefs to certain assumptions in the Indian world view. As a secondary goal, I have attempted to relate those beliefs and assumptions to selected social realities of life in Santiago El Palmar. In the main, I believe that the elements of the belief system which I have described are congenial with, and to some extent even expressive of, those social factors I have chosen to stress. I do not, however, entertain the conviction that all elements of a belief system must necessarily be highly compatible with all elements of social reality. Nor do I think that we can predict belief systems from a knowledge of social structure, or social structure from a disembodied knowledge of belief systems. I do think, however, that in any viable society there must be an appreciable amount of correspondence between the two, although I have avoided in this paper any attempt to come to grips with the theoretical issues involved in a discussion of such correspondence.

To an extent, this paper represents a selective response to an assertion made by Wisdom (1952: 122), who, after identifying *nagual* as companion animal, went on to say that "Nagualism has by now got confused with the animal transformation of sorcerers and witches. It is relatively unimportant anywhere, and seems to be confined to Mexico and the Guatemalan highlands." I am not of the opinion that the beliefs usually subsumed under the rubric "nagualism" are "relatively unimportant anywhere."[3] Without embracing an extreme functionalism, I would say that beliefs of this sort are quite likely to be important if only because they exist. Though sometimes their meaning may be obscure and their importance oblique, it is the task of the anthropologist to penetrate the obscure and to appreciate the oblique.

[3] Among the studies demonstrating the importance of "nagualistic" beliefs in communities less acculturated than Santiago El Palmar, one of the most emphatic is that of Villa Rojas (1947), who indicates clearly how, among the Oxchuc Tzeltal, such beliefs relate to kinship and social control.

6 THE SOCIOLOGY OF SORCERY
IN A CENTRAL AFRICAN TRIBE

M. G. Marwick

THERE IS AN extensive literature on beliefs in sorcery and witchcraft, both as they occur in contemporary, non-literate societies and as they occurred historically in our own society. Although much of what has been written on the sociology of these two related fields of belief is not always explicit, it is possible to derive from the literature certain hypotheses that the writers at least seem to have at the backs of their minds, and in some instances put forward explicitly. What I propose to attempt in this paper is to present material I collected among the Northern Rhodesian Cewa[1] in such a form as to facilitate its being checked against these hypotheses.

I shall not try here to set out and develop the hypotheses explicit or implicit in the literature. Although I had them in mind when I collected and analyzed my Cewa case material, I feel that my main argument will be more intelligible in a short space if I simply describe the various social contexts in which beliefs in sorcery occur among the Cewa and, then, towards the end, try to sum up their common features, leaving the reader to judge the extent to which the generalizations that emerge agree with the formulated and unformulated propositions of those anthropologists, psychologists and historians who have written on witchcraft and sorcery. I am adopting this course, not in an attempt to fol-

Reprinted from *African Studies* 22 (1), 1963: 1–21, by permission of the author and the editor, *African Studies*.

[1] This paper was read at a meeting of the Royal Anthropological Institute in London on October 11, 1962, and presents the main argument of Marwick. My fieldwork was financed by the Colonial Social Science Research Council to whom I take this opportunity of recording my indebtedness.

low the methodologically questionable procedure of inducing generalizations from specific instances (see J. O. Wisdom 1952; R. A. Fisher 1935: 6 ff.), but rather as a means of making what I have to say more easily digestible.

I shall start, then, by summarizing the way of life and world of belief of the Northern Rhodesian Ceŵa; next, I shall present, in varying detail, the various social contexts in which suspicions of sorcery arise and in which accusations of sorcery are made; and I shall end by trying to abstract the elements common to such contexts.

The Ceŵa are a matrilineal Bantu-speaking people who live on the plateau where Northern Rhodesia, Nyasaland and Moçambique meet. About a million in number, they make up some two-thirds of the so-called Nyanja-speaking peoples and about a third of the African population of the area bounded by the Luaŋgwa in the north-west, the Zambezi in the south and lakes Nyasa, Ciuta and Cilwa in the east. The Nyanja-speaking peoples are descended from a tribe or federation of tribes, known as the Maravi, or Malaŵi, a name now familiar because of its association with the political party led by Dr Hastings Banda, himself a Nyasaland Ceŵa. Portuguese records from the early seventeenth century onwards refer to the Maravi as inhabiting the country between the Luaŋgwa in the north-west and the boundary of Portuguese Crown Lands on the left bank of the Zambezi in the south. Their modern descendants are in roughly the same area and are now differentiated into the Ceŵa (including the Cipeta and the Zimba) of the plateau, the Nyasa and Nyanja on the Lake, the Maŋanja in the Shire valley and other minor groups.

My field-work was carried out almost exclusively in Chief Kaŵaza's country in the south-west of Fort Jameson district, Northern Rhodesia, in the upper basin of the Kapoche river, whose waters reach the Zambezi via the Luia. Chief Kaŵaza, belonging to the Southern Ceŵa of Fort Jameson district, derived his authority from Undi, who, with his 'younger brother',[2] Cimwala, was sent to colonize the upper Kapoche basin by Kaloŋga,

---

[2] *Mphwace*, "his younger sibling of the same sex" (honorific plural, (w)aphwawo) may in some contexts mean any junior matrilineal male relative, and could include younger own brother, genealogically junior classificatory brother, sister's son, etc. See Figure 1.

who is believed to have led the Ceŵa away from the other Malaŵi peoples and parcelled out the country that they now occupy. Undi's modern descendant—who has the same name because succession to chieftainship (and lesser headmanship) involves name-inheritance—is now Paramount Chief of the Fort Jameson Ceŵa. Other chiefs deriving their titles directly or indirectly from Kaloŋga's subdivision include Mkanda and Mwase.

When, in 1831–32, the Monteiro expedition went from Tete to the Lunda capital on the Luapula and back, its deputy-commander and chronicler, Captain (later Major) Gamitto, made excellent ethnographic notes on the tribes through whose territories the expedition passed (Gamitto 1854, Chs. 1–4), including Mkanda's and Mwase's people, whom he called *Chevas,* and Undi's, whom he called *Maraves.* Today all three groups are known as Ceŵa.

By tradition the Ceŵa are shifting hoe-cultivators. They grow their staple crop, maize, on mounds under which they bury weeds and grass, thus ensuring effective drainage and weed control in the wet season, as well as compost for the coming year. They select their soils according to the vegetation growing on them, and adapt their methods, including the relationship between cultivation and fallow, and the size of mounds, to the particular type chosen. In the last forty or fifty years, they have acquired cattle in considerable numbers, but, lacking traditional precedents regarding their ownership and control, they have found them in many ways a disturbing element in their culture.

Ceŵa villages are larger than those of neighbouring peoples, those in Kaŵaza's chiefdom having an average population of about a hundred persons. For the sake of drainage in the wet season, they are usually situated on the low ridges found in their slightly undulating country, the general monotony of which is occasionally relieved by granitic outcrops. Huts have plastered pole walls and thatched roofs. Most of them are round, though some are rectangular. In addition to huts, there are receptacles for storing maize and other crops, as well as pens for poultry, small-stock and cattle. Larger trees have generally been left, and provide shade in which women can sing and gossip as they pound maize and perform other household tasks, and where men, under a favourite tree, can discuss the affairs of state while they idly whittle or work at a productive hobby such as making baskets or reed mats.

Both men and women hoe in the gardens. Many larger tasks to be completed in a hurry, such as clearing the bush for new cultivation, or weeding a garden in danger of having its crop ruined by weeds and grass, are performed by co-operative working parties at which the traditional entertainment is beer. Although all Ceŵa are dependent on subsistence cultivation, some of them pursue specialist crafts in their spare time. Some women are potters; and some men, smiths, woodworkers and diviners. In modern times it is usual for between fifty and sixty per cent of taxable males to be away from the Reserve at work for wages. This has led to the substitution of money payments for many ceremonial gifts in kind, to an increased demand for consumer goods, especially cloth, soap and salt, and to problems such as whether property bought from the earnings of a labour migrant belongs to him or to his matrilineage. As a result partly of labour migration and partly of local developments in education, local government and the European tobacco industry, what might be called a middle class is emerging, with special tastes in clothes, houses and beverages.

Although, in terms of the available technology, the Ceŵa environment is a bountiful one, it is also one favourable to the vectors of serious diseases, such as malaria, hookworm, bilharzia, and intestinal disorders. This, taken together with poor knowledge of hygiene and a diet lacking in proteins and vitamins, results, as in other Northern Rhodesian rural areas, in an infant mortality rate of the order of 250 per 1,000 live births and a general death rate of about 30 per 1,000 of the *de jure* population (Central African Statistical Office 1952). The Ceŵa thus have one of the important ingredients in a system of beliefs in sorcery, a large number of misfortunes in need of explanation.

During the course of my field-work, I collected about two hundred cases of misfortunes, most of them deaths. I rejected a few because I had not recorded enough details about them, and I retained 194 for analysis. These give some idea of the types of beliefs in terms of which Ceŵa explain serious misfortunes. In twenty-five per cent of the cases, the misfortune was attributed to natural causes or 'deaths of God', such as the victim's suc-

TABLE I—Types of explanations offered for 194 cases of misfortunes
(mostly deaths) recorded during the course of field-work.

Type of Explanation Offered	Total	Percentage
1 Natural causes, '[acts] of God'	49	25.3
2 Acts of persons other than sorcerers:		17.0
vengeance for sorcery	11	
other acts, e.g. breach of taboo, use of property-protecting or anti-adultery magic, suicide	22	
3 Acts of sorcerers:		
sorcerers killed by own sorcery or by that of other sorcerers	6	55.1
non-sorcerers killed by sorcerers	101	
4 Acts of matrilineage spirits	5	2.6
	194	100.0

cumbing to recognizable disease, old age, or certain accidents that
were not believed to be associated with malign or sinister circumstances; in seventeen per cent, to the actions of persons
other than sorcerers, such as their breach of a taboo, their use of
legitimate property-protecting, anti-adultery or vengeance magic,
or the victim's suicide; in fifty-five per cent of cases, the misfortune was attributed to sorcery; and in three per cent, to the intervention of lineage spirits. Had my case material included minor
misfortunes, such as illnesses not likely to be fatal, their distribution in the four categories of explanations might well have been
different. In particular, there might have been a higher proportion falling into the last one.

The statistical tables to which I shall be referring in the course
of this paper are derived from the third category, misfortunes attributed to sorcery, but will take into account, not the full fifty-
five per cent, or 107 cases, but those of them, amounting to
fifty-two per cent, or 101 cases, in which sorcerers were believed
to have attacked non-sorcerers, i.e. I shall exclude cases in which
sorcerers were themselves the victim of their own or of other
people's sorcery.

To complete my hasty sketch of the background to the more
specific contexts of Cewa beliefs in sorcery that I shall be presenting, I should mention something of the prevalence of such
beliefs, of the extent to which they preoccupy people's minds,

and of their content, more particularly why I translate the Cewa term *nfiti* as 'sorcerer' and not as 'witch'.

Though objective measures are lacking, I would place the prevalence of beliefs in sorcery among the Cewa at close on 100 per cent. Preoccupation with these beliefs appears at first sight to be high, too; but there is a difference between people's general statements of belief and the beliefs that are implied in specific instances of misfortune attributed to sorcery. Thus, when one of my research assistants interviewed nineteen people individually and asked them to tell him how many out of twenty hypothetical deaths in a village would be the result of sorcery, their estimates ranged from sixteen to twenty, i.e. eighty to 100 per cent; but, as I have mentioned, of 194 cases of actual misfortunes recorded, only fifty-five per cent were ones in which sorcery was cited as the cause. Another rough measure of preoccupation is to be found in the frequency with which people seek protective treatment, such as having magical substances rubbed into incisions in the skin, or fortify their huts by weaving branches of the ordeal-poison tree into their walls before they are plastered. Such measures are often resorted to by those who have made economic advances, such as returning labour migrants and local businessmen.

As to the content of the beliefs, Cewa affirm that certain persons among them are mystical evil-doers, *nfiti* (sing. also *nfiti*). Although I have changed my mind more than once about the appropriate translation of this term, I have now come to the conclusion that it should be 'sorcerer-witch'; but that, for a convenient abbreviation, 'sorcerer' is closer than 'witch'. Briefly, my reasons are to be found in these comparisons of Cewa belief with the definitions that we owe to Evans-Pritchard (1937: 21):

1 Like sorcerers, all *nfiti* are powerless without material magical substances (*maŋkhwala*, no sing., sometimes inadequately translated as 'medicines').

2 Like sorcerers again, all *nfiti* are conscious of their actions, and most of them, designated as 'killers for malice' (*aphelanjilu*, sing. *mphelanjilu*), sixty-four per cent of my sample, are motivated by hatred and envy.

3 A minority of *nfiti*, twenty-five per cent of my sample, designated as 'real *nfiti*' (*nfiti zeni-zeni*, sing., *nfiti yeni-yeni*), are,

like witches, driven, not by malice, but by an addiction to eating human flesh, having been habituated to it in early childhood by a mother or grandmother who was an *nfiti*.

4 While the sex-ratio of all *nfiti* in my sample contradicts the expressed belief that most *nfiti* are women, 'killers-for-malice' have a higher masculinity than 'real *nfiti*', which gives the latter some resemblance to witches.

5 Some of an *nfiti's* actions are comprehensible, whereas others, designated as 'tricks' (*matseŋga*), are beyond human understanding; there is no suggestion, however, that the *mphelanjilu* is responsible for the former and the *nfiti yeni-yeni* for the latter.

Ceŵa hold sorcerers (as I shall now call them) responsible for a great variety of misfortunes: illness, death, loss of livestock to hyenas, lions and other familiars; loss of crops by their being enticed away by *nfumba* sorcery into the sorcerer's garden, or, at a later stage, into his granary; miscarriages and still-births; disturbed social relationships; and insanity. They believe that they can recognize sorcerers by their threatening and prophetic language; by their fatness from eating human flesh; by their red eyes from staying up all night; and by their having a vulture-like extra-sensory perception that enables them to know where a death has occurred in the neighbourhood before anyone else knows.

The techniques that sorcerers are believed to employ include: putting magical substances (*maŋkhwala*, into which category European poisons and medicines also fall) into their victim's food or beer; making concoctions that incorporate the intended victim's nail-parings, bodily excretions, etc.; and using these in lines (*mikhwekhwe*, sing., *mkhwekhwe*) drawn across paths to the accompaniment of an address to make them selective; attacking the victim while he is asleep; eating him while he is still alive, this being the Ceŵa interpretation of tropical ulcers; belonging to a necrophagous guild; flying around in flat winnowing baskets (*visese*, sing., *cisese*); and employing familiars, especially hyenas and owls.

The belief that sorcerers are necrophagous leads to elaborate precautions being taken whenever someone dies, including keeping his death secret until his corpse, the gravesite and the grave-

TABLE II—Types of sorcerers distributed: (1) By sex; and
(2) By whether or not a quarrel preceded the believed attack.

Classification of Sorcerer	(1) Sex			(2) Attack preceded by		
	Male	Female	Total	A quarrel	No quarrel	Total
'Killer-for-malice' (mphelanjilu)	43	21	64	64	1	65
'Real nfiti' (nfiti yeni-yeni)	11	14	25	6	19	25
Uncertain	4	7	11	2	8	10
	58	42	100	72	28	100
Sorcerer not identified			1			1
			101			101
Significance of association	$x^2 = 6.343$; $.05 > p > .02$			$x^2 = 64.560$; $p < .001$		

yard have been doctored; holding a vigil at the side of the grave
for two or three nights after the burial; and setting a gourdful of
magic to ensnare any sorcerers who may come when the grave-
watchers are not there.

The steps Ceŵa take to keep sorcerers at bay or to punish
them after they have killed or injured someone are: using charms
that act rather like electronic burglar alarms and, having thus
been aroused, hitting them with medicated hammers; killing them
at the graveyard by ramming a sharpened stick through the rec-
tum; detecting those that elude the grave-watchers by, traditionally, the poison ordeal and, more recently, by other methods
of divining and by periodic large-scale anti-sorcery campaigns
reminiscent of the witch-hunts of European history or of modern
McCarthyism.

Ceŵa have a clear insight into the relationship between social
tensions and believed instances of sorcery. They affirm that persons who have quarrelled 'practise sorcery against each other'.
Less often they assert that those who have quarrelled 'grasp
[i.e. accuse] each other [of] sorcery'. They maintain that matri-

lineal relatives are especially prone to practise sorcery against each other because, being unable to express their disagreements openly or to have them adjusted in the Chief's court, they develop smouldering hatreds that flare up in attacks by sorcery. They regard the matrilineage as the natural arena for quarrels over headmanship and property, and believe that a man's divided loyalties towards his children and his sisters' children may lead to quarrels culminating in sorcery.

The exceptions that they allow to the rule that sorcerers attack their matrikin are, firstly, that polygyny causes many deaths by sorcery because of the jealousies it arouses; and, secondly, that persons competing for the favour of a superior, such as a chief or, in modern times, an employer, practise sorcery against each other.

Ceŵa believe sorcery to be on the increase, and, though they attribute this mainly to the suppression of the poison ordeal, they nevertheless show much insight into the link between this belief and increasing social tensions. As causes of specific cases, they cite jealousy over newly acquired riches or over cattle, which, as I have mentioned, are a relatively new element in Ceŵa life.

Having presented an outline of the Ceŵa way of life and world of belief, I shall now describe the social contexts of believed instances of sorcery, and, as I do this, try to build up a picture, though inevitably an incomplete one, of Ceŵa social organization. I shall give more detailed attention to relationships between matrikin, since, as I have noted, this is a context of sorcery about which the Ceŵa themselves have a remarkable degree of insight. I shall deal more summarily with other contexts, such as relationships between spouses, co-wives, affines and unrelated persons. And, before trying to tie up loose ends, I shall make some brief reference to sorcery as a conservative moral force. Some of the contexts, such as matrilineal relationships, are positive, in the sense that they seem to encourage the formulation of tensions in terms of sorcery; others, such as marriage, are negative, in that they do not.

The basic social group among the Ceŵa is a matrilineage-remnant from three to four generations in depth, to which for convenience I shall refer as a matrilineage. This group is important in Ceŵa social organization as the core of the residential unit, as the setting for norms of prescribed behaviour among kinsmen, and as the unit that sues or is sued in the Chief's court.

As to social composition, a Ceŵa village consists typically of a number of kinship units, not necessarily related to one another, occupying the same site. These sections, as I shall call them, may be joined by various possible links. The village headman is the headman of the founding section, and the other sections may be linked to his through common matrilineal descent, common matriclanship or some other form of kinship, e.g. that involving a father-child link; or they may be unrelated to his section but associated with it as a result of historical accident or administrative decision, or simply because they like the headman or the village.

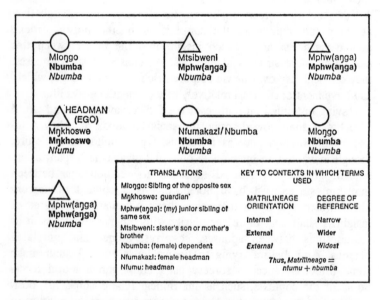

Fig. 1. The Unity of the Ceŵa Matrilineage Reflected in Kinship Terminology.

Each of these village sections has a matrilineal nucleus, consisting typically of the headman, his sisters, his sisters' children, his sisters' daughters' children—and so on. To this nucleus are appended the spouses of matrilineage members, the majority of them husbands, since marriage is predominantly uxorilocal, and the children of locally domiciled male members, these children belonging to the matrilineages of their mothers. Sometimes this general pattern is modified by there being a higher proportion than usual of virilocal marriages.

The relationship between leader and followers, better than any other aspect of its structure, throws light on the organization and the integration of the Ceŵa matrilineage. There is no word that Ceŵa use exclusively for the matrilineage as a whole, but there is a pair of terms which, when combined in a formula, make up the matrilineage, i.e. the headman and his dependants, *A nfumu ndi nbumba zawo,* this formula being applicable when the speaker's orientation is external to his matrilineage and when the term *nbumba* refers to all the headman's dependants and is not limited, as it is in narrower contexts, to his female dependants or even his sisters' daughters.

Like other human leaders, the Ceŵa headman has lieutenants, both male and female. As to the latter, in every generation, each woman of the matrilineage is the source, and in a sense the president (symbolic rather than executive) of her own group of uterine descendants within it—her children, her daughters' children, and so on. She is the 'ancestress' (*kholo*) of this group, which, since she has metaphorically suckled its members, is referred to as her 'breast' (*bele*). The status of her 'breast' or segment in the matrilineage as a whole depends on a number of circumstances. Firstly, the generation to which she belongs determines the depth of her segment and therefore its span. Secondly, her order of birth will make her segment senior or junior to that of her own sister, and the order of birth of her mother, her mother's mother, and so on, will determine the status of her segment in relation to those of her female collaterals of the same generation, such as her ortho-cousins. This genealogical seniority, depending on the birth-order of the ancestress herself or of her lineal ancestresses, is designated by saying that a segment is a 'big breast' (*bele lalikulu*) or a 'little breast' (*bele laliŋono*) in relation to any other segment of the same order with which it may be compared.

The Ceŵa succession rule is to the effect that matrilineage headmanship (which may coincide with chieftainship, village headmanship or section headmanship) should remain in the sen-

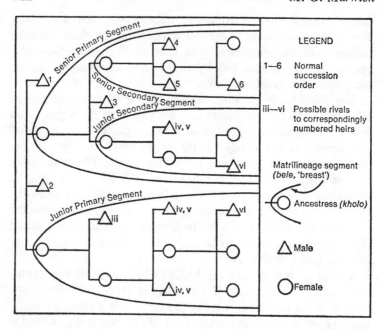

Fig. 2. Segmentation of the Ceŵa Matrilineage and Succession to
its Headmanship.

ior segment, or 'big breast' ('biggest' might be more precise, but
I am following the Ceŵa expression). In other words, a headman
should be succeeded, firstly, by his own (as opposed to classificatory) brothers, then by his eldest own sister's sons, in the
order of their birth; then by his eldest own sister's eldest daughter's sons, in their order of their birth, and so on. However, it is
important to note that the succession rule is often disregarded
when a genealogically junior candidate is believed to have personal qualifications superior to those of a senior rival.

Because the headman's female lieutenants are, as Fortes would
put it (1945: 32), the growing points of the matrilineage, their
'breasts' or segments tend to form the units into which the matrilineage differentiates as it expands. This brings us to the headman's male lieutenants; for the tendency for the matrilineage to
divide and for each separated segment to seek its own destiny is
encouraged by the fact that these men are distributed in the

various segments and that they have ambitions to lead. Every man is the 'guardian' (*mŋkhoswe*) of his own sisters, younger brothers and sisters' children; and to him the headman, who in this context is referred to as the 'senior guardian' (*mŋkhoswe wamkulu*), delegates some of his responsibilities, especially those relating to marriage and to consulting diviners about dependants' illnesses. In this delegation of authority lie the germs of fission.

It is matrilineage segmentation that provides one of the most important contexts for beliefs in sorcery. As the matrilineage grows and becomes unmanageable in terms of ecology and leadership, it divides, usually along its natural planes of cleavage, those between segments. Beliefs in sorcery express this inevitable but nevertheless disturbing process in that they provide a means of formulating tensions between the segments. In terms of the hypothesis I put forward in 1952 (Marwick 1952: 232–33 *et passim*), Ceŵa beliefs in sorcery are, *inter alia*, catalytic to the normal process of matrilineage segmentation in that they are a means by which redundant, insupportable relationships, which through being close and personal cannot be quietly contracted out of, are dramatically blasted away.

Tensions between segments, which may be expressed in the form of rivalry between groups, or more specifically between their leaders, pass through two phases. So long as the matrilineage remains united, segment leaders compete for its over-all control; and accusations of sorcery have the function of discrediting rivals. Once division has started, segment leaders may abandon hope of ever achieving over-all control; and accusations of sorcery then have the function of accelerating and justifying the incipient separation.

As we have seen, when a headman dies, he is succeeded in turn by his surviving younger own brothers; and, when the last of these dies, by his eldest own sister's eldest son, i.e. by the genealogically senior male member of the first descending generation. The first phase, that of rivalry for over-all leadership while the unity of the matrilineage persists, may start at any point in the succession sequence, but it is especially likely to begin on the death of the last surviving brother of the original headman. Since the succession rule may be disregarded on grounds of personal qualification or disqualification, this event may throw the

men of the first descending generation into competition. Each of
them stands a chance of succeeding if he can demonstrate his
qualities of leadership and if he can discredit his more important rivals. The virtually irreconcilable conflict of rights and interests between rival candidates, together with the fact that
headmanship is a highly valued goal, creates tension; and this
tension cannot be contained or resolved for two reasons. Firstly,
the judicial process cannot be applied to the settlement of the issue because the contestants belong to the same matrilineage. Secondly, a competitor may find an accusation of sorcery a more
effective way of discrediting a rival than any other available to
him. In these circumstances, a high incidence of accusations may
be expected between male matrilineal parallel cousins, i.e. male
ortho-cousins in this matrilineal society.

Once the headmanship has left the headman's contemporary
generation and passed to the first descending one, the second
phase begins. Hitherto one of the men of the senior generation,
through not being a member of any of the primary segments
(assuming that the ancestress of the matrilineage is his sister),
has managed to keep the group together. He has done this by
being, to borrow a term from Fortes once more (1945: 224),
the keystone of the arch. Once he falls away, the fragmentation
of the matrilineage may proceed. The successful candidate in the
junior generation, even if he is in its senior segment, may find it
difficult to weld his followers together; and tension may develop
between the various segments, the leader of each perhaps abandoning hope of ever being over-all leader. The resulting separation may be punctuated by accusations of sorcery.

Here are two cases that provide simple illustrations of what
may occur in this context. Both are in what I have described as
the first phase. In the first case, genealogical seniority wins; and,
in the second, personal qualification, though this is believed to
have been nullified by sorcery.

Case No. 1   His Uncle's Bed

A Cewa chief, whom we shall call Kabambo, had no own sister's
son, and it was generally accepted that he would be succeeded
by a classificatory sister's son: Kasinda; so much so, that Kasinda
had been given the pre-succession name associated with the

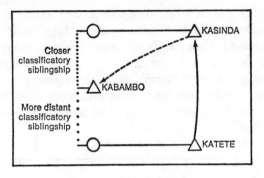

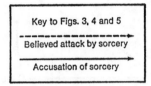

Fig. 3. His Uncle's Bed.

chieftainship. Kasinda was not, however, universally liked, and a more distantly related classificatory sister's son of Kabambo, whom we shall call Katete, who had gained an enviable reputation as an arbitrator of disputes, was regarded as a possible alternative. When, at an advanced age, Kabambo died, Katete, claiming that the old man had made a death-bed statement to him, accused Kasinda of having killed him with sorcery, adding that he had penetrated Kabambo's strong magical defences by employing the unusual technique of committing adultery with one of Kabambo's wives, an avoidance partner, thus rendering his bed dangerous to its owner. Many people believed Katete's allegation, but, although it blocked Kasinda's succession for a long period, Kasinda eventually succeeded because of his closer genealogical relationship.

Case No. 2   A Disappointed Candidate's Revenge

Thilani was the rightful heir to a junior headmanship but was passed over in favour of Ziloni, who, though junior to him both

genealogically and in years, was popular and looked upon as a
more suitable candidate. Thilani quite openly—'as if he were
mad'—threatened Ziloni, saying, 'I shall kill you this year'. He
carried out his threat, so say those who heard him make it, by
putting 'medicines' into Ziloni's beer. Subsequently he was believed to have killed with sorcery his own mother and her sister,
the mother of Ziloni, both of whom had sided with Ziloni against
him.

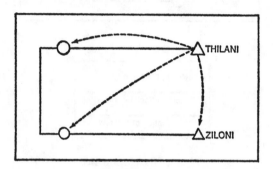

Fig. 4. A Disappointed Candidate's Revenge.

My third case illustrates what may happen in what I have
called the second phase, when, the matrilineage having started
to break up, an accusation has the function of justifying the
separation. This case does not, however, represent tensions between male ortho-cousins, but between a young headman, threatened with the diminution of his following, and one of his female
ortho-cousins belonging to a small group of women who lacked a
male guardian in their own segment and whom he wanted to live
in his section.

Case No. 3   The Diminished Following

A young married woman, Elena, had no brothers or mother's
brothers. She and her mother, Cimalo, had been living in Gombe's
village, to the headman's section of which they had long standing
ties of friendship, though not of kinship. Elena's mother's sister's
son, Galami, persuaded them to move to a village in which he
was headman of a small section. They were not, however, happy

there, and came back to Gombe's village. Their leaving Galami and thus diminishing his following led to a violent quarrel between him and Elena, during which she alleged, by way of excuse for leaving his section, that his wife was practising sorcery against her younger sister. Elena fell pregnant soon after their return from Galami's village-section, and feared that Galami had concocted,

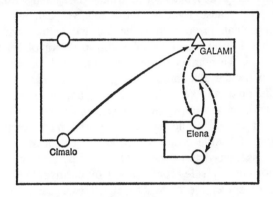

Fig. 5. The Diminished Following.

using soil on which she had urinated, a form of sorcery known as *kalamatila,* which makes child-birth difficult. When her time came, it was reported to me that she had been in labour for four days. I rushed her to the nearest mission hospital, but she died there of a ruptured uterus—probably the result, the doctor told me, of bearing down too hard, which I assume could have been caused by the fear that her classificatory brother's sorcery would prevent her from giving birth to her baby. The day after Elena's funeral, her mother, Cimalo, accused Galami of having killed her with sorcery.

To what extent is the function of beliefs in sorcery that these cases illustrate reflected in the statistics derived from summarizing the attributes of all the cases collected? The first column of Table III shows the distribution in relationship categories of believed attacks, i.e. sorcerer-victim coincidences; and the second, that of accusations, i.e. accuser-sorcerer coincidences. At first sight these two distributions seem to confirm the impression that believed attacks and accusations are more common between members of different matrilineage-segments than between members of the same segment. But such a conclusion may be the result of a reckless interpretation of statistics; for it involves a comparison of absolute numbers (even though transformed into percentages) and not of standardized rates. It does not eliminate the possibility that believed attacks and accusations of sorcery occur more frequently *between* matrilineage-segments than *within* them simply because Ego has more relatives belonging to segments other than his own than he has within his own. I must confess that I have failed to solve this problem of relating, on the one hand, the number of occasions on which persons belonging to a particular relationship category are brought together in the hostile dual role of sorcerer and victim or of accuser and sorcerer and, on the other, the universe of interaction characteristic of that category; and as a last resort I have compared the distribution of hostile accuser-sorcerer coincidences with that of affiliative accuser-victim ones. This comparison gives some, though not entirely safe, confirmation of the hypothesis that accusations of sorcery, even when related to accuser-victim relationships, are more frequent between segments than within them; for among members of the same segment there is a significantly larger proportion of accuser-victim than accuser-sorcerer coincidences; the opposite is true of members of different segments, though the percentage difference is not statistically significant.

What of the third sub-division of matrilineal relationships in Table III—ones in respect of which relative segment membership is indeterminate? This sub-category comprises very largely persons in the relationship of mother's brother and sister's son. It resembles that comprising members of the same segment in having a larger number—at the same level of statistical significance —of affiliative accuser-victim than of hostile accuser-sorcerer coincidences. This finding is somewhat at variance with the impression I formed, from what people said, of the considerable degree of tension between partners in this relationship. It is possible that, in the unsystematic collection of people's opinions, I heard more of their quarrels than of their quiet but faithful performance of avuncular and nepotal duties, such as those that an accuser performs for the victim whose cause he has espoused.

The table gives us leads for some very brief references to the

TABLE III—Links between: (1) Sorcerer and victim; (2) Accuser and sorcerer; and (3) Accuser and victim—distributed by relationship category (with full counting of 'multiple' cases*)

Type of Social Relationship	Percentage Distribution of Links between: (1) Sorcerer & Victim (N = 115)	(2) Accuser & Sorcerer (N = 112)	(3) Accuser and Victim (N = 90)	Difference (2) − (3) and its Significance†	Ratio (2)/(3) where Difference is Significant
Related:					
Matrilineally:					
same segment	17.4	13.4	33.3	−19.9‡‡‡	0.40
different segments	29.6	33.0	22.2	+10.8	—
segment indeterminate	11.3	3.6	22.2	−18.6‡‡‡	0.16
(a)	58.3	50.0	77.7	−27.7‡‡‡	0.64
Not matrilineally:					
spouses	5.2	1.8	4.4	− 2.6	—
co-wives, actual or potential	1.7	0.9	—	+ 0.9	—
other affines	11.3	31.2	8.9	+22.3‡‡‡	3.51
others	13.9	7.1	7.8	− 0.7	—
(b)	32.1	41.0	21.1	+19.9‡‡	1.95
Unrelated (c)	8.7	8.9	1.1	+ 7.8‡	8.05
Relationship unknown (d)	0.9	—	—	—	—
Total (a + b + c + d)	100	100	100	0	1.00

* i.e. cases in which there were more than one sorcerer, victim or accuser.

† The code for statistical significance is as follows:—

Unmarked: $p > .05$

‡: $.05 > p > .01$

‡‡: $.01 > p > .001$

‡‡‡: $p < .001$

other contexts of sorcery. It does not confirm the Ceŵa dictum that polygyny is an important cause of friction leading to sorcery, since the proportions of co-wives, or even of spouses, linked as sorcerers and victims or as accusers and sorcerers are very small. It shows, too, that both believed attacks and accusations between unrelated persons make up less than ten per cent, but that this small proportion of hostile links is still significantly higher than that of affiliative accuser-victim coincidences in this sub-category.

What is it that accounts for the low frequency of believed attacks or of accusations between spouses, even though polygyny may be involved? The main characteristics of Ceŵa marriage are that it is, initially at least, uxorilocal; and, while the movement involved in it is asymmetrical, in that the husband goes to live with his wife's matrilineage, he is not incorporated into it as a bride is incorporated into her husband's patrilineage among the Zulu. Since the system is matrilineal, there is no need to ensure by means of bride-wealth that the children of the marriage will belong to their father's descent group, and marital stability as a by-product of bride-wealth is lacking. In one of my samples, Barnes's Ratio B (1949: 44–45) was seventy-three per cent, i.e. seventy-three per cent of completed marriages had ended in divorce; twenty-seven per cent, in death, a divorce rate about three times that of modern Americans and about five times that of South African whites.[3] Thus easy and frequent divorce may account for the low incidence of believed attacks and accusations of sorcery between spouses. If tension develops between them, they can easily part before it reaches a dangerous level. Furthermore, the high divorce rate, far from being an index of social pathology as it might be regarded in Western society, is more likely a necessary condition for the high degree of integration of the effective social unit, the matrilineage; for any person faced with a conflict of loyalties towards his spouse and his matrilineage can usually resolve it by getting rid of his spouse. The Ceŵa have a type of social organization that Linton would have classified as consanguineal rather than conjugal (1936:

[3] Barnes (1949), Table III, cites some American rates comparable in method of computation but not in date; and those for South African whites (for the period 1938–44) are given in Union of South Africa 1913–44.

159), their social unit being a nucleus of blood relatives surrounded by a fringe of spouses, the fringe being, in the absence of bride-wealth with its consequent paternal rights, insecurely tacked on.

The discovery that nearly a third of accusations were between affines came as a surprise to me after I had noted in 1952 that, in a sample of twenty cases, there was not a single instance of either a believed attack or an accusation involving affines. While allowing for the possibility that a sample as small as twenty could have missed accusations or suspicions between affines, I suggested, in line with Radcliffe-Brown's analysis, that their incidence was low because, firstly, avoidance relationships would prevent the development of tension between affines of proximate generations, and, secondly, joking relationships would permit of the harmless discharge of tensions developing between affines of the same or of alternate generations (Marwick 1952: 227). With the extension of my sample of cases from twenty to 101, the proportion of accusations between affines rises from zero to thirty-one per cent, rendering the explanation I gave in 1952 unnecessary, and pointing to the dangers of generalizing from too few observations. The extended case material suggests that affinal relationships are so tense that the traditional circumscription of behaviour between affines, which is an important feature of Cewa social organization, is not adequate as a means of controlling hostility; and that this is expressed in accusations of sorcery. My cases indicate that attachment to a sibling, to a child or to a spouse may break down the barriers erected by the prescription of interaction between affines. Or, if the guilt of the sorcerer is clear because of something he said or did, an affine may be the one to formulate the accusation.

The rare instances in which unrelated persons accused each other of sorcery or were believed to have practised it against one another had a common thread, strong motivation. In virtually all of these cases a quarrel had preceded the believed attack or the accusation; and, though there were many instances of quarrels having preceded attacks and accusations between related persons, there was a statistically significant tendency for unrelated persons to have quarrelled over issues different from those over which related persons quarrelled. Of the two main issues, love and politics, that preceded believed attacks and accusations between unrelated persons, the following two cases provide illustrations:

Case No. 4 Revenge Taken Rather Far

Zechariah betrothed a girl and then went to work in Southern Rhodesia. After he had been there three years, the girl said, 'How's this? When he left me, I was but a child. Now I am a grown woman.

TABLE IV—Quarrels preceding: (1) Believed attacks; and (2) Accusations of sorcery.

Attack or Accusation Believed to be Linked with:	(1) *Sorcerer and Victim*			(2) *Accuser and Sorcerer*			
	Related	Un-related	Total	Related	Un-related	Relation-ship Unknown	Total
Quarrels over: social obligations, cattle and other property	31	1	32	29	0	10	39
other issues, including sexual jealousy and politics	32	8	40	23	9	8	40
No Quarrel	27	1	28	18	0	4	22
	90	10	100	70	9	22	101
Victim not identified			1				
			101				
Significance of association	$x^2 = 7.411$; $.05 > p > .02$			$x^2 = 15.626$; $.01 > p > .001$			

Now I'll form a liaison with a man'. This she proceeded to do, with Abelo. Zechariah received a letter from his sister in which she reported the infidelity of his betrothed; and he wrote back to her,

'How is it that my betrothed has taken up with Abelo? Did he not know that I had betrothed her? She will see [i.e. experience] something!' And he signed his letter with the drawing of a lion. After a month, lions came and took one of Abelo's beasts. Next day they caught another; and, the following day, yet another. But when the lions came to catch Abelo himself, they failed to get him, and went back again to Southern Rhodesia where they were received by their master [Zechariah]. Zechariah now procured magical substances which he sent through the air, and with them he killed Abelo's mother, three of his sisters, two of his mother's sisters, two of his younger brothers, his mother's mother and his mother's brother. The accuser, Abelo, did not need to make enquiries; to him it was obvious who the sorcerer was.

Case No. 5   *Supporters of Rival Candidates*

As we saw in Case No. 1 (His Uncle's Bed), Katete and Kasinda were rivals for a chieftainship, that of Kabambo. One day a messenger reported to one of Katete's friends, Filipo, that one of his rival's supporters, Cimteŋgo, on hearing of the Paramount Chief's intention to support Katete's candidature, had said that he disagreed; that Katete might have a right to succeed, but only after the death of Kasinda. He had added the threat, 'If Katete doesn't die, there'll be a war'. Subsequently Filipo was informed by some of Katete's relatives that they had overheard Cimteŋgo saying, 'The moon is old. If Katete is alive by the next moon, he will be lucky.' Filipo claims that Cimteŋgo has been attempting to kill Katete with sorcery.

It is interesting to speculate on the part played by the Ceŵa judicial machine in keeping down the frequency of believed instances and accusations of sorcery. There seems to be some support for the Ceŵa insight that, because the matrilineage is a jural unit, the Chief's court cannot settle disputes between members of the same matrilineage and that they therefore have to resort to practising sorcery against each other or to accusing each other of such practices. Perhaps more crucial to my argument are the cases in which this machine, normally successful in adjusting relationships between members of different matrilineages, fails to reconcile them. I could generalize the handful of cases in which sorcery expressed an unresolved conflict between members of different matrilineages by saying that this happened when the machine was incompetently used, as when a chief, involved in a dispute himself, sat in judgment of it; or that ill-fortune intervened, as when a cow awarded as damages for adultery died before those to whom it had been awarded could enjoy the benefits of owning it; or that the miscreant escaped, as when an adulterer ran away to Southern Rhodesia before the case against him could be heard; or that the conflicts involved, by their very nature, could not be resolved, as when motives were strong or norms conflicting.

Before trying to wind up, I should like to refer to a context of sorcery and witchcraft about which many writers are relatively explicit. This is the moral one. Perhaps it is not a context so much as an aspect of every context. It is widely held that beliefs in witchcraft—and the same would hold for sorcery—are an effective means of dramatizing social norms in that they provide, in the person of the mystical evil-doer, a symbol of all that is held to be anti-social and illegitimate. This conservative function of beliefs of this kind is thrown into prominence when, as a result of social change, indigenous values are threatened by intrusive ones, and indigenous social relationships are displaced by new ones or at least fundamentally altered by new conditions. The moral aspect of sorcery sometimes has reference to the victim in that his misfortune may be retrospectively attributed to his own foolishness or failings. My case material provides many illustrations of these principles, though it is not every case that has moral implications. My material shows, for instance, that about half of the sorcerers first mentioned in the 101 cases had anti-social traits before the suspicion was entertained or the accusation made; that about sixty per cent of believed victims or their close associates had been considered guilty of a misdemeanour directly related to the attack made on them. It also shows that modern objects of competition, such as cattle, money and other property, crop up in over half the cases of accusations; and that new relationships, such as those between unrelated fellow employees, are sometimes involved, or that indigenous conflicts, such as a man's divided loyalties to his children and his sister's children, may be exacerbated by his owning modern forms of property.

I have provided barely enough grist for the mill of analysis, but space is limited. What are some of the conclusions we can draw from the material I have presented?

First and foremost, beliefs in sorcery are a means of formulating tense relationships. This statement holds whether we adopt the viewpoint of the people themselves and think in terms of the imaginary relationship between sorcerer and victim; or whether, as objective observers, we concentrate on the real relationships between accuser and alleged sorcerer.

What do the contexts we have examined tell us about the ingredients in the tensions that are expressed through beliefs in sorcery? A common element seems to be competition for a highly valued goal connected with such fields of aspiration as leadership, property, love or tribal politics. Such competition can take place and can generate tension because of uncertainty or conflict, associated, perhaps, with a lack of clear normative prescription or definition of the situation in which it occurs. There may be a conflict between the claims of genealogical position and those of personal qualification; or a conflict between a headman's traditional right to dispose of his matrilineage's property and the claims of those of his followers who have gone to the labour centres, where they have been exposed to individualistic values, and who have contributed their earnings to its accumulation.

Some conflicts, such as the last two mentioned, are often insoluble, either by their very nature or because of the particular context in which they occur; and it is these that tend to be expressed through the medium of beliefs in sorcery. Others may be resolved by judicial arbitration or by what the Wilsons call social separation (1945: 60–61), a good example of the latter being the apparent link between the high divorce rate and the low incidence of believed attacks or of accusations between spouses. In other words, there are alternatives to sorcery as a means of articulating and relieving tensions springing from competition for valued goals in an ill-defined situation. It is usually when these alternatives are inapplicable, as, for instance, when Cewa judicial machinery cannot control the internal working of the matrilineage, or when they work inadequately, leaving discontent, or when motives are too strong to be contained by them, that sorcery is invoked.

A final common element in the contexts of Cewa sorcery should not escape us because, like Chesterton's postman, it is so familiar that it is invisible. In all the cases I have recorded and possibly in all cases of believed witchcraft and sorcery that have ever been recorded, the relationship between the characters involved has been a personal one, one in which they have exposed in their mutual interaction not merely single facets of their personalities but all facets. Their relationships have been what Gluckman calls multiplex (1955: 19) and what some sociologists call total as opposed to segmental (e.g. Coser 1955).

This last point may provide the answer to the question why beliefs in witchcraft and sorcery, in the form in which they exist in many contemporary non-literate societies, have disappeared from our own society. We may attribute their disappearance, neither to the growth of religion, nor entirely to the rise of rationalism, but rather to the development of a society in which a large proportion of our day-to-day relationships are impersonal and segmental ones in which tensions may be isolated and compartmentalized, and expressed in forms very different from those of a society small enough in scale to be dominated by the idea of personal influence.

7 WITCHCRAFT AS SOCIAL PROCESS IN A TZELTAL COMMUNITY

Manning Nash

WITCHCRAFT BELIEF and practice is a pervasive aspect of Tzeltal and Tzotzil Indian communities in the southeastern highlands of Chiapas.[1] In the community of Amatenango, a Tzeltal speaking municipio, men are frequently killed for being practicing witches. In the nine months that I spent in Amatenango, and for three additional months for which I have data, every two months a man was murdered for being a witch.[2]

The theory of witchcraft in Amatenango is a fairly coherent body of conventional understandings. Amatenangeros believe that some men have animal counterparts, called *nawales*. The nawal may be a common domesticated animal like a horse, dog, or bull, or it may be one of the wild animals that roves the hills, such as the mountain lion or deer. It is never a fantasy animal. The nawal is a source of power for its owner, or possessor. The possessor of a nawal may, on whim, but only at night, transform himself into the animal and roam the streets of the pueblo or travel the hills near the community. As the nawal he may converse with other nawales. The nawal is the source of power in medical practice, and all curers must have at least one nawal in their possession. A man is born associated with, or possessor of a nawal. The nawal is revealed to him in a dream. He does not necessarily announce this to the community, or act any special way because he has an animal counterpart.

Reprinted from *American Indigena* 20, 1961: 121–26 by permission of the author and the editor, *American Indigena*.

[1] Paper read at the Central States Anthropological Society, May 13–15, 1959.
[2] Field work was financed by the National Institute of Mental Health. I am also indebted to the Instituto Nacional Indigenista for aid and support.

Sometimes men with nawales may get vicious and use their power, which is essentially a medical and curing power, to bring illness rather than to cure it. These men are witches. Possessors of animal counterparts who use the special medical power that such animals confer to inject illness into others or to eat souls are witches. The nawal who walks by night may pass a sick person's house and night by night "eat" a bit of his soul, until the body has no strength and the bewitched victim dies.

Two things must be stressed about the nawal witch belief system. First all curers have nawales, but some men with nawales are not known to the community. Secondly, possession of a nawal does not necessarily mean that a person is a witch or practicing witchcraft.

As a body of cultural theory then, the witchcraft system leaves open the empirical definition of *who* is a witch. Cultural theory does not tell anyone who a witch is, and gives no particular, immediate rules for the logical or empirical establishment of a witch. This I take to be a characteristic of any functioning system of witchcraft belief. Since witches are practitioners of aggressive and deadly magic and are continual threats to the social order, and operate in violation of the moral rules of a society, it is not possible to have a set of cultural beliefs which provides general and immediately verifiable rules for the identification of a witch. If such operational witch theory did exist it would mean that no witches would, for nobody would suffer their presence.

It is this general characteristic of a system of witch beliefs that makes the study of witchcraft a study of social process. For one of the issues perennially at stake in a society with a cultural theory that includes witchcraft is the identification of witches and their elimination.

The identification of a witch is a social process of validation of somebody's aggressive activity against a witch. A society with witchcraft beliefs must have some social machinery to decide when a man, or group, or the whole society eliminates a witch they have served as executioners, not murderers. The problem of social order rests on the consensual meshing of public opinion about an act of violence which is either a favor to the society as a whole, or the most flagrant violation of its moral equilibrium.

Viewing witchcraft from the side of the victim, that is someone who feels that witchcraft has been exercised against him, is a convenient perspective for seeing how the social process of identification, and validation is conducted. A man or a member of his family gets sick in Amatenango. Like us, he assumes it will pass. He may take a bottle of the home brewed *trago,* a medicinal herb, some aspirin, and forget about it. The illness, however, does not pass. He needs the services of a specialist. He calls one of the curers, of which there are about a dozen. A curing ritual is carried on. Time passes and he worsens. He calls the curer again, this time asking if he is under the spell of a witch. A ceremony of pulsing and blood letting is carried on, and foreign objects are sought in the man's blood. His blood is asked to "talk" to the diviner and say what kind of illness he is afflicted with.

He gets sicker and sicker, no curing ceremony helps, no herbs relieve, no liquor eases, no penicillin brings abatement. It is witchcraft, certainly. As he sickens, he cannot work, his assets melt away, he cannot look after his animals, and they are lost. All this is a further sign of witchcraft. His pressing problem is to get the spell lifted, to identify the witch who is causing this trouble. He calls all the curers together in a major curing ceremony. Each one pulses, each one says he is trying to cure the man. Nobody will name a witch. The man is dying and no one knows who is behind it.

He may invite one of the curers with whom he is especially friendly or in whom he has confidence, ply the man with liquor and attempt to get a name from him. Failing this, he will review the reasons why anyone would hold a grudge against him. Was it envy for his good crop? Was it an argument in a brawl? Was it a refusal to offer liquor to a curer? Was it stickiness in a marriage negotiation? Was it his hauteur in treating a poor villager? These are the kinds of questions he asks.

He then makes a decision that someone is doing him in. He asks one of the curers to send his nawal around to talk to this man's nawal and tell it that no harm, envy, or hatred is held by the sick man. If he recovers soon thereafter, the affair is closed. But say it is one of his children and the child dies. He then holds a grudge against a witch. He may not be sure enough to act, but he keeps looking for evidence. He watches his suspect, keeps asking, keeps worrying the idea, and he begins to sound public opinion about the man, and perhaps spread news of his growing suspicion. If a further misfortune hits him in short order, he acts.

In Amatenango killing a witch is always an affair of ambush, is always a group of men against the witch. Amatenangeros may or may not be brave as we measure bravery, but only a fool will pit his ordinary self against a man he suspects of being a powerful witch, and only a fool will even seek vengeance when his intended victim is in command of his powers. The killing of a witch then is an ambush, with the man to be killed set upon when he is drunk, and set upon by a group of men. The most usual method of killing is to poke a shot gun through the wattle and daub wall of the suspect's house when the man to be killed is in an alcoholic stupor, pull the trigger, and disappear into the night. Other killings of which I have knowledge include cutting a witch to pieces with a machete, kicking him to death with the heavy cleated *caites,* and shooting in the back with a pistol.

The crucial factor here is that a man, together with a small number of his friends or kinsmen, have decided to kill another man as a witch. The problem facing the community is was the killing justified? That is did a witch get destroyed, and therefore a source of potential evil removed, or did a man indulge a personal grievance, or a drunken impulse? This is what the trials after a killing are concerned with. It is rarely a question of who did the killing; that is almost immediate public knowledge. The question is one of the validity of the slaying, and that validity turns on the problem of identification. Identification is a social decision as to the character of a dead man, and as to the character of his slayer. For after all, it is nearly as uncomfortable a situation to have a murderer about in a small community as it is to have a witch. Both share the trait of irresponsible evil making.

Here I want, in part, to describe, a trial after the killing of a man. The suspected slayer was brought before the assembled officials of Amatenango in the building which houses the civil officers. The accused man was seen drinking with the dead man the night before. They had quarreled, the accused had called the man an 'ak chamel—a caster of sickness—and had cursed him for bringing misfortune. The now dead man had laughed and staggered away to his house. So much was common knowledge.

Witnesses were assembled. They included the immediate family of the accused, the widow and brother of the dead man, and the father of the dead man. Several of the neighbors of the dead man and several neighbors of the accused were also on hand inside the *juzgado*. Outside many people of the dead man's barrio hovered near the entrance to the juzgado. Everybody in the community was talking about the recent death. The people in the dead man's barrio came to view the body, which was under the charge of the officers of the civil hierarchy.

The questioning went something like this. The judges addressed remarks to the accused. Did he drink with the deceased last night and did he insult him? Yes, he did both. Why the insult? The accused recounted the death of one of his children, from witchcraft. Then he said the dead man had told him at the time of the funeral that death was not finished yet in that household. Two weeks later another member of the household died. The man's wife supported the story. Neighbors said they had heard the threat at the funeral. Neighbors then went on to say the dead man was becoming *muy bravo* as he learned to be a curer. He was not as humble as a beginning curer should be, but demanded much.

The judge then turned to the dead man's family, who had heard all this testimony, which established two important things: First the dead man was a novice curer and this meant that he had a nawal, and second that he was regarded as *bravo* or aggressive by the neighbors and did not properly abide by the age respect rules of Amatenango social interaction.

The kin of the dead man then began a line of testimony which carefully and systematically severed their social relations with the deceased. The dead man's wife testified that her husband was often gone nights, drinking, or doing she knew not what. She did not know of his special powers—had she not recently lost a child from what appeared to be witchcraft too? She established the fact that her husband was a mystery to her and that she did not know of his violation of respect relations or his beginnings in curing. Effectively she denied her social relation as wife. The dead man's brother then testified that he was a friend of the accused and that they had been drinking the night before and in fact were together when the killing took place, but were far from the site of the slaying. Now every one knew that the dead man's brother had been so drunk that he could not with reliability testify to anything. What he was affirming was his confidence in the accused and his unwillingness to assert the claim of sibling for revenge. He too severed social relationship with the dead man.

It was now clear to the judges, and to me, who was amazed and confused by the trial, that nothing was going to happen to the accused. He was free. His just grievance had been established, his neighbors had called him a *cumplido*, honorable man. And the dead man was singled out as a violator of norms, his wife and brother had publicly cut their connections to him and had established the basis for a verdict. The judges decided the slain man had been in fact a witch. The slayer was in fact an executioner, not a murderer. Community consensus was quickly reached on this killing.

When the Mexican police came the next day to investigate a killing, they were presented with a minute description of the position of the dead man, the time of the killing, the size of the hole in his head, etc. But they were not presented with any suspects. To the outside world, nobody in the community had the slightest suspicion of why the man was killed, or the remotest idea of who did it. The police took notes, went home, muttering about inditos and their ways.

Not all killings reach this level of agreement. Some men are killed and many people have reservations about the justice of the slaying. In a case of a curer who was killed by the rest of the curers for what essentially was a violation of guild rules, many people in the community thought an injustice was committed. Nor do the families of the victims always cut off social relations with the deceased in a public display. Some women mourn their dead husbands long after they have been slain as witches, and continue to say that a murder was committed. The consensus making mechanism is not always perfect, and witchcraft leaves many unresolved strains in the community and generates cause for further violence. This too is one of the built in hazards of a system of witch belief having *post hoc* identification as a necessary corollary.

The process of identification of a witch is one of consensus, and a man runs a risk of death if he misjudges the character of the victim, or if he is not well integrated into his neighborhood and kin group. Having witches about who can only be identified after the fact is a necessary condition of a viable theory of witchcraft. But the *ad hoc* identification is not an invitation to indulgence or to wanton killing. The constraints of communal judgments about the character of the persons involved, both slayer and slain, set the limits of witchcraft action. And in a small face-to-face community, no one can for long pretend to or fake virtues and social status as a moral man.

8 A SOCIOLOGICAL ANALYSIS OF WITCH BELIEFS IN A MYSORE VILLAGE

Scarlett Epstein

THE OPERATION of witch beliefs in African societies has been amply recorded by anthropologists. By contrast the lack of reference to witch beliefs in anthropological accounts of present-day Hindu societies is most striking. Yet there is ample evidence of the existence of witch beliefs in traditional Hindu societies (Thurston 1906, Lyall 1899, Crooke 1926). Unfortunately, none of the cases quoted in the ethnographic literature provides us with sufficient information to analyse the social relations involved between the victim and the accused. For instance, O'Malley reports the case of "one Kari, a man of a very low caste in the Saran district of Bihar, who was troubled by an evil spirit, and on consulting an exorcist, learnt that it had been sent by a neighbour called Gokhul. Kari made haste to come to terms with his enemy and an agreement was drawn up in which Gokhul undertook to recall the evil spirit and never let it trouble Kari again. Should it do so, Gokhul promised to pay a penalty of Rs. 25. The agreement was carefully recorded on a formal document with the signatures of witnesses. Kari, however, found that he was still vexed by the evil spirit and accordingly brought a case against Gokhul charging him with cheating" (O'Malley 1935).

In order to make a sociological analysis of this case we would need to know the relationship between Kari and Gokhul, the knowledge that the exorcist had of it and the constitution of the court to whom Kari put his case against Gokhul. When Kari approached the exorcist to find out whose evil spirit was bewitching

Reprinted from *The Eastern Anthropologist* 12 (4), 1959: 234–51, by permission of the author and the editor, *The Eastern Anthropologist*.

him, the latter obviously produced an answer which was acceptable to him. The exorcist may have arrived at the accusation
against Gokhul in the same manner as "a Cewa diviner is able to
arrive at an acceptable answer by (a) being a keen student of
local friendships, animosities and kinship ties; (b) insisting on an
interval between the opening of a case and the actual consultations
or seance; (c) requiring that the client should be accompanied by
a relative or close acquaintance; and (d) skilfully drawing the
client into arguments he has with his divining apparatus" (Marwick 1952: 216). Judging from the literature on witchcraft accusations in Hindu societies it appears that here, too, an exorcist
names the witch responsible only if he is well acquainted with the
social relationship between the victim and the person he accuses
of witchcraft. If he is an outsider he usually points only to a category of people among whom the witch may be found as, for instance, that the witch is a woman living in the same village as
the victim. This leaves the actual choice of the accused to the victim, and thereby narrows down the circle of people from among
whom the witch will be chosen to persons with whom the victim
has strained social relations.

The apparent contrast between the ample evidence of witch beliefs given in the ethnographic literature on traditional Hindu societies and the lack of it in anthropological accounts of modern
Hindu societies raises the question whether witch beliefs have
disappeared. In this paper I set out to show that witch beliefs are
still flourishing in a Mysore village.[1] Wangala[2] is a multi-caste
village composed of 192 households of which 67% belong to the
peasant (Okkaliga) caste. Landholding is highly dispersed and no
one household owns more than 15 acres of land. 89% of all the
land owned by Wangala villagers belongs to Peasants. The numerical and economic dominance of Peasants in Wangala accounts
for my concentration on their social organisation and pattern of
witch beliefs in this paper.

The village is situated about four miles south of Mandya. Its
lands were irrigated in 1938 from a major canal irrigation scheme

[1] Material for this paper was collected during two years' fieldwork
(1954–56) in Mysore villages.
[2] I have changed the name of the village slightly, using the initial "W"
to remind the reader that it is a wet village.

originating at a dam over the Kaveri river at Kanambadi about 25 miles south-west of Wangala. Prior to irrigation the village economy could be described as being largely subsistence. Sericulture provided the only major source of cash, but was not widely practised. Irrigation, accompanied by the establishment of a sugar factory in Mandya, enabled farmers to grow sugarcane as a cash crop: in this way the village became linked to the wider cash economy. Because the cultivation of sugarcane requires a lot of working capital only the richest peasant farmers could venture into cane-growing immediately after irrigation. Thus irrigation re-emphasised the economic predominance of the richest farmers. It was among the group of "middle-farmers" that irrigation created a struggle for status. Among this group new criteria of prestige developed. They vied with each other in arranging the most elaborate weddings for their sons. They also began to regard the sort of life a farmer provided for his wife as a matter of prestige. The more a man relieved his wife from work on his lands and the greater independence he allowed her, the higher his prestige, other things being equal. Some farmers went so far as to buy their wives a buffalo whose milk yield provided the latter with an independent source of income. Others again gave considerable money presents to their wives before they themselves died, to ensure the status of their wives even after their own death. This enabled some women to enter the money market by becoming lenders of small short-term loans. The interest on these loans is much higher than that charged by men on larger long-term loans. Women money lenders charge one anna per rupee per month, which amounts to an annual interest rate of 75%, while men charge only 12% interest per year. However, debtors usually borrow only a few rupees at a time from a woman moneylender which they repay after a few months, whereas from men they borrow larger sums for many years. Indebtedness among Wangala Peasant men runs along traditionally established patron-client relations and debts are usually inherited like the other strands of social relations which link patrons and clients. By contrast, the lending of money by women to other women as well as to men created a new type of social relation which did not exist in the pre-irrigation subsistence economy. The fact that women have entered the field of struggle for economy status quite independently of their menfolk adds an element of tension to social relations. Men do not like the idea of getting indebted to a woman, but necessity often forces them to do so. Moneylending by women provides a fresh stimulus to situations which give rise to harbouring a grudge. I shall argue that the tensions created by women having become moneylenders are projected into witchcraft accusations because they can find no other medium of expression in Wangala's present-day social organization.

Wangala Peasants do not distinguish as clearly between witchcraft and sorcery as the Azande, who believe that "a witch performs no rite, utters no spell and possesses no medicines. They [the Azande] believe also that sorcerers, may do them ill by performing magic rites with bad medicines" (Evans-Pritchard 1937: 21). On the contrary, Wangala Peasants believe that 'witches are women who administer poison to their victims, but cannot help doing so. Women who give poison cannot control the evil spirit within themselves that makes them poison other people.'[3] In Wangala witches never profess to exercise witchcraft. They therefore differ from those described by Sir A. Lyall in a review of the Indian evidence. He defines a witch as "one who professes to work marvels, not through the aid and counsel of supernatural beings in whom he believes as much as the rest, but by certain occult faculties and devices which he conceives himself to possess' (Lyall 899: 106).

Wangala Peasants distinguish between poison (*maddu*) which will result in sickness and poison (*visha*) which will result in death. Wangala witches are believed to be "*maddu*-givers" only. 'If they do not attempt to poison somebody within a certain period of time such "*maddu*-givers" will have to die. Therefore, from time to time they have to poison somebody. If a witch invites a number of people for a meal and puts poison in the food for the whole lot but only wants one person to be poisoned the poison will go only to that person.' In most of the cases I recorded Wangala Peasants did not consult a diviner or oracle as to what witch had poisoned them. They simply stated it as a fact that they had been poisoned by a certain woman. For instance Kempamma,[4] a young Peasant

---

[3] Single quotation marks indicate statements made by informants.
[4] All names are fictitious, though I have chosen customary Peasant names.

woman accused Lingamma, an old widow who was her relative and neighbour, of having poisoned her. Kempamma had been feeling sick for several weeks and when she went to see a native doctor in another village, who gave her some medicine which made her vomit, she was shown some small black pills, which were supposed to be the poison she had been given and which she had now vomited. Kempamma immediately remembered that she had a meal at Lingamma's shortly before she had become sick. So when Kempamma returned to Wangala and met Lingamma outside her own house she accused the latter of being the witch who had poisoned her and kicked the old lady to the ground. When Lingamma fell she hit her head against a stone and became unconscious. By this time a crowd of onlookers had gathered. The villagers had become accustomed to asking my medical aid whenever somebody was sick or had had an accident. On this occasion, however, when I wanted to apply a smelling bottle to Lingamma, they told me not to interfere but let the old widow lie. She was lying unconscious and did not seem to react to any efforts made by her sons to revive her. Some of the village elders tried to make the sons carry their mother, who was lying on the porch of Kempamma's hut, to their own house, but the sons insisted that they did not want her in their own home; if the old lady were to die she should die under the roof of her attacker. However, in spite of the sons' protests the village chairman ordered some men to carry Lingamma to her own home, where she was received by her daughters-in-law.

After Lingamma had been removed from the scene her younger son, Puttegowda, was wailing loudly, complaining that such misfortune should have befallen his mother who had always been an honest and forthright woman. Onlooking Peasants just sneered at his remarks and said that Lingamma was a witch. This infuriated Bhoomegowda, his elder brother, who threatened to take the case to Mandya court if anyone brought any witchcraft accusation against his mother. Bhoomegowda requested the village chairman to write a report of the whole incident so that he could take it to Mandya police. The chairman agreed to do so but at the same time requested the two parties to the dispute to settle their quarrel within the village and not to take it to the police. The elders agreed to hold a *panchayat* meeting the following morning to try and settle the dispute.

Although Kempamma, a young woman, had obviously attacked and caused bodily harm to Lingamma, an old widow, an action which they would normally condemn, Wangala Peasants all sympathised with Kempamma. I heard people whisper among themselves that Lingamma was an evil person, that she had attempted to poison other people already and therefore she well deserved the beating she had received from Kempamma. Kempamma's sister's husband came over to tell me that Lingamma had already tried to poison his own wife Chennamma about seven years ago, when she presented poison with betel leaves and nuts to Chennamma. However, the latter had fortunately detected the poison and it was shown to the village *panchayat*. Lingamma was then called before the *panchayat*. When shown the poison she said in her defence that she had bought the betel leaves and nuts and had no idea how any poison came into them. Since no damage had been done the *panchayat* members decided to drop the case at the time, but all villagers well remembered the incident.

The following morning a *panchayat* meeting was held while Puttegowda loaded his mother, who still seemed to be unconscious, on to a cart and started on his way to Mandya to take her to the town hospital. This meant that her sons were openly threatening to take the case to Mandya police, for if the old lady were admitted to the hospital a report would have to be made to the police. Yet to show that they were willing to compromise and settle the dispute within the village, Bhoomegowda stayed behind for the *panchayat* meeting. Remembering Bhoomegowda's threat, nobody at the meeting even mentioned any witchcraft accusation against Lingamma and only the matter of compensation due to her sons was discussed. One of the elders, an expert in deciding the amount of compensation due to an injured party, ruled that if Lingamma were to die Kempamma would have to give Rs. 350 to Bhoomegowda and his younger brother. But as long as Lingamma was alive and only slightly hurt by Kempamma Rs. 25 compensation would be sufficient. Bhoomegowda was not prepared to accept Rs. 25 as compensation and refused to go and fetch his brother back, who was on his way taking his mother to Mandya hospital. Kempamma, on the other hand, who was represented by her husband Chaudegowda, pointed out that they were too poor and could not possibly afford to pay Rs. 25 compensation. Chaudegowda complained that he and his wife were already heavily indebted. The expert arbitrator then approached Kempamma's brothers, who were slightly better off than Chaudegowda, and asked them to pay compensation on behalf of their sister. After further argument Bhoomegowda finally agreed to accept Rs. 35, which were paid over to him by Kempamma's brothers, on the understanding that he would receive a further Rs. 315 if his mother were to die of the injury caused her by Kempamma. Bhoomegowda then quickly left on his bicycle to intercept his brother and mother before they reached Mandya and bring them back to the village. Lingamma was thus brought back to Wangala where she recovered after a few days in her own home. The case was thereby settled though Kempamma and most other Wangala Peasants are still convinced that Lingamma is a witch.

I shall now examine the factors which led Kempamma to accuse Lingamma of witchcraft and which made other Wangala Peasants concur in her accusation, and shall try to explain the reasons which prevented them from levelling this accusation openly in front of the village *panchayat*. Lingamma's husband had been one of the richer "middle-farmers"; he had bought his wife a buffalo to supply her with an independent source of income and shortly before he died about ten years ago he gave her a present of Rs. 500. This enabled Lingamma to become a moneylender, which she has been ever since. She is known in the village for her ruthlessness against her debtors and no-one turned to her for a loan unless he or she was absolutely forced to do so. Kempamma was one of her debtors. She had borrowed Rs. 100 about three years ago from Lingamma to help her husband purchase a pair of bullocks, but she had not paid one single anna interest on her debt in spite of the pressing demands from Lingamma. Kempamma's father was the adopted brother of Lingamma and Lingamma's own husband was a putative brother of Kempamma's husband's father (see chart 1). In other words, Kempamma and Lingamma both belonged to the same lineage and had also married into the same lineage. Thus Kempamma regarded Lingamma as one of her close kin and therefore considered the loan from Lingamma as a rightful claim on her part to help from her own kin. Lin-

gamma's insistent demands for interest payments on the loan led
to tension between the two women. Kempamma was basing
her claim to support from Lingamma on the custom prevalent in
the traditional social system of Wangala Peasants whereby kin
were obliged to help their needy relatives. Lingamma, on the
other hand, was basing her demand for interest payments on the
practice prevalent in the modern economic system whereby interest is considered the proper reward for a loan and the personal
relationship outside the immediate family between debtor and
creditor is disregarded. Here we have a clash between the values
which stem from the traditional social system and those of the
new economic system. The traditional social system is based
on personal relationships, whereas the modern economic system
is characterised by impersonal relationships. The ascribed status
system which was part of Wangala's traditional social organisation
prescribed the relationship between Kempamma and Lingamma
and obliged the latter to help the former. However, the introduction of a money economy undermined the customary system of
ascribed status and this resulted in the tension between the two
women. There was no institutionalised pattern of behaviour which
would have allowed Kempamma to give vent to the aggression
generated in her social relation with Lingamma. Accordingly when
Kempamma was sick she sought an explanation in witchcraft.
The belief in witchcraft is deeply rooted among Wangala Peasants.
They believe in the full and explicit Hindu mythology concerned
with explaining all the natural phenomena in the world: the creation of man and animals, the origin of death and disease and so
forth. At the same time they argue that just as good can and does
appear in the shell of a man—and there are several such mediums
in Wangala—so evil spirits manifest themselves through witches.
Thus they harmonise witchcraft accusations with their general
Hindu religious beliefs. Even my Brahmin research assistant told
me that he too had been poisoned by a witch who was his neighbour and was jealous because he gained admittance to university
whereas her own son had failed in this. He was sick and, like
Kempamma, went to a native doctor who made him vomit and
then showed him two small black pills which were supposed to
have been the poison he had been given by the witch. Thus we can
see that even some of the urban Brahmins subscribe to witch

beliefs. Therefore, Kempamma's witch beliefs were in accordance with more general Hindu beliefs. The native doctor certified her beliefs by showing her the little black pills which were supposed to have poisoned her. Who could mean her ill but Lingamma who was constantly pressing her to pay her long overdue interest and who was disregarding her 'rightful' claim to support?

In this case we see therefore the familiar situation where the concatenation of personal misfortune and the existence of a grudge is given expression in witchcraft accusations.[5] Yet no mention of witchcraft was made before the *panchayat*. When I enquired from Kempamma why she had not brought her accusations of witchcraft before the *panchayat*, she said that she had been afraid that if she did this Bhoomegowda would take the case to Mandya police, as he was threatening to do, and there she would be most heavily fined or put into prison. She realised that the magistrate's court would not listen to any witchcraft accusation and would only condemn her for having hit the old lady. The elders with whom I discussed the case also said that though they were convinced that Lingamma was a witch they had not mentioned witchcraft to prevent Bhoomegowda from taking the case to Mandya police and outside the jurisdiction of Wangala's *panchayat*. When Chennamma had brought her case against Lingamma before the *panchayat*, they could and did discuss the witchcraft accusation because Lingamma had not been attacked then and therefore had no grounds to take the case to the magistrate's court. They dropped the case against Lingamma at the time because no damage had been done.

The existence of an external political authority enabled Bhoomegowda to threaten Wangala Peasants that if they mentioned any witchcraft accusation against his mother he would take the case to the Mandya police. Thus it was the pressure from the external political authority which prevented Wangala Peasants from discussing the witchcraft accusation openly.

Nevertheless, the general belief held by Wangala Peasants was that Lingamma really was a witch. This general condemnation of

[5] E. E. Evans-Pritchard says: "In a study of Zande witchcraft we must bear in mind, firstly, that the notion is a function of situations of misfortune, and, secondly, that it is a function of personal relations." (Evans-Pritchard 1937: 106.)

Lingamma indicates the persistence of the value Wangala Peasants still attach to generosity to one's kin. A sociological function of witch beliefs widely recognised in the literature is their tendency to support the system of values and thus to sustain the social structure (see Hunter 1936, Kluckhohn 1944). Lingamma in short is condemned for being a greedy and grasping woman. At the same

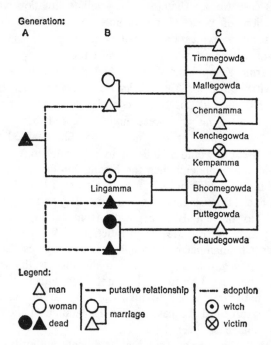

Chart 1. Genealogy Showing the Relationship Between Kempamma and Lingamma.

time such a condemnation is a re-affirmation of the traditional social structure in which women did not enter the field of money lending. Their economic relations were with their own family or with their employers. The ideal Peasant woman, according to the traditional set of values, was a woman who worked hard on the lands of her husband and in her home, who bore many children, in particular many sons, and who was obedient to her husband and affines and generous to her kin and beggars. The obligation of mutual aid between kin is well documented for many subsistence economies. This emphasis on sharing in subsistence economy can be readily explained by the fact that an individual householder can do little else with his surplus but share it with his kin or neighbours. The introduction of cash and the link with a wider market makes economic differentiation on the basis of a greater variety of possessions possible. Under such conditions the emphasis on sharing will give way to a competitive system. "It can be stated as a theorem valid in a high percentage of cases, that the greater opportunity for profit in any social-cultural situation, the weaker the ties of extended kinship will become" (Linton 1952: 84). However, there appears to be a time lag between changes in the economic, political or general social sphere and changes in the set of values held by a society. Wangala's economic system changed from subsistence to cash about twenty years ago, while some of the values held by Wangala Peasants are still in line with the traditional subsistence economy. Although the joint family system has been superseded by the nuclear family, Wangala Peasants still set a value on lineage unity. They uphold generosity in a woman as a value and condemn the grasping ways of Lingamma, which are after all in accordance with the working of the modern cash economy. She is not the only woman who is thus condemned and accused of witchcraft.

There was, for instance, the case of Hanumegowda and Halgamma. Hanumegowda was an immigrant to Wangala. He was a landless Peasant employed as labourer on the nearby factory-owned sugarcane plantation. Halgamma was a young Peasant widow who had been married to a "middle-farmer" in another village. Since she had no children and her husband had been an only child she inherited most of her husband's lands on his death. She decided to sell the lands and return to Wangala, her native village, where she now lives with her brother. With the money she got from the sale of her husband's lands she ventured into money-lending. Like Lingamma she is very insistent on getting interest payments on her loans and gives little attention to the ability or otherwise of her debtors to pay interest. Hanumegowda borrowed Rs. 50 from Halgamma about two years ago and has not been able to pay any interest yet. Whenever Halgamma met Hanumegowda in the street she stopped him and demanded payment of the long overdue interest. He was not the only one to whom she did this; she kept stopping many other Peasants in the village streets and shouted at them demanding payment of interest due to her.

One day I met Hanumegowda when he had been sick for several days and unable to go to work. When I enquired after his health he told me that he had just returned from a visit to a native doctor in another village who had given him some medicine, which had made him vomit the poison that had made him sick and he was now beginning to feel better. When I asked who had poisoned him he was at first very hedgy, but after some time he admitted that he was sure it was Halgamma. There were a few other Peasants present who all nodded their heads gravely and said that they too thought that Halgamma was a witch. 'She could not help but poison other people. She must do it so as to bring prosperity on herself and her family. If she stopped poisoning other people something bad would befall herself.'

Here too, as in the case of Lingamma, Halgamma was generally accused of being a witch and the relationship between her and her accuser was one of creditor-debtor. Wangala Peasants sided with Hanumegowda against Halgamma, though he was an immigrant and Halgamma a native of the village. He had their sympathy because she was a creditor to many other native Peasants who had also suffered from her meanness. Through the imputation of witchcraft her greed and bad temper was publicly condemned.

Whether or not the imputation of witchcraft is commonly accepted seems to depend largely on the status of the accuser and the number and status of people involved in economic relations with the accused. For instance, they did not concur in Mallegowda's witchcraft accusation against Timmamma. Mallegowda was a young Peasant. His father had immigrated to Wangala about twenty years ago when Mallegowda was a small boy. The family had chosen to move to Wangala because irrigation attracted labourers and farmers and it could establish a kinship link with some Wangala Peasants (Mallegowda's mother's mother was a native of Wangala). When the family first moved into Wangala they had no house and therefore went to stay with Mallegowda's mother's mother's father's brother's daughter's daughter Timmamma and her husband Kempegowda (see chart 2). This sort of far-distant relationship through the female line is hardly ever remembered among the patrilineal Peasants. It was only the needs of the emergency which induced Mallegowda's parents to activate the relationship. Timmamma and her husband Kempegowda promised to help Mallegowda's parents but instead of receiving help they found that some of their own vessels disappeared in Timmamma's household. So Devamma, Mallegowda's mother, quarrelled with Timmamma and after only about one month's stay she and her family moved out of Timmamma's house to build their own hut. Since that day relations between Mallegowda's family and Timmamma have been hostile.

During my stay in Wangala a typhoid epidemic broke out in the village and Mallegowda was one of the victims. Being an employee on the nearby factory-owned sugarcane plantation he was entitled to free medicine from the factory dispensary. Therefore he sent for some medicine as soon as he was taken ill. Since the medicine did not cure him within a few days his mother's mother, Chennamma, sent for a *pujari,* a priest belonging to the Ostaman caste, living in a neighbouring village. The *pujari* came and performed a number of rites over Mallegowda 'to free him from the evil spirit which was causing his disease.' When the *pujari* had finished with his rites Chennamma asked him who the evil spirit was that had caused Mallegowda's disease. The *pujari* then took out ten small shells and threw them on the ground like dice. He examined the position of the shells in relationship to each other and nodding gravely said that the evil spirit was a woman. Once more he threw the shells down and after examining again their position he pointed to the village and said she lived in Wangala. Whereupon Chennamma nodded knowingly. She then enquired from the *pujari* whether this was the same witch who had already poisoned herself, her daughter and Mallegowda on previous occasions. After throwing the shells on the ground once more and examining their position the *pujari* answered in the positive.

In this case the diviner was not from the same village as the victim. He was not familiar with the local friendships and animosities and therefore did not venture to specify the person he accused of witchcraft. He simply stated a category, namely women in Wangala, from whom the victim could choose the accused. Knowing that Wangala Peasants believe that only women are witches and aware of the fact that strained social relations are more likely

to occur within the village, he made a fair guess when he suggested
that the witch was a woman from Wangala. When I enquired from
Chennamma whom she suspected to be the witch responsible for
Mallegowda's disease she said that she knew it was Timmamma.

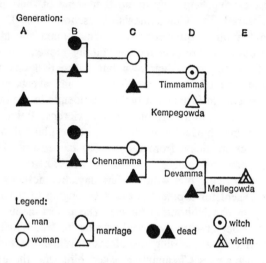

Chart 2. Genealogy Showing the Relationship Between Mallegowda and Timmamma.

Timmamma had come to their hut the day before Mallegowda was
taken ill, but she had not entered it because they were not on
speaking terms. This must have been the occasion when Timmamma's evil spirit made Mallegowda sick. On previous occasions when Chennamma, her daughter or Mallegowda had been
sick it was usually immediately after Timmamma had appeared in
the vicinity of their hut. At each instance they had called a *pujari*
and after he had performed some rites to counteract the evil spirit
the victims were soon alright again. In this instance, too, Mallegowda soon recovered from his attack of typhoid after the *pujari*
had performed his rites. As far as Chennamma knew Timmamma
bewitched only her family and no one else in the village.

In this case no actual poison was supposed to have been administered, rather the evil spirit of a woman was believed to have
caused the disease. The victim's relatives consulted an exorcist

and asked him to divine who the witch was. But here too the accusation arose out of the social tension existing between the accused and the victims' family. Again we find the lack of generosity being the cause of the conflict between the two parties involved. Chennamma felt that she had a claim to support from Timmamma who was her relative; instead she found that Timmamma actually stole some of her vessels. This she could never forgive her. As with Kempamma so Chennamma and her daughter Devamma thought that they had a right to expect help from Timmamma. But whereas in the case of Kempamma almost the whole Peasant community of Wangala sided with her in regarding Lingamma as a witch, in the case of Mallegowda, who was an immigrant to the village and therefore had no established lineage in it, they did not accept the accusation against Timmamma. Nor were they convinced of Chennamma's claim to hospitality from Timmamma. The relationship between the two women was too far removed: moreover, the link was traced through the female line, which made them disinclined to regard Chennamma as at all related to Timmamma. Furthermore, Timmamma was a poor woman without any money to venture into moneylending. Besides Mallegowda and his family none had suffered from her exactions and so they had no reason to concur in Mallegowda's witchcraft accusation against Timmamma. This was realised by Chennamma when she said that as far as she knew Timmamma exercised witchcraft only against her family in Wangala.

There are four aspects of Wangala Peasant witch beliefs which are of sociological interest: firstly, all witchcraft accusations are against women; secondly, they are all intra-caste; thirdly, they arise out of tension in inter-personal relations; and fourthly, Peasants recognise that witchcraft usually operates between persons whose social relations are strained.

If we examine the social tensions which gave rise to witchcraft accusations among Wangala Peasants we find that in each of the three cases stated and in many others which I cannot relate here, it was generated by the strain resulting from the "meanness" of women. In two of the three cases the accused were moneylenders, which makes the impact of the modern cash economy on witchcraft accusations quite clear. This does not necessarily mean that witch beliefs did not exist in Wangala prior to the economy changing from subsistence to cash. It simply means that many of the witchcraft accusations now made among Wangala Peasants arise from tensions generated in modern social relations. It does not prove that during the time of subsistence economy there were no —or fewer—social relations generating tensions expressed in witch beliefs of that period.

Wangala Peasants have never accused men of witchcraft. As far as I could establish only women have been so accused. In a patrilineal community, such as that of Wangala Peasants, women are outsiders. They marry virilocally into the lineage of their husbands but the absorption into it is only partial. They always maintain some links with their lineage and village of origin. In order to uphold the ideal of the unity and harmony of the patrilineal kin group in the face of conflicts arising in everyday relations between members of the group, witchcraft accusations have always been levelled against women, who are outsiders to the group. Similarly, women are always blamed for the break-up of a joint family. Brothers uphold the ideal of brotherly love and unity in the face of conflicting interests by blaming their difficulties on quarrels between their womenfolk. Thus Peasant men relieve the guilt they feel for not living up to their social ideals by projecting it on to their womenfolk.

The new economic relations created by the cash economy between Peasant men have not led to witchcraft accusations because these relations run along links of traditional social structure. For instance, to the traditional relations between a Peasant patron and his Peasant client has been added an indebtedness relationship. The many strands which make up this patron-client relationship give it an element of flexibility. If a creditor pressed too much for payment of interest his debtor might refuse to work for him when he needed the latter's help. On the other hand, if a debtor refused to pay interest to his creditor for too long a time the latter might not employ the former as farm labourer any more. Thus the mutual dependence of creditor and debtor puts pressure on both of them to be reasonable in their demands on each other. The impersonal economic relations characteristic of a cash economy have been personalised among Wangala Peasant men by being added to the structure of traditional social relations. Any tensions that arise in these social relations may be either resolved by a socially approved mechanism such as the village *panchayat* or may be projected on to women as strangers in the patrilineal kin group. The fact that economic relations among women or between women and men are new and not reinforced by any traditional social relations has only exaggerated the position of women as scapegoats for all ills in Wangala Peasant society.

It is only during the last twenty years since money has been accepted as the general medium of exchange in Wangala's economy that women have taken to moneylending. Women lend money on a purely impersonal basis not only to kin, as in the case of Lingamma and Hanumegowda. They lend money not to strengthen an already existing link such as Peasant men do, but simply and solely to make money. Here we find a conflict between the value premises of the modern money economy and those of the traditional subsistence economy; the latter lays emphasis on sharing while the former emphasises individualistic gain and competition. There are no precedents for women acting as moneylenders in Wangala prior to the establishment of a cash economy. The consequent uncertainty in the creditor-debtor relationship is one of the ingredients in the tension which becomes projected into witchcraft accusations and this is particularly the case where there is no socially approved mechanism for a debtor to air his grievance against his creditor. Neither Kempamma nor Hanumegowda could have taken their cases to the village *panchayat,* for the *panchayat* is officially bound to recognise the legal claims of Lingamma and Halgamma for payment of interest on their loans. Usually a debt is formalised by a legal document signed by creditor, debtor and witnesses. Thus creditors can always quite easily press their claims against their debtors by taking the case to the magistrate's court. However, the social pressures operating on a creditor prevent her from taking this step. In any case women are not accustomed to appear at courts and would, therefore, have to act through their husbands or sons who usually refuse to be part of such a legal transaction against one of their fellow villagers. But the existence of a legal document and the possibility of forcing one's claim against one's debtor at a magistrate's court puts pressure on the village *panchayat* to judge a dispute between a debtor and a creditor according to the legal principles laid down by the State. There is, therefore, no mechanism through which a harassed debtor can express his grudge against his creditor. The social tension arising between women creditors and their debtors has therefore no other outlet but witchcraft accusations.

Witchcraft accusations by Wangala Peasants are always intra-caste because relations between members of different castes are highly formalised and rights and duties are clearly recognised by all concerned. Wangala Peasants do not accuse members of other castes of witchcraft for the same reason as Zande people do not accuse nobles and seldom accuse influential commoners of witch-craft; not merely because it would be inadvisable to insult them but also because their social contact with these people is limited to situations in which their behaviour is determined by notions of status. As Evans-Pritchard says: "A noble is socially so sepa-rated from commoners that were a commoner to quarrel with him it would be treason. Commoners bear ill will against com-moners and princes against princes . . . Offence is more easily taken at the words or actions of an equal than of a superior or in-ferior" (Evans-Pritchard 1937: 104–5). The hierarchical structure of caste society makes for intra-caste rather than inter-caste quar-rels. Peasants are socially so separated from other castes that tension is not likely to arise in their relationship. Such tension which does arise between members of different castes can be con-trolled or resolved by regulative social institutions such as, for in-stance, the hereditary master-client relationship between Wangala Peasants and Untouchables. If a dispute arises between a Wangala Untouchable and a Peasant, the former's Peasant master will be called upon to act as arbitrator. The rivalling loyalties imposed on such a Peasant arbitrator by his membership of the same caste as one of the disputants, on the one hand, and his interest in the well-being of his Untouchable client, on the other, will bring pres-sure to bear upon him to find a solution acceptable to both parties. Whereas if a quarrel arises between a Peasant and his own Un-touchable client the pressures arising from the desire on both parts to continue the mutually beneficial relationship will lead to a settlement of the dispute fairly quickly. In other words, whenever disputes can be settled by a socially recognised mechanism the tensions generated by them will comparatively easily be resolved. It is in case of grievances or grudges where no such mechanism exists that witchcraft accusations occur.

The three cases I discussed in this paper illustrate the way witchcraft accusations among Wangala Peasants arise out of strained social relations. In a small scale community such as that of Wangala Peasants, in which people live face to face, tensions are bound to occur in their everyday relations. But not all tensions find expression in witchcraft accusation; only tensions which have no other outlet lead to such accusations. Wherever a judicial mechanism exists to settle quarrels between individuals or groups tensions in their social relations can be brought out into the open and therefore will not be channelled into witchcraft accusations. Nevertheless, we must note at this point in the argument, that notions of witchcraft are evoked primarily by misfortune and are not entirely dependent on enmities. They represent a rationalising of misfortune which is done outside the "secular" field. Thus Kempamma, Hanumegowda and Mallegowda sought to find out who wished them ill and might have bewitched them only after they had been sick. Only then did they accuse certain women of being witches.

The channelling of social tensions and grief over misfortune into witchcraft accusations enables the victim and the accused to continue their relationship. By blaming misfortune on the supernatural powers of a certain woman the victim is not really accusing the person of the witch, but rather the evil spirit which operates within her. The accounting for his misfortune by the supernatural powers of a woman with whom the victim has strained social relations provides a safety valve to the pattern of social relations among Wangala Peasants. Without such safety device the tensions generated in certain relations may threaten to upset the whole social system. If, for instance, Kempamma were to blame Lingamma herself for having poisoned her, rather than believe that Lingamma is a witch who cannot help but poison her, this would lead to an open and irreparable breach between the two women. It would also probably divide the kin of both the lineage of origin of the two women and the lineage into which they both married, into those that supported Lingamma and those that stood by Kempamma, because kinship loyalties would force some to support Lingamma. But as long as only the evil spirit within Lingamma is blamed for poisoning Kempamma the question of loyalty to Lingamma by some of her kin does not arise. Day-to-

day relations can continue unperturbed. Kempamma and Lingamma were again on neighbourly terms a few weeks after the
whole incident had occurred and Kempamma approached Lingamma for another loan but was refused. Thus the social relationship between the victim and the witch continues and so do the
tensions arising out of it.

Wangala Peasants recognise that witchcraft accusations occur
usually between persons whose social relations are strained. For
instance, most Peasants agreed that Chennamma had accused
Timmamma of witchcraft because the two women had been on
bad terms for many years. Though in this case Peasant public
opinion did not concur in the accusations against Timmamma,
simply because Timmamma's greed and meanness was exemplified
only in her relationship with Chennamma, they recognised the
connection between social tension and witchcraft accusations in
all cases. They realised it in the case between Kempamma and
Lingamma by saying that Kempamma had been unjustly pressed
for payment of interest by Lingamma and they also complained
that Halgamma was too greedy in her demands on Hanumegowda. Wangala Peasants tend to attribute witchcraft to persons
with traits they condemn, for example, greed, meanness and bad
temper.

Thus there appear to be three main social functions of Wangala
Peasant witch beliefs. Firstly, witchcraft acts as moralising agent
by condemning socially undesirable traits in individuals; secondly,
by blaming the evil spirit in a woman rather than the woman
herself, witch beliefs help to sustain the social equilibrium; and
thirdly, by upholding the traditional set of values witch beliefs
strengthen the traditional social structure in which women did
not enter the field of money lending.

9 KONKOMBA SORCERY

David Tait

THE KONKOMBA inhabit the Oti Plain in the French and British Trusteeship territories of Northern Togoland. They speak Lekpokpam, which belongs to the Gurma Dialect-Cluster of the Gur languages (Westermann & Bryan 1952: 67). In all they number about 45,000, and their culture is closely related to that of their eastern neighbours the Basare, the Kabire, and the Gurma. The Konkomba territorial and lineage system is one of small localized lineage-segments forming tightly-knit local communities that number at most some two hundred and fifty souls. The territorial unit I call a 'district', and the social unit that occupies a district I call a 'clan' (Tait 1953). Each clan is segmented into two or more major lineages; each major lineage is segmented into two or more minor lineages, which are themselves further segmented.

The Konkomba term for sorcerer is *osŭo* (pl. *bǝsuom*).[1] There is no noun that can properly be translated as 'sorcery', but there is a word, *kǝsŭo*, which refers to a class of phenomena that are evil, a class to which the activities of sorcerers belong. Unlike the Azande (Evans-Pritchard 1937: 9–10) and the Navaho (Kluckhohn 1944: 18), the Konkomba include several different kinds of behaviour under one term. There are two main kinds of activity which are ascribed to malevolent, maleficent persons—the *bǝsuom*. These activities may be called 'sorcery' and 'transvec-

Reprinted from *The Journal of the Royal Anthropological Institute* 84, 1954: 66–74, by permission of Dr. M. Tait and the Council of the Royal Anthropological Institute.

[1] The form *ŭo* is here used to indicate a sound between *u* and *o* that is nasalized.

tion'. I define sorcery as the use of magical medicines to procure the death of a selected victim. The essence of Konkomba sorcery appears to be this use of medicines. Yet, since the Konkomba are not explicit about the preparation of this medicine, it is impossible to say with certainty whether or not the use of spells enters into the technique. The medicine is known simply as _sŭoanjog_ or _osŭo a njog,_ literally 'sorcerer's medicine'. It is true that spells enter into the preparation of _idabin_ (sing. _ndabin_), and these are medicines that are used as protectives against, inter alia, _sŭoanjog._ There is, of course, no reason to suppose that any one ever in fact tries to make sorcerer's medicine, so it cannot definitely be said that spells are or are not used. By transvection I mean the flying by night of a sorcerer to attack a sleeping victim. The flying sorcerer can be seen as a moving light that is known as _sŭoŋmi,_ that is, 'sorcerer-fire'. This belief that flying sorcerers emit a light was noted by Evans-Pritchard among the Azande, and it is found also among the Akan-speaking peoples (Rapp 1935; Rattray 1916: 48) and the Tallensi (Fortes 1949: 33).

Two other methods are occasionally said to be used by Konkomba sorcerers in magical killing. In the first of these, a sorcerer is believed to be able to send snakes to lie in wait on a path until the victim comes along. It is not believed that a chance passer-by will be bitten, since sorcerers kill but they do not kill at random. It is surprising that this technique of sorcery by snake bite is seldom discussed since snake bites, even fatal ones, are not uncommon. The second of the techniques of lesser importance is that the sorcerer, instead of going himself to overlay his victim, sends his shadow to eat the victim's shadow. As the shadow in life is the ghost after death, a man whose shadow is gone dies of a lingering disease. It is probable that this particular belief is invoked only when someone has died of such a disease. The two major techniques of magical killing are both ascribed to one category of person. The technique of bad medicine is indirect in that the sorcerer does not necessarily meet his victim; transvection is direct and involves contact between sorcerer and victim.

Sorcerer's medicine can be transmitted to the victim in three ways: in beer, in a kola-nut, or by being placed on a path. When beer is being passed round in a calabash, the thumb is always kept very carefully out of the beer. It projects above the rim of the calabash and is not depressed in a way that might allow it to dip into the beer. This is because sorcerers are believed to poison their victims by putting the poison under the thumb nail and so transferring it into the beer. The thumb- and all the finger-nails are kept very short, except those of the little fingers. I know of no wholly satisfactory explanation of this short nail. The kola-nut splits down the middle. Sorcerer's medicine can be put into this split and so passed to the victim. The Konkomba do not eat kola-nuts given to them by strangers. They accept the nut, thank the giver, and, later, throw it away. Further, when kola-nuts are eaten they are first split and the two parts are eaten separately. There seems to be no protection against the medicine laid on paths. I know of no avoidance designed to help the victim not to step on it. The method is, in any case, less frequently attributed to sorcerers than are the preceding two. Again, it is believed that only the selected victim would tread on the medicine: chance travellers are not so attacked.

As a protection against transvection, the door leading into a compound is always closed at night. Even so, no one within the compound sleeps alone except, perhaps, a childless woman during the period when her husband is with a co-wife. Even then, if there are young girls in the household one or more of them will sleep with her. Any person approaching a compound after dark does so carefully, announcing his presence, since one defence against the wandering sorcerer is to snatch up a flaming stick from the fire and strike him. This drives him away. The Konkomba also put glowing charcoal by the door of the sleeping room, so that anyone entering can be seen. Finally, the Konkomba seldom go out alone after nightfall and then only during the moon's second quarter. On a dark night no Konkomba would come by himself, even a hundred yards, to set me on my way home, lest he should be unaccompanied on the way back; but two would come together. Though sorcerer-fire is greatly feared, and I have known young men turn about and go home claiming that they had seen it, the danger from it is not very clearly stated. The most precisely stated form of attack is by sorcerer's medicine and the precautions most frequently taken are those against its administration. No one would admit to knowing what ingredients go into it or how it is made. From the precautions taken to destroy the exuviae of a dead body, it may be concluded that these are among the necessary ingredients. Before burial, a body is seated on a tiny stool; the head is shaved, the nails are clipped, and the body and mouth are washed. All this is done with ordinary water. The mouth is again rinsed at the side of the grave with a ritual water called *ndzen*. At this second washing the *ndzen* runs down into the grave. After the shaving and washing, the hair and the nail-clippings are carefully burned, the water used is poured away in the bush, the stool on which the corpse sat is also burned, and the pot in which the washing water was held is broken and the pieces are deposited at a crossroads. All these precautions appear to be designed to prevent a sorcerer from getting hold of the exuviae and using them in the preparation of sorcerer's medicine. The Konkomba term for exuviae is *tədzɔ*.

One seldom hears any discussion about sorcerers, nor are accusations often made openly against individuals. More frequent, though by no means common, are general accusations of the following kind. A man discovered that some puppies, which his bitch had borne on the previous day, had disappeared. It was during the dry season and there was no nearby water into which the puppies could conceivably have fallen. The man's house was separated by a stretch of flood-plain from other houses. No path passed near his house except that leading to it. He stood before his compound shouting 'It is a sorcerer.' He thought that the puppies had been taken by a sorcerer to prepare medicine. Though the possible use of the puppies in the medicine was never fully explained to me, I believe they were to be an addition to the exuviae, an addition which would connect the active principle of the medicine, the exuviae, with the proposed victim. Now, the man was frightened. He was a big, powerfully built man in late middle-age; an active man who worked as an assistant diviner. Assistant diviners do not enjoy special ritual powers among Konkomba but are usually men who have picked up the technique in order to earn some payment in beer and meat, or they are men who simply enjoy going about visiting places (Tait 1952). While he himself was frightened, the others present, who were all members either of his household or of his lineage, were not. They sat and waited. As he himself became more and more excited and shouted the harder, the others confined themselves to brief and non-committal sentences. Nor would those I asked about the matter say whether or not they thought the puppies had in fact been taken away. The women of his household, as well as his kinsmen, were aloof and went about their business unheeding their husband's or father's shouts. The reason why the sufferer's kin did not join him in his accusations is that they themselves might be accused of sorcery.

There are general protective medicines, the *idabin,* which a man who fears that he may be the object of attack can use in his own defence; but, when once the attack has begun, it is too late to use them. The only protection then is sacrifice for rain, and the rain is asked to kill the sorcerer. The victim in this instance went to the rain-maker and asked him to carry out the necessary sacrifice and to put out the rain-medicine. The practice of sacrificing for rain as a protection against sorcerers is linked with the Konkomba belief that any person killed by a thunderbolt was a sorcerer who has been punished by God for his crimes. In 1917 Sir Alan Cardinall noted that a Konkomba shrine could be invoked to kill an enemy.[2] The only form of invocation known to me in which the aim is to bring about the death of an enemy is this invocation for rain.

An example of the accusation of a close kinsman by someone who thought himself to be attacked by sorcery is as follows. By chance, a young man and a diviner took shelter from the rain together. They took shelter in a village to which neither belonged. The young man consulted the diviner about his general well-being and was told that a sorcerer was trying to kill him. The first step in Konkomba divination is a reading of events from six cowrie shells laid on the ground. The young man asked the diviner to demonstrate to him exactly who was seeking to kill him. This was done in a second process of divination which is conceived by Konkomba as a test of the diviner's first reading. To do it, three sticks are laid on the ground and, in the diviner's absence, three questions are decided upon; each question being represented by one of the sticks. The questions once decided, the diviner is recalled. He touches one stick, and one only, with his staff to

[2] The source of this statement is an undated entry by Sir Alan in the Dagomba District Book, Yendi, Northern Territories, Gold Coast, for the year in question.

indicate that in that particular stick the truth lies—that is, that whatever was asked in the appropriate question is to be answered affirmatively. Since the questions put by this method are always of the form, 'Does the sorcerer live in village X?', it can be seen that a series of questions so put clarifies the generalities of the reading of the cowries. By putting these questions to the diviner, the supposed victim makes precise the diviner's vague accusation. In the case in point, the sorcerer was shown to be a member of the young man's own major lineage, though of a different minor lineage. I have never been present when a male sorcerer was directly accused by a victim of the same minor lineage, but there are reports that it has happened. It is even said that a sorcerer will kill his own brother, though I know of no instance of this. On the other hand, I do know of one in which a number of kinsmen joined together to accuse a sorcerer, and the accusers included one who was half-brother to the accused. The accusation was made after the death of the accused, at his Second Burial rites.

Thus, close agnatic kinsmen may be accused by their kin of being sorcerers. It is possible, then, that, when a man suspects that he is being attacked, the non-committal attitude of his kin arises from the fear that they themselves may be accused. It might be thought that they seek to dissociate themselves, in some degree, from the victim lest they too be attacked. The Konkomba themselves do not confirm this; the only time at which a sorcerer is thought to be at all likely to attack anyone, other than a carefully selected victim, is when he is obstructed by a traveller while flying by night. When a man suspects a close agnate of sorcery he does not rush away to accuse him immediately, but waits and watches the suspect. Should he fall inexplicably ill, that is, contract one of the diseases which the Konkomba do not recognize as such, then he may ascribe the illness to a sorcerer. Moreover, diviners sometimes advise their clients to take no action at once, but to await a further sign. In many instances, no doubt, nothing else happens; for example, in the case of the young man already quoted. I asked him over a year later, whether anything more had happened, and he looked very embarrassed as he muttered that 'It was all nothing'. In the end, however, an accusation may be made, and the sorcerer may be driven from his home to settle elsewhere. In one instance, a man who had been accused several times over a number of years by his clansmen was finally driven from his native district only to find that his reputation had followed him and that he had to move on again.

During my stay in the Konkomba country the number of definite accusations against men was approximately the same as against women. Among the Konkomba, whether the social structure be that of a major or a minor lineage or that of a clan, the local community is always exogamous. Consequently, the wives of that community are always members of other and possibly distant local communities. They may have no kinsmen near at hand to protect them, and certainly they have no kinsmen on the spot. In any case, since kinsmen do accuse one another there is no reason to suppose that a kinsman could or would protect an accused fellow-clanswoman. An example of the accusation of a woman is as follows. When a man of Kitiak village was told by a diviner that a particular woman sought to kill him, he went to her and, in the presence of his clansmen, placed a head of guinea-corn on the ground and an arrow on the corn. At this point the accuser used the first of two possible formulae. One can be translated as 'Eat before you die' and the other as 'Choose life or death'. The accused woman ran away that night and has not been heard of since.

In this instance, another woman also was involved in the accusation. It was believed that a second and older woman had 'given the medicine' to the one who was accused. The implication of the sentence 'She gave her the medicine' is not that the older woman gave the younger the medicine that the younger woman used on that one occasion but that she had taught her the skills of a sorcerer. Thus both the women were sorcerers, but they were not jointly charged with seeking to kill their accuser. Shortly afterwards, the older woman moved out of the village and went with her husband to another place. The husband later died there, and her children, who were young, were brought back to Kitiak, but the mother refused to come and stayed in her new home. She was afraid that, should she return, she would be accused of killing her husband. Her absence makes the likelihood of such an accusation almost a certainty. In the Second Burial rites of a dead man there is a point at which his wives appear before the group assembled to divine the cause of death, as an indication that they have nothing to fear. This woman's absence would probably be interpreted as showing that she dared not appear.

Four wives were similarly accused in 1951 in a group of villages with a total population of about 1000. Of these women, two were Kabire. The Konkomba sometimes, as they put it, 'buy' wives from the Kabire. Such women are even more alone than other Konkomba brides for they do not speak a Gurma language. In all four cases the women ran away—possibly to their fathers' homes or possibly to the south. On the other hand, some women have stayed on in their husbands' villages after being accused and have lived down an accusation made when they were young. One such woman died in 1951 and was buried with the full rites of an elder. A final example shows that a woman can be accused of killing her sister. An elderly woman had gone to visit her married daughter, and on her way home called at her natal village and died there. Her Second Burial with the rites of divining the cause of death had not been performed when I left, but her husband's clansmen were accusing her younger sister of killing her with *ndabin. Ndabin,* as I have said, is a medicine that is dangerous: it is commonly a protective one, yet, should it be misused, it may turn upon its maker. It is significant that the accusation of the younger sister does not yet say that she used sorcerer's medicine, but only *ndabin.* The dead woman was known to have gone in search of medicine for her disease, so that this accusation was more than usually vague and tentative.

All other recent instances in which persons have been directly accused of being sorcerers are similar to those already given. From the accusations recorded it is clear that close relatives, even siblings, spouses, clansmen, and clanswomen may be accused of seeking to kill one another. Accusations against women are usually made by men of their husbands' clans. I have never heard of a woman accusing one of her husband's clansmen, but it is not said to be impossible. In Konkomba thought anyone can be a sorcerer and a sorcerer may kill anyone. On the other hand, whereas women are openly threatened with death when they are suspect, kinsmen do not openly accuse one another immediately. They wait for a favourable occasion when feeling is running against the man they suspect. Again, women so threatened may make off at once to be safe. It is probably rare for a man to be driven out of his clan and district, though this does happen. Accusations by men of a clan against women married into it can be seen as an expression of hostility between the in-group of the agnatic clan towards the out-group of the wives. This view is supported by the evidence of what happened to sorcerers in the past. Before the arrival of the Germans in Togoland all deaths were first investigated on the day of death and not only at the Second Burial rites, and the sorcerer was killed on the spot. The investigation was not carried out by a diviner. In those days the body was tied to a pole and was carried round the hamlet. A similar custom was practised by the Ashanti (Rattray 1927: 167–70).

Sorcerers are known by, and only by, certain persons. First, one sorcerer 'knows', that is can see, another; secondly, a dead person knows the living sorcerer who killed him, and, finally, a diviner can point out the sorcerer who has caused, or is seeking to cause, a death. The diviner's powers are stronger after a death has occurred, because in that case his knowledge comes from the dead person. When the dead body was carried round the hamlet, it had the opportunity to point out the sorcerer responsible for the death. Where the corpse kicked a compound wall, there the sorcerer lived. The bearers then entered the compound and again the corpse would kick the wall of a room. It is impossible now to know exactly how it was done. Many living elders saw this rite when they were boys, and some have seen as many as three sorcerers discovered and killed. Such killings were not subject to retaliation and did not lead to feud. In every recorded instance the sorcerer so killed was a woman who had married into the clan carrying out the rite. While this fact can probably be taken as an exemplification of hostility between the in-group and the out-group, it might also be argued that it is a result facilitated by the structure of a Konkomba compound. The compound consists of a ring of round houses. There is a large entry room which is also a byre; behind it a number of rooms are arranged in a rough circle connected by walls to enclose the compound. Each wife has a sleeping room and a kitchen. The compound owner has no room other than the large entry room. Nor are there any other rooms in the compound, unless the head of the house has grown sons who may have a 'young men's room'. It is only in the compound of a lineage elder that a 'young men's room' is invariably found. When once a house had been selected by the corpse, it was almost inevitable that it would be one of the wives who would be exposed as a sorcerer and killed. Nevertheless, it is said that, if the 'young men's room' were indicated by the corpse, then the names of the occupants would be called over until the corpse again kicked the wall in response to a particular name.

There are no other forms of direct accusation of sorcerers known to me. The most frequently occurring accusation is the indirect one made by diviners during Second Burial rites. My records of diviners' findings at these rites show that the Konkomba conception of the cause of death varies with the age of the dead person. Though the Konkomba say that anyone may be attacked by a sorcerer, no instance is known to me in which a diviner has found that a child died by the action of a sorcerer, though there is a wide range of causes of deaths among children, most of which are ritual omissions on the part of their parents. Adults may die as the result of the action of sorcerers and, furthermore, may die because they are themselves sorcerers. The man mentioned earlier, whose brother accused him of sorcery, was believed to have been killed by the ancestors or by God, since a sorcerer is not permitted to continue his evil career indefinitely. Elders, on the other hand, invariably die as the result of attacks by sorcerers but are never themselves sorcerers, since the ancestors do not permit a sorcerer to attain to the dignity of elderhood.[3]

Though the deaths of elders are invariably ascribed to the action of sorcerers, the diviners seldom make direct accusations against individuals. Only once have I heard a diviner name the sorcerer. In this case the accused man was already believed by his kinsmen to be a sorcerer and was spoken of as such. He was a surly fellow who was also accused of sodomy.[4] During the

[3] An elder in this sense is defined as a man (or woman) who has a married daughter or, if not the parent of a daughter, then of a son of such an age that, had he been a girl, he would have been married.

[4] It is not easy to say whether or not there is a constant association in Konkomba thought between sodomy and the male sorcerer. Sodomites are supposed to creep into the rooms of sleeping youths at night. Sorcerers also are believed to creep into rooms at night. Evans-Pritchard (1937: 56) pointed out that lesbianism and witchcraft are associated in Azande

divination he sat, chin in hand, apparently unperturbed by the course it was taking. Nor did he, as others did during the long process, put questions to the diviner designed to clear himself of the accusation. In most other instances so far recorded, only vague accusations were made, or distant persons who were safe from any kind of retaliation were accused.

I have so far described the techniques employed in sorcery and have given examples of sorcery. These examples included (1) the case of a man who believed himself to be attacked; (2) the case of a youth who was warned by a diviner that he was being attacked; (3) the open accusation of a suspected woman and the covert accusation of her supposed instructor in sorcery; (4) the covert accusation of a suspected woman; and (5) the open accusation of a suspected man. In all, I discovered sixteen open and covert accusations of suspected sorcerers during the fifteen months between October 1950 and December 1951. All such accusations took place in a group of villages with a total population of about 1000. These figures do not include the vague accusations against unnamed or distant persons. An examination of the accusations shows that, with two exceptions, the accusations are made by the unmarried men against the younger married men, that is, against men who in Konkomba society are between the ages of forty and fifty years, or against young and usually childless married women. No instance is known to me in which a woman accused someone of sorcery.

The Konkomba say that anyone may be a sorcerer and that anyone may be accused of sorcery. In fact, nearly all direct accusations, either overt or covert, take place within the territorial unit that is a district, and they are either accusations against a man in middle life by a junior clansfellow or against a young wife of the lineage by an unmarried man of the lineage.[5] In other words, accusations of sorcery take place within the major unit of the Konkomba social structure. Within this unit, open aggres-

---

thought, but I have never heard of lesbian practices among Konkomba women. While I have no certain knowledge that males indulge in homosexuality, references to it are not uncommon. Wilson (1952: 88, 196) has pointed out that homosexuality and witchcraft are associated in Nyakyusa thought.

[5] It is an axiom of Konkomba marriage that a 'woman does not marry one man' but a lineage.

sion, conflict, and even loud-voiced quarrelling is prohibited by rigorous ritual sanctions. Fortes (1949: 35, 131), speaking of the Tallensi, a people very similar to the Konkomba, pointed out that among them witchcraft is linked with uterine kinship and may be transmitted by uterine descent. This fact, he points out, dissociates witchcraft from agnatic descent and disperses it along the wider ranging lines of uterine kinship. Such a dissociation protects the agnatic lineage from the disruption consequent upon accusation of witchcraft. The Konkomba lineage is not so protected: the possibility of accusing an agnatic kinsman of learning his sorcery from his father exposes that lineage to disruption. The Tallensi polygynous family, on the other hand, can be seriously disrupted by accusations of witchcraft among co-wives. Though tensions between Konkomba co-wives can be very strong, no case is known to me in which a wife accused her co-wife of sorcery.

Konkomba sorcery may be taught by a father to his son or by a mother to her daughter. Instances of both these modes of instruction are known. But other examples show that a sorcerer may learn from a person who stands in no kinship relation to him or her. The Konkomba say that not only does one sorcerer 'see' (recognize) another but that a sorcerer can 'see' a potential, commonly a youthful, sorcerer, one who has not yet 'got the medicine'. Moreover, the potential but as yet uninstructed sorcerer can see 'one who has the medicine', and so may ask that person for it. In all known cases, males have instructed males and females have instructed females, and the instructor is always senior to the pupil. There are but the slightest signs in Konkomba thought of a concept of a sorcerers' association. There is no sign at all of an association or corporation of witch-finders such as Nadel (1935) found among the Nupe and Field (1937: 130) among the Gã. Even Konkomba diviners do not form a corporate body but are a category of ritual persons, each one of whom is 'sent into the world' individually by a dead diviner of the same lineage. Every sorcerer learns from a senior sorcerer by being given sorcerer's medicine. While this medicine is fatal to the ordinary person, the sorcerer eats it not merely with impunity but in order to gain power as a sorcerer. While there are a number of categories of ritual—diviners, persons 'sent into the world' by the land or by a shrine—it does not seem that sorcerers form such a category. There is no suggestion that a sorcerer is 'sent into the world' by a dead sorcerer of his own or any other lineage.

On the other hand, there is no idea among the Konkomba of the unwitting sorcerer or of one who is so because of an inherited physical condition.[6] Sorcery is a technique to be acquired, and the sorcerer kills with full knowledge of his evil intentions. (I return to this point below.) Nor does the sorcerer work in concert with other sorcerers, though it is sometimes suggested that they employ transvection to hold sorcerers' meetings. No one is at all clear as to the purpose of these meetings: there appear to be no sabbath, no feasting, and no rites at them. Nor are they used as occasions for the instruction of novices. No qualifications, such as the murder of a sibling as among the Navaho (Kluckhohn, 1944), are required of a would-be sorcerer. The assembly, such as it is, seems to be no more than a gathering together of sorcerers before each one flies off alone in search of his intended victim. There is thus no suggestion of co-operation between sorcerers. The accusations made by men against the young women married into their lineage can be regarded as an expression of hostility between the in-group and the out-group. The accusations by young men against their seniors can be regarded as an expression of hostility towards men who exercise some authority, are possibly wealthy in cattle, and who have a number of wives but who, at the same time, are not yet senior enough to enjoy the privileges and ritual protection of elderhood.

Motives for their murders are in turn ascribed to sorcerers. I have already pointed out that the death of any elder is attributed to sorcery. In this gerontocratic society the lineage elders control most of the wealth in land, cattle, or money. The sorcerers, therefore, are said to be jealous of the wealth and power of men who are their seniors. When a younger brother is accused of killing his elder brother by sorcery, it is said that this has been done in order that the younger brother should inherit from the elder; and similarly when a woman is accused of killing her elder sister, and a wife of killing her senior co-wife. Conversely, it is dangerous for a man to succeed to a large number of cattle or

[6] Cf. Field (1937: 154) who speaks, however, of witches, not of sorcerers.

of wives at an early age, since he would then be in danger of being accused of getting them by sorcery. These are the motives most clearly ascribed to sorcerers; but specific motives are not essential to a sorcerer, because, as conceived by the Konkomba, he is evil and needs no other motive than his desire to destroy.

In these days a sorcerer is no longer killed. Women, it is true, commonly run away when accused in order to be safe. Men, when first accused, do not abandon their native clans; but, under the pressure of repeated accusations, they either move their houses to a separate part of their natal districts or go to live in a new place. The strongest penal sanction on an accused sorcerer is that of ostracism. Clansmen do not assist a suspected sorcerer in his farm work, nor do they speak to him in daily intercourse. A stronger sanction still is a ritual one: an unrelenting sorcerer will be removed by God or the ancestors. On the other hand, the Konkomba have no concept of ghostly vengeance, nor of vengeance by socially approved magic against the sorcerer. The ordinary homicide has the ritual symbol of his lineage as a protection against the ghost of the man he killed. For three nights the homicide sleeps with this symbol and a medicine horn beside him, lest the ghost appear. The sorcerer is protected by his medicine, which is at once the source of his power and a protection against ghostly vengeance. When a sorcerer dies, however, his medicine dies with him and he is buried with no more than the full rites to which his seniority entitles him.[7] Yet, during his Second Burial rites, a ritual impediment to the departure of his spirit may appear, an impediment which can be removed only by sacrifice. This ritual impediment is discovered by the diviner during the rites, and, on one occasion, it was due to the refusal of the ancestors to accept the spirit of the dead sorcerer without special sacrifice. Such an impediment does not always appear, however, and the dead sorcerer may be buried and mourned almost as though his life had been exemplary. In this Konkomba practice contrasts strongly with that of the Ewe of Hohoe, among whom a sorcerer's body is dragged to the grave in ragged clothing and is beaten with sticks before interment. The Ewe believe that sorcerers live apart from ordinary people in the afterworld, and

[7] The Tallensi also give a witch ordinary burial (Fortes 1949: 34).

that, were the spirit to arrive there unbeaten, it would be accepted neither by the spirits of ordinary people nor by those of sorcerers. (This information was given to me by students at the University College of the Gold Coast.)

The sorcerer, as I have said, is not an unwitting practitioner; he is not a sufferer from an inherited condition; he is not a person sent specially into the world by a dead sorcerer. Whence, then, comes his sorcery? He is always an individual working alone. He is one who chooses to make a deliberate approach to someone versed in sorcery to learn a technique. He is one who has asked a senior sorcerer to give him the medicine and by an act of will has eaten it in order to gain the mystical knowledge of sorcery.[8] The sorcerer can, if he will, cease to be a sorcerer. Indeed, to avoid the anger of God he must make that decision; and the problem of sorcery is therefore a moral one. Here I am concerned only with the general pattern of sorcery. On another occasion I will try to break up that pattern into smaller units. At present it can be said that the general pattern of accusations of sorcery against men of some position in Konkomba society suggests that the sorcerer is conceived as one who is rich in property or in women, or is of some status, and has used sorcery to acquire these things.

In this poor society, set in a harsh environment and with a low productive technology, there is little differentiation in wealth, and what accumulations exist are in the hands of the lineage elders, who are protected from the jealousy of their juniors by strong ritual sanctions. No means lie open to an ambitious man to achieve economic, ritual, or political power by his own efforts. The lineage elders achieve their status by simple seniority, and in them is vested supreme economic, ritual, and political power. Some ritual power, occasionally great, is vested in diviners, in persons 'sent by the land', in persons 'sent by' particular shrines, in persons 'sent by' dead ancestors, and in those who now 'hold spirits', that is, who control and use spirits for good, socially approved purposes. All these statuses are conferred by the chances of birth and by other accidents of life. None can be achieved by personal effort. The role of assistant diviner is singular in that it

[8] Cf. Fortes (1949: 35), who says that Tallensi mothers may give their children witches' medicine to eat in infancy.

does offer an individual some increase in his status. But, as conceived by the Konkomba, the role is not one of great importance, nor does it in fact lead to much ritual power, and, since even diviners exercise no political power, it is clear that assistant diviners cannot do so either.

The general pattern of accusations against women differs from that of accusations against men. Though women are 'sent by' dead diviners, 'the land' etc., the exigencies of their lives prevent them from exercising the roles proper to their ritual status. A woman 'sent by the land', for example, marries into a clan where she had no special ritual relation to the land; her status holds only in her natal district. She marries into a strange place where she is young, lonely, and of little consequence. Only with the slow passage of time and the birth of her children can she acquire the high privileged status of a cherished lineage mother. Young women accused of sorcery thus belong to a category which the Konkomba recognize as unhappy and dissatisfied. They are persons who are discontented in their personal lives and resentful of their place in society. They are often, then, accused of expressing this resentment by killing, or seeking to kill, members of the clan which is the context of their discontent.

I have suggested elsewhere (Tait 1952) that the Konkomba diviner is cast in the role of a stabilizing agent. He helps to reassure, to preserve stability, to assist continuity in life. As against him the solitary sorcerer is cast in a Faustian role. He is one who seeks to break out of the closed circle of traditional morality. He tries, by his own effort, to achieve the satisfactions of wealth and power.

10 DREAMS AND THE WISHES OF THE SOUL: A TYPE OF PSYCHOANALYTIC THEORY AMONG THE SEVENTEENTH CENTURY IROQUOIS[1]

Anthony F. C. Wallace

ANTHROPOLOGISTS have traditionally paid attention to the dreams and dream-related behavior of primitive peoples. Three sorts of anthropological interest may be distinguished: the ethnographic, the historical, and the psychoanalytic. The ethnographer describes the beliefs and customs of his subjects, including the customary way in which they regard and use dream experiences. The ethnologist may look to dreams as the point of origin for innovations, or—and I think here particularly of Tylor —he may regard primitive theorizing about the meaning of dreams as the source of fundamental and widely-distributed assumptions about the nature of the world; Tylor thought the experience of

Reprinted from *The American Anthropologist* 60 (2), 1958: 234–48, by permission of the author and the American Anthropological Association.

[1] The data presented in this paper were in part assembled in the course of a study of the Handsome Lake religion conducted while the writer was a Faculty Research Fellow of the Social Science Research Council, and were analyzed in the course of a comparative study of religious movements supported by Grants M-883 and M-1106 from the National Institute of Mental Health and Grant 1769 (Penrose Fund) from The American Philosophical Society. Research assistance was provided by Josephine Dixon; W. N. Fenton gave valued criticism.
It should be noted that I use the word "psychoanalytic" in this paper to denote a group of theories rather than a specific one. Rigorous usage would exclude many variants and dilutions which, for want of a better term, I gather under the rubric "psychoanalytic." Psychoanalytic in this usage thus includes any theory of dreams which regards the dream as the symbolic expression of unconscious wishes. As the following pages will indicate, the Iroquois theory differed from Freudian theory in regard to substantive interpretation: the Iroquois did not use the incest (Oedipus) formulation, did not give a central role to the concept of intrapsychic conflict, and did not reduce content regularly to sexual symbols. The Freudian theory of course did not use the concept of a detachable soul nor did it admit the presence of supernatural beings.

dreaming of distant or deceased persons might have suggested to early man the concept of the soul, and thus have contributed to the "theory" of animism. Finally, the cultural anthropologist of this generation has sometimes used reported dreams as data for psychoanalytic types of interpretation, with a view to determining what personality organizations might be regarded as typical of whole peoples or even of mankind, or as a portal to the understanding of the individual's relationship to his culture.

This paper is essentially ethnographic; it describes the theory and practice, relative to dreams, reported by Jesuit missionaries among the seventeenth-century Iroquois. However, the data raise questions of both theoretical and historical interest: for we find here a "primitive" people actively using a theory of the mind similar in many essentials to that expressed by Sigmund Freud and his intellectual heirs in Western European cultural tradition of two centuries later. It is at least an interesting case of independent invention (for I see no evidence of Iroquois dream theory having influenced Freud, directly or indirectly). It emphasizes again the probable importance of dreams as sources of innovation in human cultural history. And it poses an interesting question in the sociology of knowledge: what (if any) common sociocultural forces can be found to explain the existence of such similar psychological theories in two such different societies as Vienna and Iroquoia? While it is evident that Iroquoian and Freudian dream theory are not precisely the same (and the Iroquoian theory introduced an animistic thesis as well as the psychoanalytic one), the differences are not much more marked than the differences between, for instance, Jungian and Freudian varieties of psychoanalytic theory. It seems to the writer that this curious case of independent invention, in two such different cultures and in an area of culture peculiarly subject (so one might think) to functional explanations of various kinds, raises the dormant theoretical question of the nature of the psychic unity of mankind, and suggests the importance of the now unfashionable interest in the philosophical activities of "primitive" peoples for the evaluation of psycholinguistic studies and theories of "primitive" thought.[2]

---

[2] There is another area of Iroquois psychological theory which neatly parallels current psychiatric formulations: the process of mourning. In a separate paper I hope to delineate this matter too.

The black-robed Jesuit fathers began the preaching of the gospel to the Seneca nation in the year 1668. They quickly found that the Seneca were rigidly attached to Iroquoian religious traditions and were particularly obstinate in looking to their dreams for guidance in all the important affairs of life. Father Fremin wrote:

> The Iroquois have, properly speaking, only a single Divinity—the dream. To it they render their submission, and follow all its orders with the utmost exactness. The Tsonnontouens [Seneca] are more attached to this superstition than any of the others; their Religion in this respect becomes even a matter of scruple; whatever it be that they think they have done in their dreams, they believe themselves absolutely obliged to execute at the earliest moment. The other nations content themselves with observing those of their dreams which are the most important; but this people, which has the reputation of living more religiously than its neighbors, would think itself guilty of a great crime if it failed in its observance of a single dream. The people think only of that, they talk about nothing else, and all their cabins are filled with their dreams. They spare no pains, no industry, to show their attachment thereto, and their folly in this particular goes to such an excess as would be hard to imagine. He who has dreamed during the night that he was bathing, runs immediately, as soon as he rises, all naked, to several cabins, in each of which he has a kettleful of water thrown over his body, however cold the weather may be. Another who has dreamed that he was taken prisoner and burned alive, has found himself bound and burned like a captive on the next day, being persuaded that by thus satisfying his dream, this fidelity will avert from him the pain and infamy of captivity and death,—which, according to what he has learned from his Divinity, he is otherwise bound to suffer among his enemies. Some have been known to go as far as Quebec, travelling a hundred and fifty leagues, for the sake of getting a dog, that they had dreamed of buying there. . . .

Father Fremin and his colleagues were appalled: some Seneca might, any night, dream of their deaths! "What peril we are in every day," he wrote, "among people who will murder us in cold blood if they have dreamed of doing so; and how slight needs to be an offense that a Barbarian has received from someone, to enable his heated imagination to represent to him in a dream that he takes revenge on the offender" (letter of Father Fremin, in Kenton 1927, 2:191–92). It is small wonder that the Jesuits early attempted to disabuse the Seneca of their confidence in dreams, propounding various subtle questions such as, "Does the soul leave the body during sleep?" and "Can infants in the womb dream?", either affirmative or negative answers to which would involve the recognition (according to the Jesuits) of logical contradictions in native theory (Relation of Father Carheil, 1669–70, in Kenton 1927, 2:186–89).

But Jesuit logic did not discourage Seneca faith. The Quaker missionaries who reached the Seneca one hundred and thirty years later found in them much the same "superstitious" respect for dreams which their unsuccessful predecessors had discovered. "They are superstitious in the extreme, with respect to dreams, and witchcraft," wrote Halliday Jackson (1830) "and councils are often called, on the most trifling occurrences of this nature. To elucidate this—in the winter of 1799, while one of the Friends was engaged in instructing the children in school learning, a message came from a confederate tribe, eighty miles distant, stating that one of their little girls had dreamed that 'the devil was in all white people alike, and that they ought not to receive instruction from the Quakers, neither was it right for their children to learn to read and write.' In consequence of this circumstance, a council was called, the matter was deliberated on, and divers of them became so much alarmed, as to prevent their children from attending the school for some time."

This faith in dreams is still alive, although somewhat diminished in strength, in the twentieth century. For many Seneca, dreams even today control the choice and occasion of curing ceremonies, membership in the "secret" medicine societies, the selection of friends, and degree of confidence in life. At the New Year's ceremony, people still go about asking that their dreams be guessed, and a particularly vivid dream still is brought to a clairvoyant (usually a woman) for interpretation (Fenton 1953; and personal communications from M. H. Deardorff). Over the course of nearly three hundred years and probably longer, the Seneca—like the other Iroquois—have let dreams direct their lives.

The Iroquois theory of dreams was basically psychoanalytic. Father Ragueneau in 1649 described the theory in language which might have been used by Freud himself:

> In addition to the desires which we generally have that are free, or at least voluntary in us, [and] which arise from a previous knowledge of some goodness that we imagine to exist in the thing

desired, the Hurons [and, he might have added, the Seneca] believe that our souls have other desires, which are, as it were, inborn and concealed. These, they say, come from the depths of the soul, not through any knowledge, but by means of a certain blind transporting of the soul to certain objects; these transports might in the language of philosophy be called *Desideria innata,* to distinguish them from the former, which are called *Desideria Elicita.*

Now they believe that our soul makes these natural desires known by means of dreams, which are its language. Accordingly, when these desires are accomplished, it is satisfied; but, on the contrary, if it be not granted what it desires, it becomes angry, and not only does not give its body the good and the happiness that it wished to procure for it, but often it also revolts against the body, causing various diseases, and even death. . . .

In consequence of these erroneous [thought Father Ragueneau] ideas, most of the Hurons are very careful to note their dreams, and to provide the soul with what it has pictured to them during their sleep. If, for instance, they have seen a javelin in a dream, they try to get it; if they have dreamed that they gave a feast, they will give one on awakening, if they have the wherewithal; and so on with other things. And they call this *Ondinnonk*—a secret desire of the soul manifested by a dream (Kenton 1927, 1:503–4).

But the Hurons recognized that the manifest content or emptiness of a dream might conceal rather than reveal the soul's true wish. And so:

. . . just as, although we did not always declare our thoughts and inclinations by means of speech, those who by means of supernatural vision could see into the depths of our hearts would not fail to have a knowledge of them—in the same manner, the Hurons believe that there are certain persons, more enlightened than the common, whose sight penetrates, as it were, into the depths of the soul. These see the natural and hidden desires that it has, though the soul has declared nothing by dreams, or though he who may have had the dreams had completely forgotten them. It is thus that their medicine-men . . . acquire credit, and make the most of their art by saying that a child in the cradle, who has neither discernment nor knowledge, will have an *Ondinnonk*—that is to say, a natural and hidden desire for such or such a thing; and that a sick person will have similar desires for various things of which he has never had any knowledge, or anything approaching it. For, as we shall explain further on, the Hurons believe that one of the most efficacious remedies for rapidly restoring health is to grant the soul of the sick person these natural desires (Relation of Father Ragueneau, 1647–48, in Kenton 1927, 1:503–4).

According to Iroquois theory, disease or bodily infirmity could arise from three sources: from natural injuries, such as the wounds of war or physical accident; from witchcraft, by which certain foreign articles such as balls of hair, splinters of bone, clots of blood, or bear's teeth were projected magically into a victim's body; and from

> the mind of the patient himself, which desires something, and will vex the body of the sick man until it possesses the thing required. For they think that there are in every man certain inborn desires, often unknown to themselves, upon which the happiness of individuals depends. For the purpose of ascertaining desires and innate appetites of this character, they summon soothsayers, who, as they think, have a divinely-imparted power to look into the inmost recesses of the mind. These men declare that whatever first occurs to them, or something from which they suspect some gain can be derived, is desired by the sick person. Thereupon the parents, friends, and relatives of the patient do not hesitate to procure and lavish upon him whatever it may be, however expensive, a return of which is never thereafter to be sought . . . (Relation of Father Jouvency, 1610–13, in Kenton 1927, 1:7).

The Huron, Seneca, and other Iroquoian peoples ascribed to the soul several faculties which are not unlike the faculties which European psychologists of the day (i.e. the theologians) recognized. The Huron considered that the human body was inhabited by a single soul with several functions, and depending on the function which was being alluded to at the moment, a different name was used. There was a name for the soul in its capacity to animate the body and give it life; in its capacity to have knowledge; in its capacity to exercise judgment; in its capacity to wish or desire; and in its capacity to leave the body, as it might during dreams or after death. The soul occupied all parts of the body, and so had head, arms, legs, trunk, and all the rest of the anatomy (in ethereal counterpart) of the corporeal body (Relation of Father LeJeune, 1636, in Kenton 1927, 1:255–56).

Intuitively, the Iroquois had achieved a great degree of psychological sophistication. They recognized conscious and unconscious parts of the mind. They knew the great force of unconscious desires, and were aware that the frustration of these desires could cause mental and physical ("psychosomatic") illness. They understood that these desires were expressed in symbolic form by dreams, but that the individual could not always properly interpret these dreams himself. They had noted the distinction between the manifest and latent content of dreams, and employed what sounds like the technique of free association to uncover the latent meaning. And they considered that the best method for the relief of psychic and psychosomatic distress was to give the frustrated desire satisfaction, either directly or symbolically.

The dreams reported by the Jesuit fathers, and in the ethnological literature up to the present time, provide a measure of the range and types of manifest content, and to a degree of the latent content, of Iroquois dreams. Dreams involving overt sexuality were not rare, and since they were freely reported and often acted out in therapeutic orgies, they gave the fathers great concern. Normally the Iroquoian peoples were modest in dress, often rather shy in heterosexual contacts, and although premarital affairs were freely permitted to the young people and divorce and remarriage were easy for adults, chastity and marital fidelity were publicly recognized ideals. The fulfillment of dream wishes, however, took priority over other proprieties.

In 1656, at Onondaga, three warriors came to the village during the Midwinter Ceremony. They had been absent for a year in an unsuccessful campaign against the Cat, or Erie, Nation. One of the warriors "was as wasted, pale, and depressed, as if he had spoken with the Devil. He spat blood, and was so disfigured that one scarcely dared to look him in the face." This man, when he arrived, announced that he had a matter of great importance to communicate to the elders. When they had assembled, he told them that during the campaign he had seen Tarachiawagon, He-who-holds-up-the-sky, the culture hero, in the guise of a little dwarf. Tarachiawagon had addressed the warrior thus:

> I am he who holds up the Sky, and the guardian of the earth; I preserve men, and give victories to warriors. I have made you masters of the earth and victors over so many Nations: I made you conquer the Hurons, the Tobacco Nation, the Ahondihronnons, Atiraguenrek, Atiaonrek, Takoulguehronnons and Gentaguetehronnons; in short, I have made you what you are: and if you wish me to continue my protection over you, hear my words, and execute my orders.

First, you will find three Frenchmen in your village when you arrive there. Secondly, you will enter during the celebration of the Honnaouroria. Thirdly, after your arrival, let there be sacrificed to me ten dogs, ten porcelain beads from each cabin, a collar [belt of wampum] ten rows wide, four measures of sunflower seed, and as many of beans. And, as for thee, let two married women be given thee, to be at thy disposal for five days. If that be not executed item by item I will make thy Nation a prey to all sorts of disaster,—and, after it is all done, I will declare to thee my orders for the future (Father deQuens, Relation of 1655–56, in Kenton 1927, 2:80–81).

The dreamer's demands were fulfilled.

The Jesuits noted also, among the Huron, a formal ritual of gratification of sexual wishes expressed in dreams. In 1639, Father LeJeune met an old man ("in the common opinion of the Savages, . . . one of the most respectable and virtuous men of the whole country") who was dying of an ulcer which had spread from his wrist to his shoulder and finally had begun to eat into his torso. This man's last desires were "a number of dogs of a certain shape and color, with which to make a three days' feast; a quantity of flour for the same purpose; some dances, and like performances; but principally . . . the ceremony of the 'andacwander,' a mating of men with girls, which is made at the end of the feast. He specified that there should be 12 girls, and a thirteenth for himself" (Relation of Father LeJeune, 1639, in Kenton 1927, 1:388).

During the dream guessing rites at Midwinter and, on occasion of illness, at other times of the year, persons propounded riddles in a sacred game. Each person or a group announced his "own and special desire or 'Ondinonc'—according as he is able to get information and enlightenment by dreams—not openly, however, but through Riddles. For example, someone will say, 'What I desire and what I am seeking is that which bears a lake within itself'; and by this is intended a pumpkin or calabash. Another will say, 'What I ask for is seen in my eyes—it will be marked with various colors'; and because the same Huron word that signifies 'eye' also signifies 'glass bead', this is a clue to divine what he desires—namely, some kinds of beads of this material, and of different colors. Another will intimate that he desires an Andacwandat feast—that is to say, many fornications and adulteries. His Riddle being guessed, there is no lack of persons to satisfy his desire" (Father LeJeune, Relation of 1639, in Kenton 1927, 1:398).

Nightmares of torture and personal loss were apparently not uncommon among warriors. In 1642 a Huron man dreamed that non-Huron Iroquois had taken him and burned him as a captive. As soon as he awoke, a council was held. "The ill fortune of such a Dream," said the chiefs, "must be averted." At once twelve or thirteen fires were lighted in the cabin where captives were burned, and torturers seized fire brands. The dreamer was burned; "he shrieked like a madman. When he avoided one fire, he at once fell into another." Naked, he stumbled around the fires three times, singed by one torch after another, while his friends repeated compassionately, "courage, my Brother, it is thus that we have pity on thee." Finally he darted out of the ring, seized a dog held for him there, and paraded through the cabins with this dog on his shoulders, publicly offering it as a consecrated victim to the demon of war, "begging him to accept this semblance instead of the reality of his Dream." The dog was finally killed with a club, roasted in the flames, and eaten at a public feast, "in the same manner as they usually eat their captives" (Father Lalemant, Relation of 1642, in Kenton 1927, 1:455–56). In the period 1645–49, Father Francesco Bressani saw a Huron cut off a finger with a sea-shell because he had dreamed that his enemies had captured him and were performing this amputation (Bressani's Relation of 1653, in Kenton 1927, 2:42). In 1661–62, Father Lalemant describes three similar cases among the Five Nations. One man, in order to satisfy the dictates of his dream, had himself stripped naked by his friends, bound, dragged through the streets with the customary hooting, set upon the scaffold, and the fires lit. "But he was content with all these preliminaries, and, after passing some hours in singing his death song, thanked the company, believing that after this imaginary captivity he would never be actually a prisoner." Another man having dreamt that his cabin was on fire, "could find no rest until he could see it actually burning." The chief's council in a body, "after mature deliberation on the matter," ceremoniously burned it down for him. A third man went to such extremes of realism, after a captivity nightmare, that he determined "that the fire should be actually applied to his legs, in the same

way as to captives when their final torture is begun." The roasting
was so cruel and prolonged that it took six months for him to
recover from his burns (Father Lalemant, Relation of 1661–62,
in Kenton 1927, 2:74 fn.).

Some dreams were violently aggressive. One Huron dreamed
that he killed a French priest. "I killed a Frenchman; that is my
dream. Which must be fulfilled at any cost," he yelled. He was
only appeased by being given a French coat supposedly taken
from the body of a dead Frenchman. A Cayuga man dreamed
that he gave a feast of human flesh. He invited all the chief men
of the Cayuga nation to his cabin to hear a matter of importance.
"When they had assembled, he told them that he was ruined, as
he had had a dream impossible of fulfillment; that his ruin would
entail that of the whole Nation; and that a universal overthrow
and destruction of the earth was to be expected. He enlarged at
great length on the subject, and then asked them to guess his
dream. All struck wide of the mark, until one man, suspecting the
truth, said to him: 'Thou wishest to give a feast of human flesh.
Here, take my brother; I place him in thy hands to be cut up on
the spot, and put into the kettle.' All present were seized with
fright, except the dreamer, who said that his dream required a
woman." A young girl was adorned with ornaments and, unaware
of her fate, led to the dreamer-executioner. "He took her; they
watched his actions, and pitied that innocent girl; but, when they
thought him about to deal the death-blow, he cried out: 'I am
satisfied; my dream requires nothing further'" (Father deQuens,
Relation of 1655–56, in Kenton 1927, 2:69–75). During the
"Feast of Fools," the annual *Ononharoia* or "turning the brain
upside down," when men and women ran madly from cabin to
cabin, acting out their dreams in charades and demanding the
dream be guessed and satisfied, many women and men alike
dreamt of fighting natural enemies. Dreams in which hostility
was directed at members of other nations were properly satisfied
by acting them out both in pantomime and in real life; but bad
dreams about members of the same community were acted out
only in some symbolic form, which had a prophylactic effect.
Thus, someone on the Cornplanter Seneca Reservation (during
the nineteenth century) dreamed that a certain young woman
was alone in a canoe, in the middle of a stream, without a pad-

dle. The dreamer invited the young lady to a dream-guessing ceremony at his home. Various people gathered and each one tried to guess what the dream was. Finally the dream was guessed. A miniature canoe with a paddle was thereupon presented to the girl. This ceremony was expected to forestall the dream disaster from happening in real life (Skinner Ms: 13–14).

Dreams were very common in which the dreamer met a supernatural being who promised to be a friend and patron and to give his protegé special powers and responsibilities. They were often experienced by boys at puberty who deliberately sought such guardian spirits. One case was described in some detail by the Jesuits. At the age of fifteen or sixteen, the youth retired alone into the woods, where he spent sixteen days without food, drinking only water. Suddenly he heard a voice, which came from the sky, saying, "Take care of this man, and let him end his fast." At the same time, he saw an old man "of rare beauty" descend from the sky. This man approached, gazed kindly at him, and said, "Have courage, I will take care of thy life. It is a fortunate thing for thee, to have taken me for thy master. None of these Demons who haunt these countries, shall have any power to harm thee. One day thou wilt see thy hair as white as mine. Thou wilt have four children; the first two and the last will be males, and the third will be a girl; after that, thy wife will hold the relation of a sister to thee." As he concluded speaking, the old man held out to him a piece of raw human flesh. The youth turned aside his head in horror. "Eat this," then said the old man, presenting him with a piece of bear's fat. When the lad had eaten it, the old man disappeared. On later occasions, however, he frequently reappeared with assurances of help. Most of the old man's predictions came true: the youth, become a man, had four children, the third of whom was a girl; after the fourth, "a certain infirmity compelled him to . . . continence"; and, as the eating of the bear's meat augured, the man became a noted hunter, gifted with a second sight for finding game. As an old man, looking back, he judged that "he would have had equal success in war had he eaten the piece of human flesh that he refused." In his later years this man became a Christian and was baptized (Father Lalemant, Relation of 1642, in Kenton 1927, 1:453–54).

Dreams of supernatural protectors (or persecutors) also came often to sick persons, and the appropriate therapeutic ritual was deduced from the identity of the spirit. Thus, dreams of false-faces call for the curing rituals of the Society of Faces; dreams of birds (in recent years, particularly of bloody or headless chickens) indicated that the Dew Eagle Ceremony was required. Sick persons often dreamed of someone (or a relative of the sick person dreamed), and the dream was interpreted to mean that the sick person "wants a friend." During the Eagle Society Ceremony, the sick person is given a "ceremonial friend"; thereafter the two treat one another as kinfolk, and the relationship of mutual helpfulness is life-long. If a boy's friend, for instance, is an older man, he

> . . . must help the child to grow up to be a man. He must advise the boy, acting as his counsellor. . . . When one is ill, they choose a friend for him from the other side (moiety). It is believed that the ceremony of making friends merges the relatives of the two principals into one kindred unit: the relatives of the man are linked with the relatives of the child. The older man must act as an example to his junior friend. The older man's conduct shall be observed by the younger boy who considers the older friend a model of behavior. The creator has ordained that these two be friends and it is hoped the younger one will grow up to be the fine man his older partner is supposed to be. Whatever he observes the older man doing, he shall do it. The old man bears the onus of the child's future. As a reward he will see the Creator when he dies. When the two meet on the road, the older person speaks first. "Thanks you are well my friend?" The younger one answers, "Truly thank you I am well my friend." Every time he sees me, he calls me "friend" (Fenton 1953: 126; quoting Seneca informant, He-strikes-the-rushes).

The force of the unconscious desires of the individual, which are so compelling that "it would be cruelty, nay, murder, not to give a man the subject of his dream; for such a refusal might cause his death," sometimes was reinforced by the fact that in native theory they were the vehicle for expressing the desires and commands of the supernatural beings whom his wandering dream-soul had met. Some of these supernatural dreams have already been mentioned. Those involving powerful supernaturals like Tarachiawagon were apt to achieve a great notoriety, and (if the chiefs considered the dream ominous) the whole nation might exert itself to fulfill the dreamer's demands; neglect invited national disaster. In the winter of 1640, during an epidemic of smallpox among the Huron, a young fisherman had a vision: a demon appeared to him under the form of a tall and handsome young man. "Fear not," said the being, "I am the master of the earth, whom you Hurons honor under the name of Iouskeha. I am the one whom the French wrongly call Jesus, but they do not know me. I have pity on your country, which I have taken under my protection; I come to teach you both the reasons and the remedies for your misfortune. It is the strangers who alone are the cause of it; they now travel two by two through the country, with the design of spreading the disease everywhere. They will not stop with that; after this smallpox which now depopulates your cabins, there will follow certain colics which in less than three days will carry off all those whom this disease may not have removed. You can prevent this misfortune; drive out from your village the two black gowns who are there." The demon continued with prescriptions for distributing medicinal waters to the sick; but after a few days, apparently, the popular disturbance subsided and the priests were not expelled (Father Lalemant, Relation of 1640, in Kenton 1927, 1:254–55 fn.). In the winter of 1669–70, a woman at Oneida was visited in a dream by Tarachiawagon, who told her that the Andaste (southern enemies of the Five Nations) would attack and besiege the Oneida village in the spring, but that the Oneida would be victorious and that they would capture one of the most famous Andaste war-captains. In her dream she heard the voice of this man coming from the bottom of a kettle, uttering wailing cries like the cries of those who are being burned. For a time, this woman became a prophet; every day people foregathered at her house to hear her pronouncements; and all she said was believed absolutely (Father Bruyas, Relation of 1669–70, in Kenton 1927, 2:80 fn.). Of course, prophetic dreams of this kind derived much of their impact from the conviction of the community that while some dreams expressed only the wishes of the dreamer's soul, others expressed the wishes of his personal guardian spirit or of various supernatural beings—particularly of Tarachiawagon, the Holder of the Heavens, the Master of Life, he who decided the fate of battles, the clemency of the seasons, the fruitfulness of the crops, and the success of the chase.

The effectiveness of the Iroquois dream-therapy was sometimes admitted even by the Jesuits, who had neither psychological insight nor religious sympathy for the primitive dream-theory. Father LeJeune described the case of a woman who had gone to live with her husband in a strange village. One moonlit night, during a feast, she walked out from her cabin with one of her baby daughters in her arms. Suddenly, she saw the moon dip down to earth and transform itself into a tall, beautiful woman, holding in her arms a little girl like her own. This moon-lady declared herself to be the "immortal seignior" of the Hurons and the several nations allied to them, and announced that it was her wish that from each of the half-dozen or so tribes she named, a present of that tribe's special product should be given to the dreamer—from the Tobacco Nation, some tobacco; from the Neutrals, some robes of black squirrel fur; and so on. She declared that she liked the feast then being given, and wanted others like it to be held in all the other villages and tribes. "Besides," she said, "I love thee, and on that account I wish that thou shouldst henceforth be like me; and as I am wholly of fire, I desire that thou be also at least of the color of fire," and so she ordained for her a red cap, red plume, red belt, red leggings, red shoes, red all the rest.

The moon-lady then vanished and the mother returned to her cabin, where she collapsed "with a giddiness in the head and a contraction of the muscles." Thereafter she dreamt constantly of "goings and comings and outcries through her cabin."

It was decided by the chiefs that this was an important matter and that every effort should be made to give satisfaction to the sick woman: not only her wishes but those of the moon-lady were involved. She was dressed in red; the disease was diagnosed (from the symptom of giddiness) as demanding the Dream Feast or Ononwharoria ("turning the brain upside down") and messengers collected for her the articles she required. The Jesuits sounded a sour note, refusing to contribute the blue blanket she wanted from a "Frenchman," but the lady went through the five-day ritual, supported on the arms of sympathetic friends. She hobbled in her bare feet through more than two hundred fires; she received hundreds of gifts; she propounded her last desire in dozens of cabins, relating her troubles "in a plaintive and languishing voice" and giving hints as to the content of the desire, until at last it was guessed. Then there was a general rejoicing, a public council, a giving of thanks and congratulations, and a public crowning and completing of her last desire (which Father LeJeune, exasperatingly, does not describe or even hint at):

An honest man, the father was compelled to admit that all this worked:

> It is to be presumed that the true end of this act, and its catastrophe, will be nothing else but a Tragedy. The devil not being accustomed to behave otherwise. Nevertheless, this poor unhappy creature found herself much better after the feast than before, although she was not entirely free from, or cured of her trouble. This is ordinarily attributed by our Savages to the lack or failure of some detail, or to some imperfection in the ceremony . . . (Father LeJeune, Relation of 1639, in Kenton 1927, 1:393–401).

Not all therapeutic dream-fulfillments ended in even a partial cure, of course, but this was not felt as any reflection on the principles of dream-therapy. The whole village vied to give the sick person his every wish, for any frustration was a threat to life. A dying man might be surrounded by literally thousands of scissors, awls, knives, bells, needles, kettles, blankets, coats, caps, wampum belts, beads, and whatever else was suggested by the sick man's fancy or the hopeful guesses of his friends. If he died at last, "He dies," the people would say, "because his soul wished to eat the flesh of a dog, or of a man; because a certain hatchet that he wished for could not be procured; or because a fine pair of leggings that had been taken from him could not be found." If he survived, the gift of the last thing that he wished for during his illness was cherished for the rest of his life.

Looking over the material on Iroquois dreams, it is apparent that there were two major types of dreams or visions recognized by the society and separately institutionalized (although in many dreams the two types were blended). These two types may be called *symptomatic dreams* and *visitation dreams*.

A symptomatic dream expressed a wish of the dreamer's soul. This wish was interpreted either by the dreamer himself or by a clairvoyant, who for a fee diagnosed the wish by free association in reverie, by drinking a bowlful of herb teas while chanting to his guardian spirit, by consulting his guardian spirit in a dream or trance (sometimes going to sleep with a special herb under his head), by water scrying, and in later days by reading tea-leaves and cards. Anyone could become a clairvoyant and there were many in each community, some occupying roles of repute— like famous doctors—and others of more humble pretensions help-ing their immediate families (see Fenton 1953: passim; Jesuit Relations, passim, in Kenton 1927). These diagnoses served as signals for the execution of various rather conventional patterns of acting out the wish, either literally or symbolically. Some of these acting-out patterns were prophylaxes against the fate im-plicit in the wish—for example, the symbolic or partial tortures and the abortive cannibal feasts.

This sort of acting out seems to have been based on the idea that a wish, although irrational and destructive toward self or friends, was fateful, and that the only way of forestalling realiza-tion of an evil-fated wish was to fulfill it symbolically. Others were curative of existing disorders, and prophylactic only in the sense of preventing ultimate death if the wish were too long frustrated. The acting out patterns can also be classified accord-ing to whether the action required is mundane or sacred and ceremonial. Thus dreams of buying a dog, and then travelling a long distance to obtain the dog, involve no particular sacred cere-mony revolving around the wish itself, nor would a dream of go-ing on a war-party require more than participation in the normal course of military enterprise. But most of the symptomatic dreams of mentally or physically sick people demanded a cere-monial action, often not only at the time of the dream, but peri-odically thereafter during the dreamer's whole life span.

The annual festival at Midwinter not merely permitted but re-quired the guessing and fulfillment of the dreams of the whole community. There were probably several dozen special feasts, dances, or rites which might be called for at any time during the year by a sick dreamer: the *andacwander* rite, requiring sexual intercourse between partners who were not husband and wife; the *ohgiwe* ceremony, to relieve someone from persistent and troubling dreams about a dead relative or friend; the dream guessing rite, in which the dreamer accumulated many gifts from unsuccessful guessers; the Striking Stick Dance, the Ghost Dance, and many other feasts, dances, and even games. The repertoire could at any time be extended by a new rite, if the dreamer saw a new rite or a nonsacred rite in a dream, or if his clairvoyant divined that such a rite was called for; normally social dances became curative when performed for someone at the instigation of his dream. Some rites were the property of "secret" medicine societies, membership in which was obtained by having received the ministrations of the society upon dream-diagnosis of its need. Visions of false faces called for the rituals of the False Face Society; visions of dwarf spirits indicated a need for the "dark dance" of the Little People's Society; dreams of bloody birds were properly diagnosed as wishes for membership in the Eagle Society; dreams of illness or physical violence and injury were evidence of need for the Medicine Men's Society Rite or for the Little Water Society. The relationship of dreams to ritual was such that the repertoire of any one community might differ from that of the next because of the accidents of dreams and visions, and any element might at any time be abstracted from the annual calendar of community rituals and performed for the benefit of an individual (see Fenton 1936; Speck 1949; Skinner Ms; Jesuit Relations in Kenton 1927, for details on the relation of ritual and dream).

The symptomatic dreams described above displayed, in their manifest content, relatively humble and mundane matters: wanted objects such as dogs, hatchets, knives, clothing; familiar dances and rituals, and their ceremonial equipment; familiar animals, birds, and plants. However, the second category of dreams showed powerful supernatural beings who usually spoke personally to the dreamer, giving him a message of importance for himself and often also for the whole community. Sometimes these were personality transformation dreams, in which the longings, doubts, and conflicts of the dreamer were suddenly and radically resolved; the dreamer emerged from his vision with a new sense of dignity, a new capacity for playing a hitherto difficult role, and a new feeling of health and well being. Such experiences were particularly common among boys at puberty. Retiring alone to the woods, fasting and meditating in solitude, the youth after a week or two of self-denial and thought experienced a vision in which a supernatural being came to him, promised aid and protection, and gave him a talisman. In a sense, the guardian spirit took the place of the parents upon whom the boy had hitherto depended, and from whom he had now to emancipate himself emotionally if he were to become a whole man. Guardian spirits varied in character and power: some gave clairvoyant powers; some gave unusual hunting luck and skill; some gave luck, courage, strength and skill in war. Clairvoyants possessed especially potent guardian spirits which enabled the shaman, simply by breathing on a sick man's body, to render it transparent. Prominent shamans claimed the power to foretell coming events, such as approaching epidemics and other great public calamities. A few such men became known as prophets, and were "apt to acquire great influence and their advice [was] usually followed without much question." This gift of prophecy was the endowment of a particularly good and powerful guardian spirit (see Jesuit Relations, in Kenton 1927: passim; and Ely S. Parker Ms [n.d.] on medicine men and Indian dances, in Parker Collection 1802–46, in the Henry E. Huntington Library).

In Iroquois theory, a dream could thus reveal the wishes not only of the dreamer but also of the supernatural who appeared in his dream. Frustration of the wishes of a supernatural was dangerous, for he might not merely abandon or cause the death of the dreamer, but bring about disaster to the whole society or even cause the end of the world. Hence, dreams in which such powerful personages as Tarachiawagon (culture hero and a favorite dream-figure) appeared and announced that they wanted something done (frequently for the dreamer) were matters of national moment. Clairvoyants were called upon; the chiefs met, and discussed ways of satisfying the sometimes expensive or awkward demands of the dreamers (representing the powers above), or of averting the predicted catastrophe. Not infrequently this type of dream also bore elements of personality transformation for the dreamer, who in his identification with the gods assumed a new role as prophet, messiah, and public censor and adviser. Such prophets might make detailed recommendations about the storage of crops, the waging of war, diplomatic policy toward other tribes and toward the French or the English, measures to avert epidemics or famine. Rarely, however, did such prophets maintain a lasting influence.

The theory of dreams among the Iroquois is in evident accord with the theme of freedom in the culture as a whole. The intolerance of externally imposed restraints, the principle of individual independence and autonomy, the maintenance of an air of indifference to pain, hardship, and loneliness—all these are the negative expression, as it were, of the positive assertion that wishes must be satisfied, that frustration of desire is the root of all evil. But men are never equally aware and equally tolerant of all their desires; and dreams themselves, carefully examined, are perhaps the quickest portal to that shadowy region where the masked and banished wishes exist in limbo. What, if anything, can we learn about the unconscious of Iroquois Indians from the scattered dreams recorded by the Jesuits and other casual observers?

The manifest content of Iroquois dreams is probably as various as the wishes of mankind: there are dreams of love and hate, pleasure and pain, of lost loved ones and longed-for guardians; inconsequential and absurd things happen, and trivial objects are transfixed by the arrow of desire; abhorrent actions and repulsive thoughts plague the restless sleeper. Dreams as reported in the literature seem to have held a prevailingly anxious tone, ranging from nightmare fantasies of torture to the nagging need to define the unconscious wish and satisfy it before some disaster occurs. The most dramatic and most frequently mentioned dreams seem to come from three groups of people: pubescent youths (who must renounce childhood's indulgences); warriors (who fear capture and torture); and the sick (who fear to die). These are perhaps the stress points which generate desire. Adolescent conflict, dreams of battle, and the silent panic of the sick: these are things of which men of many cultures, including our own, have experience.

The manifest content, and the conscious rationale the Seneca themselves give to dreams, are largely in active voice; such passivity as shows itself is laden with pain, unless it occurs in transformation dreams, where a man may be passive in relation to a god. But the latent content, representative of the underlying wish, may be seen in the acting out which is so often passive or self-destructive. Dreams are not to brood over, to analyze, and to prompt lonely and independent action; they are to be told, or at least hinted at, and it is for other people to be active. The community rallies round the dreamer with gifts and ritual. The dreamer is fed; he is danced over; he is rubbed with ashes; he is sung to; he is given valuable presents; he is accepted as a member of a medicine society. A man whose dream manifests a wish to attack and kill is satisfied by being given a coat; a man who dreams of sleeping with a woman does not attempt to woo his mistress, he is given an available female by the chief's council. Only in the personality-transformation dreams of pubescent boys and adult prophets is passivity accepted in the dream; and these are the dreams of men in extremis.

This observation suggests that the typical Iroquois male, who in his daily life was a brave, generous, active, and independent spirit, nevertheless cherished some strong, if unconscious, wishes to be passive, to beg, to be cared for. This unallowable passive tendency, so threatening to a man's sense of self-esteem, could not appear easily even in a dream; when it did, it was either experienced as an intolerably painful episode of torture, or was put in terms of a meeting with a supernatural protector. However, the Iroquois themselves unwittingly make the translation: an active manifest dream is fulfilled by a passive, receiving action. The arrangement of the dream guessing rite raises this dependency to an exquisite degree: the dreamer cannot even ask for his wish; like a baby, he must content himself with cryptic signs and symbols until someone guesses what he wants and gives it to him.

The culture of dreams may be regarded as a useful escape-valve in Iroquois life. In their daily affairs, Iroquois men were brave, active, self-reliant, and autonomous; they cringed to no one and begged for nothing. But no man can balance forever on such a pinnacle of masculinity, where asking and being given are unknown. Iroquois men dreamt; and, without shame, they received the fruits of their dreams and their souls were satisfied.

11 SHAMANISTIC BEHAVIOR
AMONG THE NETSILIK ESKIMOS

Asen Balikci

THE PRESENT CONTRIBUTION is an ethnographic account of past Netsilik shamanistic practices in relation to Eskimo social life. Its first purpose is to describe the techniques employed by the different categories of Netsilik shamans. Second, a classification will be presented of the shamanistic acts considered as mechanisms for the control of various situations involving other individuals. Further, it will be shown that there is a basic ambivalence in the relations between human beings and supernaturals, on the one hand, and shamans and society, on the other. This may reflect the quality of Netsilik interpersonal relations, engendering suspicion antd hostility in social life. Finally, an examination will be made of the relations between some ambivalent reactions, arising partially from shamanism, and certain social phenomena, such as a high suicide rate or preferred cousin marriage. A brief analysis of Netsilik religious beliefs will help us to understand shamanism as a creative symbolic synthesis which attempts to blend elements of the natural, social, and religious universes into a meaningful unity.

Throughout this paper, Netsilik shamanistic practices will be considered as strictly social facts, and this, for two reasons: first, because the shamanistic séance is a social phenomenon involving at least two individuals ("Ce couple théorique irréductible, forme bel et bien une société": Mauss 1960: 118); and second, because there is a consensus of beliefs expressed by the com-

Reprinted from *The Southwestern Journal of Anthropology* 19 (4), 1963: 380–96 by permission of the author and the editor, *Southwestern Journal of Anthropology*.

munity in regard to shamanism in general and certain shamanistic acts in particular.

The ethnographic data presented here were collected during the winter of 1960 among the Arviligjuarmiut of Pelly Bay, N.W.T. These Eskimos were collectively converted to Catholicism in 1935, twelve years after the passage of Knud Rasmussen through the area. Informants readily described cases of shamanistic behavior they had witnessed in the recent past. The cases reflect the traditional situation of the Netsilik "tribe."

OUTLINE OF NETSILIK TRADITIONAL CULTURE

The Netsilik, or Seal Eskimos, inhabit a vast area between Simpson Peninsula and King William Island on the Arctic Coast of Canada. Rasmussen distinguished six distinct groups in this region, totaling 259 individuals in 1923, namely 150 males and 109 females (Rasmussen 1931: 84). Around Pelly Bay lived 54 people at the time. This group, the Arviligjuarmiut, in traditional times moved annually along a two phase migration circuit revealing a winter marine and summer land adaptation. In winter a large sealing camp was set on the flat ice in the middle of the bay, the men collectively hunting seals at the breathing holes. In spring, sealing was conducted from the shore camp with the help of women and children. During the short warm season large amounts of Arctic char were caught at the stone weirs. Early autumn was the time for extensive caribou drives. The herds were driven by beaters to a crossing point at Amatoq Lake on Simpson Peninsula and there speared from kayaks. Sealing, stone weir fishing, and caribou hunting by kayakers were all group activities often controlled by "superintendents." In late autumn the people congregated along the lower part of Kellett River at the bottom of the Bay and there speared char under the thin river ice. With the sea ice becoming firm enough the people prepared again for winter sealing. This brought the inland phase of the migration cycle to an end. In 1919 guns and steel traps were introduced in the area. The fur trade stimulated the rapid emergence of new forms of ecological adaptation (Balikci 1962).

Each Eskimo recognized a circle of relatives, *ilagiit,* extending bilaterally and including some affines. An individual's kindred included between thirty to fifty persons dispersed over several camps. The *ilagiit* constituted a large social sphere of personal security to the individual, who preferred to choose mates within this category of relatives.

An extended family-like kinship grouping formed the social framework for daily interaction and mutual help. This *ilagiit nangminariit* (my own relatives) consisted usually of an elderly father and mother with their married sons and their offspring. Married daughters frequently resided elsewhere. Patrilocality, culturally recognized, often knew exceptions, following situational factors. This kin group stressed the father-son relationship as an essential binding link. At the death of the old father an alignment of brothers emerged, often joined by more distantly related individuals, usually affines or tertiary relatives. The restricted *ilagiit*—the extended family grouping—tended to behave as a residential unit, the related families residing in proximity in a cluster of snowhouses or tents. The elder acted as leader of the group (*inhumataq*) and controller of the hunts. Important forms of economic collaboration, borrowing and commensality took place within this group primarily in summer when it migrated in isolation inland. This was less so at the winter camp, where several restricted *ilagiits* collaborated in seal hunting and sharing. In the fields of food acquisition, distribution and consumption the nuclear family was in all seasons superseded by larger socio-economic groupings.

The Netsilik in traditional times practiced female infanticide to a very high degree. Out of 96 births for 18 marriages Rasmussen counted 38 girls killed (Rasmussen 1931: 141). This unbalance in the sex ratio made for great difficulties in finding a mate. Many cases of wife stealing, killing a man in order to get his wife, and polyandry are remembered for the recent past. Such practices as promising mates at birth and marrying a cousin were traditionally preferred devices for solving this vital problem. Nevertheless, many hunters lived in fear of losing their wives. This was an important source of anxiety and tension in interpersonal relations. Further, the Netsilik exhibited a very high rate of suicide (Balikci 1961). Suicidal behavior in the area was interpreted as being of the egoistic type, arising from the Netsilik individual's limited range of interaction with his social milieu. Aggressive shamanistic activities were found as contributing to the social isolation of the individual.

THE ELEMENTS OF SHAMANISM

Here will be described the four Netsilik shamanistic and para-shamanistic techniques, all involving "direct intercourse with the supernatural world" (Lowie 1952: 173). Only one technique, however, was characterized by the spirit-possession trance, qualifying thus for the narrower definition of shamanism given by Nadel (1946: 25). In its main features it is identical to the classical shamanistic performances described by Danish and other ethnologists throughout the Eskimo area. This major practice will be outlined in the paragraphs immediately following. The other three techniques were labeled para-shamanistic in the sense that, although they involved direct intercourse with the supernaturals, they definitely lacked the spirit-possession trance.

The *angatkoks* were in the habit of observing the behavior of boys, to discover if some bright young man had received the call. If the selection of a boy was verified, the formal training started. Initially the novice joined the household of an elderly *angatkok*-teacher, where he observed a series of special taboos, such as abstaining from eating outdoors, from eating the liver, head, heart or intestines, or from having sexual relations. The novice, assisted by a spirit, slept intermittently and began having visions. Then he moved to a separate igloo where, during a period of several weeks, he was taught the secret vocabulary together with the shamanistic techniques and obtained his paraphernalia (a headdress and a belt) from his parents. Finally his teacher presented him with a protective spirit (*tunraq*), and they officiated together. Initially the *tunraq* was the master of the novice, and only gradually did the young *angatkok* learn to control it. Eventually, the novice became a full-fledged shaman, possessing a competence and strength apparently equal to that of his master.

The Eskimo universe was peopled by a vast number of supernatural beings with diverse characteristics, mostly malevolent. Shamans had control of only one class of spirits, the *tunraqs*. They continued to acquire *tunraqs* throughout their lives, usually as gifts from other shamans or following the spirits' own volition.

Thus Iksivalitaq, the last Netsilik shaman of importance, at the end of his life around 1940 had the following seven *tunraqs*.

(1) Kingarjuaq (Big Mountain), about 3″ long and 1″ high, with black and red spots. The shaman could remove this *tunraq* from his mouth, where it was in the habit of staying, and make it run on his hand.

(2) Kanayuq (Sea Scorpion), residing also in Iksivalitaq's mouth, whence it showed its ugly head.

(3) Kaiutinuaq, the ghost of a dead man.

(4) Kringarsarut, the ghost of a dead man, big as a needle, with a crooked mouth and one very small ear.

(5) Arlu, the killer whale, white, very big.

(6) Kunnararjuq, a black dog with no ears.

(7) Iksivalitaq, the ghost of Iksivalitaq's grandfather.

Other collections of supernatural helpers revealed a similar composition: animals, monstrous creatures with little semblance to anything living, occasionally plants, and many ghosts. *Tunraqs* usually remained in the vicinity of their "owner"; they liked to be frequently called and used.

The relations between *angatkoks* and *tunraqs* were by no means simple; they showed considerable ambivalence, because of the ethical characteristics of certain spirits and their relative autonomy of action. If it is generally true that powerful shamans were well in control of their *tunraqs,* some of the spirits, however, seem to have been very independent. Such was the case of the spirit called Orpingalik, who used to attack his master Anaidjuq suddenly from behind and pull out his genitals; the unfortunate shaman, after much yelling, could recover these during a trance.

It was well known that many classes of malevolent supernaturals could bring misfortune to the Eskimo. Among the Netsilik evil ghosts were particularly dreaded. These were the wandering souls of men who died in bed believing they were killed by magic; they questioned the officiating shamans, accused neighbors, and obviously feared death. But nobody feared the ghost of the hunter who met violent death. *Tupiliqs* were another important kind of evil spirits. Round in shape and filled with blood under considerable pressure, they caused sickness. Most dreaded, however, were the *tunraqs* themselves. When a shaman dispatched one of his spirits on an aggressive mission and the *tunraq* failed to achieve its task, it became a "reversed spirit" or *tunraq kigdloretto,* a blood-thirsty being, blinded by anger, totally out of control, who generally turned against his very master and relatives, and brought sickness and death into the camp. Under these circumstances, other shamans had to intervene and with their more powerful *tunraqs* harness the *kigdloretto.*

Sickness was always caused by evil ghosts and spirits, usually angered by a breach of taboo. These attacked the patient in group formation and took abode in his body. The shaman was then called to chase them away. In a typical performance the shaman, adorned with his paraphernalia, crouched in a corner of the igloo or behind the sleeping platform and covered himself with a caribou skin. The lamps were extinguished. A protective spirit called by the shaman entered his body and, through his mouth, started to speak very rapidly, using the shaman's secret vocabulary. While the shaman was in trance, the *tupiliqs* left the patient's body and hid outside the igloo. The shaman then dispatched his protective spirits after the *tupiliqs;* they, assisted usually by the benevolent ghost of some deceased shaman, drove the *tupiliqs* back into the igloo through the entrance; the audience encouraged the evil spirits, shouting: "Come in, come in, somebody is here waiting for you." No sooner had the *tupiliqs* entered the igloo than the shaman, with his snow knife, attacked them and killed as many as he could; his successful fight was evidenced by the evil spirits' blood on his hands. In case the patient died, it was said that the *tupiliqs* were too numerous for the shaman to kill or that after the séance additional evil spirits attacked the patient again.

The main para-shamanistic technique, called *krilaq* (head lifting), was widely practised in the Netsilik area. The *krilasoktoq* (practitioner of *krilaq*) did not require any special training; his technique, although involving the manipulation of spirits, lacked the trance. His spirits, *aperksaqs* (helping spirits), were weaker than the *tunraqs* and not his "property." Head lifting was performed generally on the *krilasoktoq's* wife or on his own leg or on a stone. A thong was tied around the hooded head of the woman; then the *aperksaqs* were called. The *krilasoktoq* pulled on the thong; an easy answering pull meant a negative answer from the spirits, a heavy pull the contrary. The helping spirits, which were the ghosts of the shaman's deceased relatives, were called in the following order: father, mother, brother, grandparents, sister.

Typical curing consisted in questioning the helping spirits with a view to discovering a broken taboo. This accomplished, the evil spirits were supposed to leave the body of the patient. The *krilasoktoq* repeatedly assured the patient that he was getting better. *Angatkoks* apparently never practised *krilaq;* they disdained the lack of sharp vision and the dilatory action of the *krilasoktoq.*

Angatkungaruks (lesser shamans) constituted a third class of curers. Their para-shamanistic technique consisted in perceiving the evil spirit and localizing it in the patient's body. They were helped by some of the weaker *tunraqs,* who never possessed them. The *angatkungaruk* would sit calmly near the patient and after many hesitations declare that he saw the evil spirit and that the latter was leaving the patient. Because of the *angatkungaruk's* lack of keen vision and inability to control powerful supernaturals, the diagnostic treatment and his encouragements to the patient had to be often repeated. This class of shamans received no special training, practised very rarely the *krilaq* technique, and was incapable of foreseeing future events.

Different from the shamanistic and para-shamanistic techniques described so far was a form of magical practice called *ilisiniq.* It is probable that numerous persons could engage in this evil art in order to bring calamity, paralysis, or death to a secret enemy or to a person disliked or envied. Many manipulative techniques were known, most of them based upon connecting something associated with the enemy to the dead or to menstrual blood; animal bones brought in by the enemy might be stolen and placed in a graveyard; the enemy might be touched with the mitt of a dead man; some fur from a graveyard might be obtained and placed in the kayak of a fast kayaker in order to slow him down; menstrual blood might be mixed with the seal meat brought in by the enemy, etc. Some practices were simpler: breaking the bones of the enemy's seal or spitting in front of him. It was essential for all such acts to be accompanied by mental wishes specifying the evil aim desired. The role played by spirits in *ilisiniq* remains obscure, mainly because of lack of information, despite Rasmussen's assertion that *ilisiniq* occurred only in combination with shamanizing (Rasmussen 1931: 299). Further, Rasmussen noted for the Igloolik Eskimos that *tupiliqs* were used in evil witchcraft (Rasmussen 1929: 143). Among the Netsilik, how-

ever, *ilisiniq* appeared as a rather mechanical or peripheric shamanistic art. However, too aggressive *ilisiniq* acts could rebound
and harm their very practitioner.

THE ACTS OF SHAMANISM

The preceding discussion has attempted to describe the basic
Netsilik techniques of manipulating supernatural spirits and to
illustrate these activities with curing practices. But a classification
based upon the objectives ostensibly pursued by shamans—curing,
putting down storms, calling the animals to be hunted, providing
help in obtaining a mate, etc.—obscures any understanding of the
relations between the shaman, as an individual, and the group
(Lévi-Strauss 1949a: 401). Shaman-group relations can be
described by examining the shaman's efforts at manipulating the
social life of his people. Accordingly, the practices of the shaman
will be discussed below in terms of his attempts to control (a)
environmental threats endangering the group, (b) individual or
group crises, (c) interpersonal relations, and (d) his own prestige
among his people.

(a)   Shamanistic control aims at maintaining a balance between people and environment, usually in cases of disaster. Shamanistic practices of calling the game, seals or caribou, belong
to this category. Whenever game was unavailable, the *krilasoktoq*
was asked to discover, with the help of his spirits, where the
animals were located, while the *angatkok's tunraqs* more actively
directed the game towards the hunters. Frequently, a breach of
taboo brought the community to the verge of famine, and the
shaman had to invite people to make confessions. His spirits
informed him in advance of a breach of taboo. It was essential,
however, that culprits confessed of their own volition. Further,
seals could be killed by *tunraqs* in the open sea and brought
ashore, under the guidance of the shaman.

Shamans could control thunder and put down snow storms.
They accomplished this either by dispatching a *tunraq,* or, in a
trance, tying thongs around the child-like weather god Narsuk.
Shamans could even stop the cracking of the ice, as is illustrated
in the following case.

At the winter sealing camp, built on the flat ice, a young girl had a hole in her boots, repaired them, and thus broke a sewing taboo. Soon followed an extraordinary snow storm; the ice started cracking and breaking, endangering the whole camp. The people, terrified, gave presents to the *angatkok* and begged him to stop the oncoming disaster. The séance took place in the *kagske,* the large ceremonial snowhouse, after putting down all the lamp lights. The *angatkok,* in trance, cried, "It is coming," pointing to a young caribou (a spirit) he saw running about. Everybody except the young girl started confessing, admitting breaches of taboo. When the spirit came near enough to be seen by the girl, she admitted her fault, and the ice cracking stopped.

(b) Shamanistic acts controlling individual or collective crises, not necessarily stemming from the physical environment, belong to this category. Crises are generally engendered by breaches of taboo which anger the spirits and cause them to attack humans. All cases of curing may be grouped under this category. A sickness should not be considered, however, a purely individual misfortune; it is a collective crisis. Such is the dependence of people on each other in an extremely harsh environment within a small community that a hunter in bed means probable hunger for the family and lessened chances for the group to kill seals; conversely, a sick wife leaves the husband with nobody to cook the meat and mend his clothes.

Evil spirits and various classes of monsters might try to attack the people. The whole community often lived in dreadful fear, surrounded by malevolent beings. The intervention of several shamans then became imperative. Rasmussen described such a case for a Southampton Island community (Rasmussen 1929: 144), and several additional cases are known for the Netsilik area.

Harpoons, ice chisels, and iron needles were important tools, highly prized and difficult to replace. Loss of any of them created a crisis calling for the shaman's help. Harpoons and ice chisels often fell into the sea through seals' breathing holes. The shaman recovered them either by jumping supernaturally into the water through the narrow ice hole, in front of a credulous audience, or by tying them with a thong lowered through the breathing hole; the helping spirits did the rest. Lost needles were directly found by *tunraqs.*

(c) Numerous shamanistic acts and *ilisiniq* practices were meant to control interpersonal relations. All aggressive acts, usually involving the shaman himself in a competitive or otherwise hostile relation, belong to this category; here, too, are included his supernatural aid in selecting a mate and in achieving blood revenge.

Interpersonal tensions may be caused by many different factors. Jealousy, however, seems to have been a frequent motivation for aggressive shamanizing.

(1) Irqi was the mother of a grown son, a very poor seal hunter. This boy's meat-sharing partner, Krasovik, used to catch many seals. Krasovik was a much faster runner. Irqi grew jealous and made *ilisiniq* against Krasovik. The latter, protected by powerful amulets, got only some pains in the legs. The aggressive act turned against the witch and killed her son.

(2) Kanayuq, an *angatkungaruk,* was jealous of Qaqortingoaq, a much faster caribou hunter, and did *ilisiniq* against him. Qaqortingoak, as a result, had a paralyzed leg. Much later Kanayuq admitted that his witchcraft turned against him and paralyzed him too.

(3) Having lost a child, Irkinoark grew jealous of another woman's child and made *ilisiniq* against the boy. The aggressive act turned against her and she felt sick. An *angatkok* told her she has done something very bad. Despite her admission of having done so, she died, became an evil ghost, and as such managed to bring sickness to the envied boy. The latter was cured by a shaman.

(4) Ululu and her husband, Nahurnaksaq, were camping with the Kagernermiut, among whom were powerful shamans. The visitors excelled in the ball game; the Kagernermiut became jealous and bewitched them. On their way back Ululu got a crippled leg and her husband died.

(5) Kaormik was a better bear hunter than Amaoligardjuk's son, so Amaoligardjuk, a shaman, became jealous and sent his *tunraq* polar bear against Kaormik. The bear scratched the left side of his face severely but failed to kill him. Amaoligardjuk added after: "This man is hard to kill!"

(6) Tavoq, a shaman, grew jealous of Angutitak, an excellent hunter, and scolded him repeatedly. Angutitak, a quiet and fearful man, never answered, until one day he accused Tavoq of being a mediocre and lazy hunter. Tavoq avenged himself by dispatching his *tunraq* to raise a snow storm just at the moment when Angutitak was stalking caribou.

A certain external difficulty may irritate an individual and lead him to aggression.

> Atkrartok, a shaman, and Nulialik were travelling together on rough ice. Nulialik became irritated because of the difficult journey and apparently wanted to turn back, to which Atkrartok objected. A fight with knives ensued; they decided to stop using knives but to continue fighting with supernatural means. Nulialik did *ilisiniq* against the shaman, believing that his opponent was trying to kill him with his *tunraq*. The evil act turned against Nulialik and killed him.

Constant quarreling may be a cause for supposed shamanistic aggression.

> Inaksak, an ambitious *angatkungaruk,* and Qagotak, a shaman, both very bad tempered, were constantly quarreling, Qagotak was in trance one day, officiating, when Inaksak saw under Qagotak's feet a dark shadow. Inaksak thought this was his own soul Qagotak was trying to steal from him in order to make him sick. Being an *angatkungaruk,* Inaksak knew how to defend himself.

In traditional times, as was previously noted, the high incidence of female infanticide caused a considerable sex-ratio imbalance to exist. This made for great difficulties in finding a wife. Steenhoven (1959: 40) notes several cases of the murder of husbands by men who wanted to steal their wives. Such murders could be accomplished with supernatural means.

> Kaumadluk, a shaman, desired Inuksak's wife. So Kaumadluk decided to kill Inuksak. He did so with the help of his *tunraq,* who turned over Inuksak's kayak; the latter drowned. Unfortunately for the murderer, his victim's wife did not want him and married another man.

In the following cases evil shamanizing was used to avenge frustrated lovers.

> (1) After the death of her husband, Arnapak, a shaman, moved with her sons among the Kagnermiut, where she wanted to marry again. The young man she had her eye on had no desire for her, presumably because of her age. Then Arnapak decided to take revenge by sending her *tunraq* caribou against him. Seeing a caribou on an island one day, the man went after it; the caribou attacked him and he was killed. The people saw this and also noticed that Arnapak was smiling; they consequently realized what had really

happened. Shortly after, the Kagnermiut put Arnapak and her sons to death by shooting them with arrows from behind.

(2) M, a girl, refused to marry S, who desired her greatly. Instead she married A. The family of S was angered, and S together with his paternal uncle, a lesser shaman, killed A with supernatural means.

(3) U opposed the marriage of his son to S's daughter. S avenged herself by doing *ilisiniq* against U and killing him.

Some shamans considered lying with a particular woman as a necessary part of a shamanistic act. The audience assumed this was a desire of the *tunraq*. Often, however, the shaman's propositions were rejected.

(1) The people asked Igarataitsok to stop a particularly violent snow storm. The shaman first desired to lie with two girls. The father of the first agreed immediately, but the husband of the second said: "a *tunraq* can not copulate with women."

(2) Iksivalitaq had difficulties curing Kovertelik, a woman. He said to her: "If I lie with you, I will cure you." He did so and cured her.

This attitude was not general with all shamans. Informants agreed, however, that a shaman who desired a particular woman would readily menace her with imminent sickness in order to attain his aim.

It was important for shamans to discover cases of incest, which could be a source of calamity.

Avataut, son of the woman Nuutlaq, was sick for a whole winter. Both a *krilasoktok* and an *angatkok* tried to discover the cause of this sickness, without much success. The patient and his mother refused to admit their sin. Ivaiarak, the shaman, finally said, pointing to both: "Your wife and your husband." Nuutlaq violently denied the charge. The *angatkok* repeated the accusation several times, with the same result. Avataut, near death, said: "I waited for somebody to speak, but nobody did, so I better say something before I die." And Nuutlaq added: "Oh, I remember. I love my son so much that when he asked me I slept with him once." Despite the confession, Avataut died.

In a recent paper Steenhoven (1959: 61), after analyzing several Netsilik murder cases, failed to see any evidence of blood revenge in the historic data. Steenhoven's cases refer exclusively to physical murder. I collected some cases in which murder was committed by supernatural means for the purpose of blood revenge.

(1) Kotirjoaq and her husband were quarreling. The latter became angry at his wife and in his anger hanged himself. Kotirjoaq remarried soon to Neharaisok and had a baby. Armadluq, the first husband's mother, decided to avenge her son's death; with her *tunraq* she killed Kotirjoaq soon after the birth of the child.

(2) Moraq, a dangerous shaman, killed the brother of Itiitoq, another shaman, with his *tunraq* polar bear. Itiitoq decided to avenge his brother's death. When the two met, they had a friendly conversation; they both went to sleep in their igloos. In the middle of the night Itiitoq said to his daughter: "Wake up. Moraq is out of his bed." Indeed Moraq was lying on the ice floor of his igloo; he had been immobilized there by Itiitoq's *tunraq* at the moment when Moraq wanted to go deep underground and attack Itiitoq, while asleep, from below. Moraq's wife went to implore Itiitoq to help her husband. At that moment Itiitoq got frightened, believing that if he killed Moraq, the latter might become an evil ghost and bring disaster to his family. So he decided to let Moraq live.

(d) In this residual category we shall place the large number of shamanistic performances, the obvious or hidden objectives of which are to control the shaman's own position in society, to enhance his prestige. Fights between shamans as a test of supernatural strength have this end in view.

(1) Utaq was a *krilasoktoq* and Inutsaq an *angatkok*. They were wrestling partners and frequently engaged also in friendly competitions with *tunraqs* in tests of supernatural strength. One day, after a bitter quarrel, Utaq dreamed that Intusaq's *tunraq* polar bear was on a mission to kill him. Utaq immediately dispatched one of his own helping spirits to stop the *tunraq*, which, overpowered, became a *kigdloretto*. Utak made a polar bear out of snow and turned it against Inutsaq. The bloodthirsty evil spirit turned back and later killed its own master.

(2) Iksivalitaq and Isargataitsoq were both great *angatkoks*. In the sealing camp Iksivalitaq was boasting about his supernatural powers, so he sent his *tunraq* in the form of a dark monster under the breathing hole attended by Isargataitsoq, who, after some hesitation, refused to strike it. Then by supernatural means Isargataitsoq stuffed his opponent's breathing hole with seaweeds.

Other cases of shamanistic competition lacked this aggressive element.

(1) Two shamans of different camps had a competition in flying with the help of their *tunraqs*. The one who flew higher and passed over the other had the power to ground him. After many circumvolutions one shaman was immobilized on the ground. "If I leave him on the ground, he will freeze to death. So I will bring him up again," decided the victor.

(2) Atkrartoq, a shaman, asked Neptaroq, a *krilasoktok:* "Do you think I can pass through this tea cup?" Following a negative answer the shaman first pushed his head through the cup, then his whole body, and finally disappeared underground with a rumbling noise. He came back the same way.

In other situations the shaman performed strange and wonderful acts upon his own body, and this always in front of an audience. Iksivalitaq used to shoot himself with a gun, Qagortingnerk removed his own leg, and other *angatkoks* preferred to pierce themselves with spears or grow beards in a second. People who claim to have seen such performances still speak with awe and admiration about the ability of these shamans.

Finally, there is the large class of outstanding shamanistic achievements, such as journeys to the underworld, travels to the moon, or meetings with strange monsters, which fill the pages of Rasmussen's reports. These were feats of the most important shamans, to whom they brought considerable prestige. At the time of Rasmussen's journey through the Netsilik area the shamanistic art was already in decay, and probably very few shamans could claim such successes.

SHAMANISM AND THE BASIC RELIGIOUS BELIEFS OF THE NETSILIK

Although numerous traits (concrete specificity of goal, substitution of technique, irregularity of séances, malevolent practices, etc.) orient Netsilik shamanism towards the magical pole of the magical-religious continuum (Goode 1951: 53), there are important links between shamanism and the basic religious beliefs of the Netsilik. These links make of the shaman the integrator of many religious conceptions.

The relations between shamanistic practice and the ghost cult can be simply identified. As was mentioned previously, ghosts counted among a shaman's *tunraqs* and were continuously utilized by him in the fight against evil ghosts. Further, it was the shaman who discovered if a recently deceased person had become an evil ghost. Often it was in his relation with the *angatkok* that a patient showed potentialities to turn himself into an evil ghost: "The man who died in a bad way worried about the *angatkok,* saying, 'Why didn't he cure me?'" And it was already noted that the *ilisiniq* technique frequently utilized graves and dead men's objects.

The Netsilik recognized three afterworlds: one in the sky, one just under the surface of the earth, and the third deep down under the ground. All three were visited by shamans who described to the living the adventures of the dead (Rasmussen 1931: 314–19).

Shamanism and the belief in various souls, human and animal, were closely connected. The shaman's soul was considered to be particularly strong. Whenever a sickness resulted from loss of the soul, the shaman could bring it back. He was able to strengthen another person's soul or steal it. Some shamans even had their souls temporarily stolen by their *tunraqs.* The shaman could act upon the numerous and sometimes malevolent animal souls, the bear's soul being particularly dangerous. He also had the power to give name-souls to patients in order to protect them against sickness.

Shamans interacted with the major deities and played an important role in myth. Although the knowledge of myth was not limited to shamans, it is probable that they knew more traditions than the simpler folk. It was no mere chance that Nâlungiaq, who told Rasmussen the most important Netsilik myths, learned these from Unâraluk, a shaman (Rasmussen 1931: 207). Further, shamans often appeared in essential myths, such as those depicting the earliest time on earth and the creation of mankind (Rasmussen 1931: 209). It was mentioned above that shamans tried to restrain Narsuk, the weather god. They also attempted to control Nuliajuk, the most powerful deity of the Eskimo pantheon, the mother of animals and mistress of both sea and land. Some shamans achieved this at a distance with the help of their *tunraqs,* while others did not hesitate to "rush down [to the bottom of the sea] to her themselves to fight her, to overcome her and appease her" (Rasmussen 1931: 226).

The role played by the taboo system in shamanistic practice has already been suggested. Most misfortunes were attributed to breaches of taboo, and it was the shaman's function to have these admitted openly through confession. In a sense the taboo system provided the shaman with an important rationale for supporting his practices.

SOCIAL FUNCTIONS OF NETSILIK SHAMANISM

At the simplest possible level of analysis, that of informants' opinions, shamans were considered generally "good" by their camp fellows. Informants showed gratitude for shamans' help in varied situations. Feelings of fear and respect were added, however, in consideration of the *angatkok's* superior skills and aggressive capabilities: "people never used to make *angatkoks* mad." In the case of reputedly evil shamans, society reacted mainly in two ways. It was believed that the evil spirits used by dangerous shamans turned against their owners, bringing them a quick death. If this did not occur, a good *angatkok* intervened in an attempt to control the evil ones supernaturally. In other cases execution or expulsion from the camp took place.

The most striking characteristic of Netsilik shamanism and associated beliefs was the fusion of good and evil elements. Although the Netsilik distinguished clearly an evil shamanistic act from its positive counterpart, it was the same shaman who was capable of both. Thus, although most shamans were good, at some time in their career they committed aggressive acts; and the very few reputedly evil shamans were considered bad only during a limited period. Further, a considerable ambivalence or blending of ethical qualities characterized the protective spirits and ghosts themselves. Good spirits and ghosts could undergo metamorphosis and evolve into malevolent beings, and an opposite change could also affect evil spirits. This fusion of good and evil had important social consequences.

The possibility of *angatkoks,* lesser shamans, and probably simple people to influence supernaturals for aggressive purposes was a contributing factor to the emergence of interpersonal suspicion and hidden hostility. The cases cited above clearly show that many factors might motivate an evil act; malicious intentions, however, were carefully concealed behind amiable attitudes. On the surface, camp life proceeded peacefully, while secretly vicious attacks took place with the help of supernaturals: "an action, apparently the most innocently meant, and not worthy of a second thought, may be the cause of remorseless persecution" (Rasmussen 1931: 200). The individual lived in an atmosphere of suspicion and fear, dreading both the attacks of his camp fellows and the spirits who might initiate an evil action of their own volition. This attitude contributed to the isolation of the individual from society, and it partially explains the high rate of egoistic suicide in the tribe (Balikci 1961).

Further, this suspicion, applied most commonly to nonrelatives at the large winter camp and in a particularly heavy measure to strangers, was a contributing factor to the emergence of strongly preferred cousin marriage in the area, a pattern of rare occurrence in the Arctic. Genealogies indicate that in traditional times numerous first cousin marriages occurred. Informants unanimously considered a first cousin as an ideal husband "because non-relatives may harm the girl." The close relatives among whom aggressive use of supernaturals would be excluded was the safest social circle in which a young girl could be established.

The ambivalence in the ethical characteristics of shamanistic practice had yet another effect. The concept of control, which was employed for categorizing our cases, may be interpreted as an effort to enforce norms or reestablish harmonious relations between environment, people, and supernaturals. If many cases fulfilled such an aim, the aggressive acts surveyed here show that the ready recourse to supernatural helpers sometimes worsened social relations and intensified interpersonal hostilities. The shaman rarely had full control over the spirits; they could acquire autonomy, attack some individual blindly, and create new enmities in a greatly confused situation. Thus, in the imbroglio of fears and accusations not only existing enmities found free expression but entirely new hostilities could emerge.

Shamanism, then, can be regarded as reflecting concrete tensions and existing environmental or social maladjustments in crisis situations. Through its ambivalent character and the resulting atmosphere of suspicion, shamanism was also a potent factor in the emergence of certain social phenomena, such as preferred cousin marriage, the high suicide rate and, at another level, new interpersonal hostilities.

Yet in most vital matters concerning the survival of society special mechanisms could operate to control the ambivalent role of the shaman and the diffuse interpersonal suspicion already mentioned. The complicated taboo system and the seal-meat sharing rules were such mechanisms. Theoretically it is possible to consider the numerous Netsilik food taboos and other similar restrictions as reflecting anxieties about some uncontrollable vital issues (Radcliffe-Brown 1959: 148). But why are some shamanistic acts accompanied by public confession about breaches of taboo while others are not? Our cases indicate that the taboo system is involved in most of the situations endangering social life (lack of game, sickness, bad weather, evil spirit attacks, incest) and apparently controlled by the shaman. The people break taboos; this angers the spirits, who strike and bring misfortune. The shaman confesses the audience, discovers the breach of taboo, and officiates. Here society itself is the source of evil. Through the taboo system society provides a precise framework which supports the shaman in his search for evil causes. The taboo system appears thus as a control mechanism through which society limits the inherent ambivalences in shamanistic practice. This control mechanism is applied to the most vital issues of a collective character; the other cases show the full development of the shaman's ambivalent role.

At the summer camps inland, composed of a circle of closely related people, no rigid meat-sharing rules existed (Rasmussen 1931: 173; Balikci 1962: 60). But seal hunting at the winter camp, composed primarily of unrelated extended families, was accompanied by very precise and rigorously applied sharing patterns binding several families together (Van de Velde 1956). It is well known that the winter camp was the preferred locale for shamanistic performances (Mauss 1906: 96). The presence of unrelated people at the winter camp—people who feared and suspected each other—was the ideal setting for the emergence of ambivalent and aggressive shamanistic acts. Rigid meat-sharing rules thus functioned as a mechanism transcending interpersonal hostilities and assuring certain vital collaborative activities. They were an effort of man to adapt to man and only secondarily reflected ecological stringencies.

Thus far the relations between supernaturals, shamans, and

society have been analyzed in segments, emphasis being put on the hidden influences of the shamanistic complex upon social life. But shamanism should be considered as a totality with reference to its symbolic content. Both the components and acts of shamanism indicate that for varying aims a multiplicity of elements were brought together and fused during the shamanistic performances. Elements of nature, the animals of land and sea, snow storms and thunder, cracking ice, etc. were brought under the shaman's power. The world of the dead was also present during a séance: deceased relatives were utilized as protective spirits, and evil ghosts fought. Society was also represented, and in two ways; often an audience participated directly in the shamanistic performance, and all shamanistic practices involved the presence of an audience. The basic religious beliefs were also included in the shamanistic complex. In varying situations and for different purposes the shaman integrated these diverse elements into a dynamic unity: "Toutes les opérations magiques reposent sur la restauration d'une unité . . ." (Lévi-Strauss 1960: xlvii). In his role as integrator, in a stream of symbolic effusions, the shaman gave new meanings to a multiplicity of situations which would have remained inexplicable to society without his intervention.

12 DIVINATION IN BUNYORO, UGANDA

John Beattie

DIVINATION, "the endeavour to obtain information about things future or otherwise removed from ordinary perception, by consulting informants other than human,"[1] has been practised in all human cultures and in all ages. With the extension of knowledge of natural causation and so of control over nature, especially in the field of human health and disease, recourse to it has nowadays greatly diminished in most countries, but among many preliterate or only recently literate communities it is still widely practised, and may be a highly important social and cultural institution. In this article I describe some of the techniques of divination employed in rural Bunyoro at the present day. These are worth recording both because divination still plays an important part in the everyday life of most Nyoro peasants, and because the techniques used are comparable with similar techniques reported from other peoples in Africa and elsewhere. But they may also be of some interest as exemplifying in a contemporary context some of the modes of divination (for example through possession by gods or spirits) with which we are familiar from classical literature.

Like other people, Nyoro consult diviners when they are in trouble, and want to know the cause of the trouble, and what they should do about it. The commonest kind of trouble is illness, and most consultations relate to a client's health, or that of his child or other close relative. In rural Bunyoro miscarriage during

Reprinted from *Sociologus* 14 (1), 1964: 44–61, by permission of the author and the editor, *Sociologus*.

[1] H. J. *Rose* (1911). Rose's typology of kinds of divination is still valuable, and I make some use of it here.

pregnancy is frequent, and many women consult diviners to find out why they have miscarried. People also consult diviners to discover why they are impotent or barren, why spouses no longer love them, and to ascertain the identity of a sorcerer or a thief. Whatever the affliction, the diviner is likely to diagnose one or other of three possible kinds of agencies, sorcery by some living person, the activity of a ghost, or the agency of one of the numerous non-human *mbandwa* spirits. Whichever kind of agent is disclosed, Nyoro culture prescribes specific ways of dealing with the situation; I have given accounts of these elsewhere.[2]

In Bunyoro most diviners (*baraguzi,* singular *muraguzi;* the verb *kuragura* means "to divine") are men. Women may practise some of the simpler kinds of divination, but I have never heard of one doing so for a fee. Men are thought to possess more wisdom (*magezi*) than women, and diviners are commonly thought of as being wiser than ordinary people. Consistent with this, most diviners are old or middle-aged; if a young man were to set himself up as a diviner the more traditionally-minded would think him presumptuous, though in recent years some have done so. Most diviners know several of the methods of divination which I describe below, but some of these, especially those involving spirit mediumship, are the preserve of experts, and may be extremely costly. When I was in Bunyoro in the 1950's the simpler kinds of divination cost from fifty cents (the equivalent of sixpence in English currency) to a few shillings, depending on the resources of the client and the reputation of the diviner, but divination by *mbandwa* spirit possession might cost fifty or a hundred shillings or even more, and might also entail the sacrifice of a fowl or goat.

There are a few men in Bunyoro who have made big reputations as diviners, usually through spirit mediumship (I record a case concerning one of them below), and such men may travel about the country and make a good deal of money. But most diviners are part time. They are known to be diviners, and they may be consulted two or three times in a month, or more or less often, but for most of the time they are engaged in subsistence and cash farming like their neighbours, and in everyday life they

[2] Beattie 1957, 1960, 1961, 1963, and 1964, chapter 7.

are not regarded with any particular respect or awe. Most diviners are "doctors" (*bafumu*, singular *mufumu*) as well; they can provide treatment, for example by furnishing recipes for magical medicines or by initiating patients into the mediumship cult, as well as diagnosis. But sometimes a diviner will advise a client to consult another *mufumu* who is an expert in dealing with the particular condition diagnosed. Also, if they can afford it clients often consult two or more diviners in order to obtain confirmation of the original diagnosis.

In this paper I take divination to involve the performance by the practitioner of some positive act to obtain the information required. Thus I do not here discuss Nyoro ideas about dreams, omens and other portents, though they certainly have such ideas. Actual techniques used by Nyoro diviners fall into three broad classes. First, there are those "mechanical" modes of divination which involve only the manipulation of material objects and the operation of what we should call "chance." Secondly, there is divination by augury which, for my present purpose, I take to mean the observation, in specially prepared conditions, of the behaviour or some other aspect of animals. And, thirdly, there is divination by reference to "spiritual" powers or forces with quasi-human attributes, sometimes mediated through techniques of spirit mediumship, sometimes involving the use of ventriloquy. It is convenient to consider Nyoro techniques of divination under these three broad headings.

I   "MECHANICAL" METHODS OF DIVINATION

I have notes on seven of these, but I do not doubt that there are many more. By far the commonest is divination by cowry shells (*nsimbe*), and this is the only technique which I have myself witnessed several times and of which I have a fairly full account. But before I give a detailed account of this method, the other six may be briefly dealt with.

First, there is divination by throwing small strips of leather (called *nkaito*, a word which also means sandals) on to a skin spread on the floor. The *nkaito* are about four inches long and three inches wide, and they are decorated with cowries or beads on one side. Two or three of them are thrown at a time, and the diviner determines the answers to his questions, for example whether his client will recover or die, by examining the way they have fallen.[3]

Second, some diviners are said to use the juicy leaves of a plant called *muhoko* (*Phytolacca dodecandra*[4]). The operator squeezes the leaves in his hands, and the amount and disposition of the drops are examined.

Third is the method called *Egonje* or *Nkonje*. *Egonje* is a species of large, sweet banana. The diviner cuts off the stem of a young plant, and puts a grain of millet on the exposed surface. If the juice which exudes from the stem does not displace the millet seed the prognosis is favourable; if the seed falls off, it is unfavourable. This is evidently the same method as that mistakenly said by Roscoe to be used by "*Mulaguzi wa Mayembe.*"[5] Actually *ihembe* (plural *mahembe*) means "horn," and divination by means of animal horns is a very different and much more dangerous procedure; I describe it below.

Fourth, some *baraguzi* divine by means of wooden charms (*ngisa*), called *misinga*. These are five small twigs, about three inches long, with the bark peeled off. In the only instance of this type of divination which I observed, the *mufumu* held the bunch of twigs close to his mouth and whispered to them that they should divine well. He then spat lightly on them. Next he dropped them into a basin about a quarter full of water, and he read off the answers to his client's enquiries by examining the pattern in which the five twigs settled on the water, i.e. separately, adhering together in groups, and so on.[6]

A fifth kind of "mechanical" divination is by means of a rubbing stick oracle (*segeto*). The diviner uses a short piece of wood, perhaps a section of a spear shaft, which he holds between his toes. The stick is moistened, perhaps with the blood of a goat slaughtered for the purpose, more usually just with water, and the diviner grasps it between his finger and thumb and runs his

[3] Cf. J. *Roscoe* 1923: 39; also H. K. *Karubanga* 1949: 42.
[4] For this and other plant identifications I am indebted to M. B. *Davis* (1938).
[5] *Roscoe* 1923: 39.
[6] *Roscoe* 1923: 40. Roscoe asserts that nine, not five, small sticks are used. It is possible that the number used is at the option of the diviner.

hand up and down it. The point at which his hand sticks indicates the oracle's answers to the questions put to it.[7]

Sixthly, a relatively recent type of divination, said to be practised by Moslems, is by means of the Koran. Some informants claimed that this method was particularly effective in establishing the identity of a thief. One practitioner had a small oblong piece of wood, on all six sides of which Arabic characters were inscribed. His client was told to whisper (inaudibly) the name of a suspect to the stick, and then to drop it on a mat. The diviner examined the sign on that side of the stick which had fallen upwards, and then consulted the section of the Koran to which the sign directed him. He then read, or pretended to read, a few sentences, and interpreted the words he read as confirming or contradicting his client's suspicions.

Other types of mechanical divination have been described for Bunyoro,[8] but those listed above, and the cowry oracle, to which I now turn, are the only ones of which I was given direct accounts by informants in the field.

Divination by means of cowry shells is by far the most widely used method. Cowries formerly served as currency in Bunyoro as in many other parts of Africa, and although they are no longer so used, there are still a great many in the country. They usually have their convex side levelled off, so that when they were used as currency a string could be passed through them; it is an incidental consequence of this that if they are thrown on the ground they are equally likely to fall with one side or the other uppermost. A diviner uses nine shells, which he holds in his left hand. After his client has explained what his trouble is, and has put some money "for the shells" in a small bowl provided for the purpose, the diviner holds the shells up to his mouth and says: "this is a thing of my forefathers; all were diviners: it is a traditional thing, not something I have made up for myself." He may also ask the shells to divine well. He then scatters them on a mat or skin spread on the ground between him and his client; some-

[7] Cf. *Roscoe* and *Karubanga*. This device employs in a simpler form the same principle as the Zande rubbing-board oracle (E. E. *Evans-Pritchard* 1937: 362).

[8] E.g. by sprinkling or pouring various substances, such as the ashes of the burnt leaves of certain plants, on water, and studying the ensuing patterns. Cf. *Roscoe* 1923: 35, 36.

times the client is invited to throw the shells himself. The shells are thrown a number of times, and the diviner interprets the pattern in which they fall at each throw.

There are conventional meanings associated with certain positions of the shells: it is good if they fall with the cut-off side up, bad if the other way round; one shell resting on top of another portends death; if they are widely scattered a journey is imminent; if three or more form a straight line the traveller will return safely. But, on the whole, my impression is that diviners are free to give their own interpretations, usually based on their local knowledge of the case and on clues unwittingly provided by their clients.

Two first-hand accounts of consultations will give a clearer representation of what actually happens than any amount of general description. Here is a translation of an account written in Lunyoro by my research assistant, the late Mr Lameki Kikubebe, who was a young man with secondary education, of a consultation with a diviner.

> I went to this diviner, in the course of my research, and asked him what it was that was making my sister's child ill. When he was ready he took from his house a barkcloth bag containing his shells, and a black goat-skin. He spread the skin on the ground under a barkcloth tree (*mutoma*, a species of fig—*Antiaris Africana*), about ten yards from his house. We knelt down one on each side of the skin, and he took out his nine cowry shells. He began by holding them in his left hand, and spitting lightly on them. He then said something to them which I could not hear [probably the invocation mentioned above], and began to drop them on the mat. When he picked them up he was very careful not to drop one accidentally; he told me that if he did so it would cause him to die that very year.
>
> Then he asked again what I wanted to know, and I told him about my sister's child's illness. I did not tell him the child's real name, but gave a false one, Rwakaikara, instead. Then he picked up the shells again, spat on them very lightly, "tup, tup, tup," and said: "is that Rwakaikara going to die, and leave men behind eating this year's millet?" He dropped the cowries again, and scrutinized them from all angles. Then he picked them up and dropped them again, saying "truly I have refused; truly, you will not kill him!" After he had thrown the shells a few more times, he said that the answer was negative, and that the child would not die.
>
> He then asked the shells "is it a ghost that is killing the child?" The shells answered affirmatively. The diviner looked carefully at the scattered shells and passed his finger between them as they lay, and

said to me: "you see! you see, father! The shells have shown the way!" He asked again several times whether the child would die, and the answer was "no".

Then, still throwing the shells, he tried to find out what kind of ghost was responsible. He said: "this is a man's ghost; boys, what sort of a man is it? Ha! What man has died recently in your lineage? Pai! My divination shows that it is a man's ghost; whatever way you look at it, it's a man's ghost! Is your father alive?" I replied that he was, and went on to suggest that the ghost might be that of our father's brother, who had died a long time ago when we were small children. I had heard that he had died on bad terms with us. Another possibility was our grandfather; when he died I was at school, so I did not know on what terms he was with us when he died. The diviner continued to throw his shells, and then he said: "It is your father's brother's ghost which is catching that child Rwakaikara; and look; the shells show that it is very angry. It wants to eat, and to have a little hut built for it, and then for the child to be washed with medicines."

I said, "now, boys, who can finish off all these things for us?" He replied, "I'll come and do it for you, if you can provide a black he-goat and fifty shillings." Then he asked me if I was married—I think he asked me this because he knew that if people of my age have money they are likely to be married. "Have you a wife? The shells here are showing me that you have a wife!" I replied, untruthfully, that I had. Then, continuing to throw his shells, the diviner said: "I see that the shells are showing that she has something inside her (i.e. is pregnant): they are cutting a skin (to carry the child on its mother's back), but it will never be carried in it. That wife of yours is pregnant, but unless you trouble yourself about the matter the child will never be born alive. That woman longs to be bathing her child, but unless you do something about it she will never bear one."

The diviner went on to tell me that there was also a woman who had practised sorcery against that child Rwakaikara by putting medicine in his food, and this, too, was making him sick. He should be given a medicine to make him vomit up that poison. The diviner was saying all these things to show me how skilled he was. He thought that by speaking about things that I did not want to tell him openly, he would convince me, and so get a lot of money from me. Of course he did not know that I was pulling his leg.

Then he told me to go home and think the matter over. When I had collected the goat and money for him he would come and catch that ghost.[9] He also told me the names of a lot of people who had been attacked by ghosts and whom he had cured. But unfortunately

[9] For an account of techniques of ghost-catching, see Beattie 1964.

all these people lived in Bugangaizi (about fifty miles away), so I could not ask them about him.

Though this was not, strictly speaking, a genuine consultation, since the client was a sceptic and was only pretending to need the diviner's services, the case does show how skilfully diviners may elicit small items of information which will enable them to offer convincing diagnoses. It also illustrates the manner in which a diviner may insert into his client's mind further doubts and worries (in my informant's case, about his wife's pregnancy), quite unconnected with the initial consultation. These may then call for additional magical services by the diviner, to his greater profit. A second case of divination by cowry shells, at which the same informant was present, but this time as an observer not a client, further illustrates the diviner's technique. This case concerned a different practitioner, and in it the client *was* a believer in the diviner's power. Again, I have translated my informant's written text.

I accompanied to the diviner a woman who had been having miscarriages; I had promised to pay the fee. We arrived at the diviner's house at dusk, and started the consultation at once. The diviner spread a calf-skin on the floor inside the house, and we sat around it. First the *mufumu* divined for himself. He spat lightly into his closed hand in which he held the nine cowry shells, and prayed (*kurama*) as follows. "Is Kahwa (his name) going to die and perish, leaving (other) men eating this year's millet?" Then he dropped the shells on the skin. He was smoking a clay pipe and spitting copiously. After he had divined for himself—he did not tell us what the answer was—he asked the woman, whose name was Kagole, to spit very lightly on the shells. Then he began to throw them. First he asked, "Is Kagole now going to die and perish, leaving (other) women eating this year's millet?" He did this several times, and then pointed to some of the cowries on the skin. He said, "Look! Look! These cowries have closed the way, and these ones are cutting barkcloths (for burial). Ha! Ha! Terrible things are threatening: this pregnancy is going to cause great trouble!"

He went on: "let me try it again, boys, so that I may see what it is!" And he started dropping the cowries again. But this time he spoke different words. "Truly (literally 'by your stomach') you shall not kill her; truly you shall not kill her; I have refused; no, you shall not kill her! You shall not kill her; I shall give you a fowl: truly you shall not kill her; I shall give you a fowl. Truly you shall not kill her; I shall give you a goat: truly you shall not kill her; I shall give you a goat. Aaa! Accept, by your stomach; Thank you! Thank you! Thank you! Accept, by your stomach!" With each prayer he threw the cowries again and studied the way they fell. Then he turned to us and said: "very good! The cowries are laughing, and they have got up and gone. To begin with I saw that they were carrying (a corpse) on the way to bury it."

By this time that woman Kagole was really frightened by the diviner's words. Then he went on to tell her that the thing which was attacking her wanted a goat. He said that he would find out what it was that was causing her to miscarry; perhaps it was a ghost, perhaps a sorcerer. He then told her to say the names of any people whom she suspected of having planted horns at her home or collected dust from her footprints—these are two ways of practising sorcery. She named about ten people, eight women and two men. As she spoke each name the diviner threw his shells and spoke as follows: "so-and-so, is it you that have been making sorcery against Kagole? Is it you that have been making sorcery against her and killing her, so that she must leave other women eating this year's millet harvest?" But the shells gave a negative answer to each name.

Next the diviner asked the shells if a ghost was responsible. "Is it a ghost that is causing Kagole's abortions and is trying to kill her? I know not. Is it someone who has died, and is causing Kagole to leave the women eating this year's millet?" He then tried the names of three of Kagole's deceased relatives whom she named to him, and the cowries showed that it was her father's ghost which was causing her miscarriages. The diviner asked Kagole if she had yet built a shrine for her dead father's ghost, and she replied that she had not.

My informant's text ends here, but probably the diviner offered, for a substantial fee, to arrange for a sacrifice to be made to the ghost and a spirit hut made for it, also for a spirit séance at which Kagole would be possessed by the ghost, after she had been initiated as a member of the mediumship cult.

In both of these cases it is reported that the diviner himself threw the shells. Some informants told me, however, that often, especially where sorcery is suspected, the diviner hands the cowries to his client to throw, telling him to whisper inaudibly to the shells the name of the person he suspects. The diviner then reads off from the shells whether they confirm or contradict his client's suggestion. Often a client will "test" the shells by naming to begin with people whom he does not suspect at all. By allowing his client to throw the shells and then reading off the answer they give, a diviner can avoid the charge that he has himself imputed sorcery to any individual. To make such accusations is a serious matter, but if the shells are seen merely to confirm a client's unspoken suspicions the diviner himself can hardly be held responsible for their verdict.

II DIVINATION BY AUGURY

In Bunyoro there are two kinds of augury, the first involving the observation of the behaviour of animate creatures, the second the examination of dead ones. I give one example of the first type: it differs from the mere reading of omens (not here considered) in that it involves a practical technique; the setting up, so to speak, of an experimental situation.

This kind of divination is called *etondo;* Roscoe gives an adequate account of it.[10] A small forked stick of *ngusuru* (a small shrub with yellow poisonous fruit; a colocynth), or alternatively a tall stem of flowering grass (*rukonzi*), is planted in the ground, and a little of the patient's saliva is placed on one branch of it. Then a small beetle, called *etondo,* is placed on the stem, and its movements are observed. If it goes towards the saliva, this is a good sign; if away from it, the prognosis is bad. This insect (which I have not seen) is said to have long antennae, and an informant told me that a further refinement of this technique involves the close observation of the movements of these antennae. As in other forms of divination the first diagnosis may be confirmed by a further test, especially if it is unfavourable. This would depend in part on the resources of the client, who in any case would be required to provide his own beetle and stick.

The second broad type of augury is by haruspication, the examination of the entrails of dead animals. This mode of divination was of course familiar to the ancient Greeks, and has been reported from many cultures throughout the world. It is said that in ancient Bunyoro oxen might be used, and Nyoro traditional history tells how the departure from the country of the Chwezi hero-kings, and their replacement by the Nilotic Bito from the north, were foretold by this means by a Nilotic di-

[10] *Roscoe* 1923: 39.

viner.[11] "In recent times, however, the creature used for this type of divination is generally a chicken, as elsewhere in Africa.[12] Here is an elderly informant's account, dictated to me in Bunyoro, of the procedures involved; in the main it corroborates Roscoe's brief account.[13]

Divination by means of a chicken is one of the more powerful methods. A man who wants to use it must bring two chickens to the diviner, so that if the first one gives an unpropitious diagnosis the other one may be tried. Only young birds, whose tail feathers are just beginning to show, are used.

Before the diviner begins, a small quantity of the sick person's saliva is placed by the client in the chicken's beak—if the sick person is not himself present, his saliva will have been brought wrapped in a leaf. As he does this, the client addresses the chicken, saying "I shall die? I shall never recover? I shall never leave this place?," and so on. Then he hands the fowl to the diviner.

The diviner may then tell his client to collect some couchgrass (*rumbugu*) and some leaves of the barkcloth tree (*mutoma*). These are spread on the ground. Then the diviner addresses (*kurama*, literally "prays to") the chicken: "so-and-so says that he is going to die; now show us whether he will die or recover." He then lays the bird on its back on the leaves and grass, and cuts it open from beak to tail. He must be especially careful not to break the breast-bone (*muhini*, literally "handle"; the bone is shaped like an old-fashioned hoe handle); if he does break it he may die, though not necessarily at once. This is why most diviners are afraid to divine by cutting open chickens. He must also be careful not to cut the intestines, for the same reason.

The diviner then spreads out the opened body of the fowl, and also extends its tongue. Its organs are now visible. He looks especially for small, white spots (*nkebe*) on any of them; if any of these are seen it is a bad sign. Such spots may also be called "that which does not want to eat with children" (*"nyamutalya nabwana"*); this may be a way of referring to the unfavourable prognostication. The diviner begins by examining the cavity where the liver lies (*rusika*, literally "room"); if there are *nkebe* there it is a sign that his client will die. He also examines the liver itself (called *ngabo*); the broad part of the intestine (*ihirra*); its middle part (*bwetegero*); and its

[11] For an account of this incident, see Mrs. A. B. *Fisher* 1911: 106–7. Despite its absurd title (for which the author was not responsible), this book contains the best account in English of Nyoro myth and traditional history. Cf. also John *Beattie* 1960: 15.

[12] Cf., for example, J. *Roscoe* 1911: 340.

[13] 1923: 35.

lower parts (*biranga*); also the part where the gizzard is (*kabuku*). The way in which these organs are lying is also important. If the anus is swollen (*ecunzire empihi*) this also is a bad sign.

If there are no spots, and the intestines are lying in their normal positions (*biranga bibyamire*, literally "the intestines are lying down"), and there are no abnormal swellings, then the patient will recover.

If the prognosis is favourable, the diviner says that if he has read the signs wrongly he will eat the chicken (*"nyowe baicumba nazinena"*)—traditionally men did not eat fowls. The patient then takes the remains of the chicken, or perhaps just some of its skin and feathers, and these are wrapped up in grass. He then takes them home, and may keep them by his bed. Sometimes the body of the chicken is just left in a deserted ant-hill. If the diagnosis is unfavourable the chicken is just thrown into the bush. Then the second chicken may be tried. But only two may be used at one session; if it is desired to consult another (that is, if both of the first two prognoses have been unfavourable) a week or two must elapse first.

As in ancient Greece, the principle in Bunyoro seems to be that any abnormality, especially of the liver, is a bad sign. There is no evidence, however, that for Nyoro haruspication (or extispication) is a sub-rite associated with sacrifice, as has been claimed in regard to the Greek practice,[14] nor does this appear to be the case among other East African peoples who practise it.[15]

III   DIVINATION BY MEANS OF SPIRITS

The technique of divination through possession by a god or spirit was also known to ancient Greeks. Bunyoro has a traditional cult of spirit mediumship, originally centred on a pantheon of mythical hero-gods called the Chwezi, who are believed to have ruled the country for a generation or two in ancient times, and then to have disappeared as mysteriously as they came. In former times these Chwezi spirits were associated with the well-being and fertility of the numerous clans into which the Nyoro people are divided: they were not and still are not concerned with divination. But in recent generations a great number of new spirits, many of them deriving from Bunyoro's Nilotic neighbours to the north,

[14] E.g. by W. R. *Halliday* 1913: 193.
[15] Cf., for example, Peristiany's account of haruspication among the Pastoral Pokot of Kenya (J. G. *Peristiany* 1951: 198–200).

and, more recently, from the new forces of social change due to contact with the Western world, have been added to the traditional pantheon. And some of these, when "in the heads" of their mediums, may divine for clients if a sufficient fee is paid. One of the most famous of these non-Chwezi spirits is Irungu, the spirit of the bush and of wild animals, believed to be of Nilotic origin. Here is a brief account of a mediumistic séance at which Irungu was mediated. My informant, who dictated it to me in English, was a secondary schoolboy, who had attended the séance some years earlier.

One morning I went to the house of a neighbour called Ndolerire; I was with my mother and my mother's sister. We found several other neighbours there, and when I asked what they had come for, my mother told me that a well-known diviner called Binkamanyire was visiting the village, and that people had come to consult him about their various troubles.

We stayed there all day, and in the evening Binkamanyire arrived. He was a tall man in late middle age. After we had eaten, everyone sat in a big semi-circle around the fire-place in the front room of the house. The fire was burning brightly; it had been fed with *ngando* wood, which burns with a clear white flame. Then Binkamanyire came into the room; he was dressed in a bark-cloth, and was wearing a bark-cloth headdress (*mukako*) decorated with cowry shells. He was carrying a bag made of skin. He went up to an old lady from our village and sat down on her lap; she also was a member of the *mbandwa* spirit mediumship cult.[16] Then he took a gourd rattle (*nyege*) out of his bag, and began to shake it rhythmically in his right hand, and to sing one of the songs associated with spirit mediumship. Everybody knew this song, and all joined in. As soon as everyone was singing Binkamanyire became silent, but he went on shaking his rattle. People sang loudly and fervently. I do not remember whether different songs were sung, or whether the same song was repeated over and over again, but the singing went on for about half an hour, without the spirit rising into Binkamanyire's head.

Then his rattle began to shake very quickly and violently, and suddenly he fell off the old woman's knees where he had been sitting, and fell forward on the ground, where he lay face downwards, with his face buried in his hands. As he fell he flung his rattle away from him. Everyone stopped singing, and there was complete silence. After about ten minutes he began to utter small, high-pitched

[16] To sit on another's lap signifies very close attachment and dependence; here it shows the close bond that unites fellow initiates in the mbandwa spirit mediumship cult.

moans, still without moving from where he was lying. Then the old lady raised him to a sitting position, but he did not return to sit on her lap. He then began to speak in a small, falsetto voice, like a woman's; he was using words which I could not understand, as they were of the special vocabulary used by mediums.

So people knew that the spirit had come into his head, and they began to ask him questions. He would look at a certain person, and then that person would ask a question. If two people started to speak at once, one would stop: everyone was respectful and polite, as in church. There was no smoking or drinking. But people could come in or go out as they liked, quietly and humbly. Many people asked questions; I can only remember a few of them.

A woman called Kaitamitano said "my husband hates me, and I do not know why." The spirit said, "your husband has another wife besides you." She agreed. The spirit went on, "well then, she has made sorcery against you; if you don't take care she will kill you. You had better use your wits and leave your husband and go home, if you want to be safe."

My mother Isoke asked: "one day some time ago my dress (*kikoye*) disappeared from my house. I want to know if it was stolen by a thief, or by someone who wanted to use it to make sorcery against me." The *mbandwa* spirit was silent for a long time, and then it said "I do not know how it was taken, or by whom."

The head of that house, Ndolerire, said: "one day I got up very early to go to another village, and when I got to the entrance to the path to my house (*masangani*) I saw some magical medicine lying there in the middle of the path. This magical thing (*kyonzira*) consisted of a bundle of leaves of a kind which I did not recognise, tied up with cowry shells and with a special kind of flowering grass (*nkonzi*). I want to know who it was that put that thing there in my pathway." The spirit thought and said: "one day at a beer party you fought with a certain man, and it was he who brought the *kyonzira* so that bad luck should come to your home and somebody should die there. But you had no fault against that man, so the medicine had no effect."[17]

The spirit which was in Binkamanyire's head answered many more questions, but after about two hours it became evident that it was leaving him. His voice and appearance were returning to normal. The spirit which was possessing him was Irungu: I know this because Irungu is associated with wild animals and the bush, and when I wanted to leave the house to go and sleep in another house nearby,

---

[17] It is believed that such a charm might cause the first person to step over it to become ill and perhaps die. It is of interest that, for Nyoro, there is a moral element even in sorcery; it is thought that although a man with a perfectly clear conscience is by no means immune, he has rather less to fear from it than one who knows that he has been at fault.

my mother refused to let me go by myself, saying that there would certainly be leopards and other wild beasts outside. I do not know what this diviner was paid, but I am sure that he received a lot of money. Also, he would require some of his clients to sacrifice an animal such as a goat, and he would get one leg of such an animal. Famous diviners like Binkamanyire obtain a great deal of meat.

This account gives a broad picture of how a séance, held for purposes of divination, is conducted. The occasion is a serious one: there is a powerful spirit present, and modesty and respect are appropriate. Important also (though this is not brought out in my informant's account) is the theatrical aspect of such occasions. The medium is not attired in his ordinary clothes, but in a distinctive and striking costume. Some of the headdresses worn by mediums, which may be fringed with black and white colobus monkey skins and decorated with beads and shells, lend them a very weird and extraordinary aspect. As far as his audience is concerned, a medium *becomes* the spirit which is supposed to be possessing him. Like all ritual, spirit possession is a drama, an "acting out" of anxieties and problems with which the culture provides no other manner of coping.

The last mode of divination which I consider here, divining by means of specially prepared magical horns or other "fetishes,"[18] does not involve possession. Supra-human powers are imputed to the horn (*ihembe*) or other object used, which is supposed to be able to speak like a person, and to answer questions put to it. This kind of divination is said to be a fairly recent thing in Bunyoro. Also, it is thought to be particularly sinister and dangerous, for horns are much used in sorcery and are especially associated with it.[19] Such magic horns and other fetishes have their own personal names. Often they are brought from far-away regions like the Congo, where people are thought to have more powerful magic than is known at home. They may be extremely costly. Sometimes a horn may require periodic sacrifices from its owner or "master" (*mukama*), if it is not to cause him injury. It is said that some horns, when offended, have "turned on" their purchasers and killed both them and their families. But in spite

---

[18] In the present context I mean by "fetish" ("something made") an object specially prepared or made by men, to which magical powers of a quasi-human kind are attributed.

[19] Cf. Beattie 1963: 38–39.

of the danger, to possess a powerful and fearsome *ihembe* may be a source of great local prestige, as well as being of considerable profit to the practitioner who is expert enough and brave enough to control it. At any rate, some men are willing to take the risk.

Here are two brief texts which give some account of this technique: in the first, my informant, a young man with some secondary education, describes a consultation made by himself. It can be seen that he is really impressed by the horn's performance. I have translated his text from Lunyoro.

Once I lost some money, and I went to consult a *mufumu* who could divine by means of a horn called Igondo or Mpebwe, which could talk. I wanted to know if I should find my money again, and, if it had been stolen, who had taken it, or whether I had just dropped it somewhere. If it had been stolen, I wanted advice about how I should get it back, perhaps by frightening the thief so that he would return it to me.

When I got to that diviner's house, at about seven in the evening, I told him what I had come for. He asked me how I would like him to divine, as he knew how to do so with cowries, as well as by means of the horn Igondo. He did not use Igondo often, both because it was more expensive than cowries (at least two shillings, instead of fifty cents or so), and because it was thought to be a very fearsome thing (*eryekitinisa*). I asked him to use Igondo.

First he asked me to pay two shillings, and I did so. Then he explained to me about the horn. "You have come to divine by Igondo. Everything you ask it, it will answer truly. It can tell you where your money is hidden, whether indoors or outside, and it can go itself to where the thief is. Even if he himself is a magician-diviner, Igondo can speak to you and find him out." Then the diviner stood in the inner doorway of the house, looking into the inner room, and called out "Igondo"! And I heard it answering "Sir!" (*"waitu"*) in a small voice. I could see the diviner all this time, and I am sure that it was not he who answered. I was astonished at this. Then it asked him, still in the same tiny, falsetto voice, to fetch it so that it could come and greet the visitor, that is, myself. And the diviner went in and fetched it; it was kept in a special, very beautiful basket (*ndiro*) called *Yamahembe*, which means "for the horns." The horn itself was inside a skin bag made of the hide of a small cat-like animal called *kamundagi;* the bag was shaped like a live animal, but its legs had been cut off. The horn greeted me, and I replied. It spoke just like a person, and the diviner was holding it right up in front of me.

Then the diviner told it what I had come for, and asked it to say what had happened to my money. Igondo explained that it had been stolen by a fellow-clansman of mine while I was staying in his house. And it told me exactly what had happened, that I had meant to slip my money into the inside pocket of my jacket when I was getting up, but it had fallen on to the floor without my knowing. And when I later asked about it in that house, everybody denied having seen it. All this was quite true, and I had not told these details to anyone. So I asked Igondo where the thieves had put the money, and it said that they had buried it in an ash heap by a *muhohi* tree at the back of the house. But, it continued, it would be very difficult for me to find it, as I could not very well go poking around another man's house. So it would go there for me that very night, and would find out everything about the money. It told me to come back the following morning, and it would tell me everything.

I waited expectantly until the morning, and I returned to that diviner's house at about 7 a.m. He brought Igondo out again, and asked it what it had seen at my relative's house. Igondo replied, "that man's wife has been begging him to buy her a new dress, and he has told her to wait for a few days and he will buy her one, since he has had some good fortune." It went on to say that I had better purchase from it some medicine which would cause lightning to strike and kill the thief, and to uncover the money.[20] Later I consulted other diviners, and they said the same thing.

I wanted to know if all this was really true, so one day some time later I quietly asked that man's wife about the matter, and she admitted that it was her husband who had stolen from me, and no one else. She even agreed that they had had a conversation about a dress, as Igondo had said; I was very surprised. In the end I did not buy the lightning sorcery medicine from Igondo, for that would have been murder (*obuisi*); I just left the matter. But the experience taught me that the skill (*magezi*) of diviners is very wonderful.

In the second text, the instrument of divination was not an animal horn (though Nyoro include it in the general category of *mahembe*); it was a small, wooden object, called *nyakarondo*, about two inches long and shaped rather like a short whistle. Such "fetishes" are sometimes tightly covered in animal skin, and informants say that like horns, *nyakarondo* are very dangerous. In the text which follows, the connection between this kind of divination and sorcery is very plain. This text, too, was written for me in Lunyoro, by a schoolboy.

[20] It is believed that the kind of sorcery which causes people to be struck by lightning is especially effective against thieves, and when people are killed by lightning it is often thought that they must have been guilty of theft.

One day I went with a relative of mine, a woman called Nyakato, to visit a man who had a thing called *nyakarondo*, which he used for divining, Nyakato wished to find out about a child of hers who had died. The diviner, whose name was Barongo, kept this *nyakarondo* in a bottle; it can speak like a person.

When the time came to divine, at about 8 p.m., when it was quite dark, all the doors and windows of the house were shut, so that it was pitch dark inside. The bottle was brought, and Barongo, who was smoking a pipe, blew smoke into the bottle and then stopped it up, with the *nyakarondo* inside. The bottle was placed on a goat-skin which was on the floor.

Before it began to speak, the bottle began to rise up into the air above the goat-skin, and then fell back violently, owing to the power of Satan which was in it. I was very frightened. But soon it became quiet, and greeted everyone present in a small, falsetto voice. Then it said, "sing a song, and I shall sing and dance!" So everyone began to sing some of the songs of *runyege*, which are associated with spirit possession. And the *nyakarondo* joined in; it sang very well. You could feel the ground shaking near the mat, because of its dancing. Everyone clapped their hands in time with the singing.

When the song was finished, it asked the names of those who were present. But when it asked me who I was I was afraid to answer, and its "owner" Barongo said to it, "it's Mikairi; he's afraid of you!" Then it said, "isn't that the son of Yoneki?" I answered "yes," but I was very much astonished that it knew who I was.

Then it said to the people who had come to divine: "what brings you here to Amoti's place"; Amoti was Barongo's *mpako* name.[21] I was surprised that it should call its master by this name. Then my relative Nyakato said, "I've come for you to finish my affair." The *nyakarondo* asked her what the matter was. She replied that her child had died, and she wanted to know who had practised sorcery against him. It replied by naming a particular village and said that the sorcerer came from there, but it did not say what his (or her) name was. Instead it asked her to pay fifty shillings for the consultation, and told her to return on Saturday with a goat. Then it would tell her the name of the person who had killed her child, and it would give her medicine so that she should be able to kill that person. What was remarkable was that this *nyakarondo* spoke by itself; its master Barongo hardly said anything, but just sat listening to what it said. From time to time it would ask Barongo, "you there, is not what I am saying true?", and Barongo would reply, "it is true, Abwoli!"—Abwoli was the mpako name of that *nyakarondo*. All this I saw and understood well.

[21] The ten or so mpako names, one of which is given to every Nyoro child soon after birth, are of Nilotic origin, and their use implies both intimacy and respect. Cf. J. P. *Crazzolara* 1950: 97–100.

Barongo told us afterwards that he had bought this *nyakarondo* in Bugoma, a remote part of Bunyoro; these magical things are commoner in that country. He got it through a friend with whom he had once made a blood pact (*kunywana*). He was told to be very careful of it, for if he were careless it could escape and return to its own place. Its name was Mijago, and it could travel from place to place by itself; I myself think that it does this by flying through the air. A *nyakarondo* can charge anything it likes of people who come to divine, even up to a hundred shillings, and sometimes a goat or beer as well. Its "owner" does not get any of this money, only about fifty cents "for the mat" (*za kisato*).

In this case Nyakato did not return to that diviner, as she could not obtain the money which *nyakarondo* had demanded.

In both of these cases of divination by *mahembe* or "fetishes," the association with sorcery is explicit. In the first, the horn Igondo offered to sell its client sorcery medicine to strike the thief with lightning, and in the second the *nyakarondo* Mijago offered, for a price, to supply lethal medicine for its client to avenge her child's death. Roscoe was correct in remarking that divination by *"mayembe"* (*mahembe*) "was not looked upon as a legitimate form of augury," and that its practitioner "was called a wizard" (Roscoe 1923: 39), even though, as I noted above, he confused this method with another quite innocuous one. Divination through possession by certain *mbandwa* spirits such as Irungu and Kifaru may also sometimes be connected with sorcery.

I think that it is plain enough why this should be so. Unlike cowry shells, charms, animal entrails and so on, spirits and "fetishes" are essentially "personalized"; they are represented as being able to speak and act in some degree like people. Thus the *nyakarondo* Mijago could and did sing and dance, and both it and Igondo could move from place to place without human aid. So, as well as divining, these powers are thought to be able to act as "familiars" to their masters, and to carry out their bidding. And, since they only become culturally relevant in the context of the interpersonal suspicions, fears and rivalries which are the matrix of sorcery, their power is naturally thought to be primarily malevolent.

Indeed they are thought to be so powerful as to be dangerous to their "owners" as well as to those against whom he may send them. I was told that a man who owns a *nyakarondo* cannot get rid of it or chase it away even if he wants to do so: it will use all its skill to find its master again, and may punish him for his imprudence by making him ill. Such powerful "fetishes" may indicate to their owners, through dreams, that they require some living thing, such as a chicken, a goat, or even, it is said, a human being (though I have no detailed evidence of this) to be made over to them by sacrifice, and if they do not get what they want, they may kill their "masters" and their whole families. I have heard several tales of the disastrous consequences of neglecting or thwarting such *mahembe*.

There are other techniques of divination in Bunyoro besides those which I have described, but these are the most commonly used and spoken of. What, then, are we to make of this proliferation of divinatory techniques, and why do they enjoy such continuing popularity?

This is a question which can be asked of all magical behaviour, and many answers have been given to it. No doubt it fills in gaps in people's knowledge of causes and effects, and provides recipes for action where inaction would be intolerable. And it may be assumed that with increase in the general social well-being, and the spread through education of a clearer understanding of scientific causation, especially in the sphere of medicine are public health, recourse to magical types of explanation and behaviour will decline. But I think that this is only part of the answer. A full understanding of the persistence of magical beliefs and practises requires that a clear distinction be made between the expressive and the instrumental aspects of ritual. Like all magic, divination is a rite: it is not just a way of doing something; it is also, and essentially, a way of saying something.[22] Certainly the client who consults the cowry oracle, or has the insides of a chicken examined by an expert, or attends a séance and asks questions of a mediated spirit, wants to know the answers to the questions which he has in his mind. But, through the ritual performance which divination entails, he is also giving overt expression to his doubts, suspicions and fears. And this, at least in some measure, is an end in itself.

[22] Cf. *Halliday* 1913: 22: "the *raison d'être* of all ritual . . . is, in the long run, nothing more nor less than the attainment of a distinctive mode of expression."

There is a markedly dramatic quality in much of the ritual of divination, as there is in all ritual. This is especially striking in spirit possession. Mediums take on the character of the spirit which they are supposed to be mediating, often with vivid effect, and all present join in the singing and dancing which accompany a séance. The cases last quoted show that ventriloquy is a skill much used in divination. Often, then, divination involves a vivid dramatic performance, in which, usually, all present can participate. Like other magico-religious ritual, divinatory rites have a cathartic quality. They provide a way of expressing, and so of relieving, some of the interpersonal stresses and strains which are inseparable from life in a small-scale community.

In Bunyoro, as elsewhere, divination is not a would-be "practical" technique, subject to experiment and modification in the light of experience. If it were simply this, it would be hard to see why Nyoro, or anyone else, should persist in practising it. Like other forms of magic (and quite unlike "scientific" procedures, however unsophisticated), divination is a rite, and so is essentially dramatic and expressive. This is the central reason why, even though diviners are sometimes wrong, divination is not thereby discredited. A Western theatre-goer does not ask whether a play is "true." He asks, rather, whether it aptly communicates what it is sought to communicate. And, often, divination is a drama no less—perhaps more—than it is a technique.

13 DIVINATION AND
ITS SOCIAL CONTEXTS

George K. Park

IN A GOOD MANY societies studied by anthropologists divination holds, or has held, a fairly exalted place; yet the argument is not often put forward that the working of any particular social system has hinged in any critical way upon the performances of its diviners. In a general way, diviners are to be classed with the native herbalist and the shaman as private practitioners of an art to which natural science lends little support; and when it is once assumed that the 'doctor' does not do what he manifestly claims to do—that a diviner does not, in fact, divine—reason would seem to suggest that on the whole he is likely to do as much harm as good. In particular would that reasoning seem to apply for the many societies in which the diviner is most conspicuously employed in the finding of witches, and where a normal consequence of his fallible accusations may be the destruction of innocent persons.

There will be occasion to examine a few such cases in later sections of this paper, where I shall argue that their crueller aspects tell us less about the nature of divination than about the general problem of order in human societies. But first I should like to present, in the light of some less dramatic facts, an argument for taking divination seriously as a characteristic social institution of which our understanding needs to be improved. From the study of divining, I think we may properly expect to gain some insight into the working of other, and perhaps more reputable, institutions also exhibiting the phenomenon which I shall call 'procedural intervention'. It will be a thesis of this paper that developed

Reprinted from *The Journal of the Royal Anthropological Institute* 93 (2), 1963: 195–209, by permission of the author and the Council of the Royal Anthropological Institute.

systems of divination should not be regarded as mere excrescences upon the body politic, doing none of its work; but that the diviner, with all his peculiar skills and his characteristic paraphernalia, does in a controlled way intervene in and affect the social process with rather definite and socially useful results. I do not suggest that the consequences of any given act of divination are more likely to be just than unjust; nor shall I claim to have become convinced, by an examination of cases, that witch-doctors usually help to rid their societies of disagreeable deviants. But I shall argue that, quite apart from such considerations as these, divination has as its regular consequence the elimination of an important source of disorder in social relationships.

I

Divination is always, I think, associated with a situation which, from the point of view of the client or instigator, seems to call for decision upon some plan of action which is not easily taken. Even the urban addict to fortune-telling is probably no exception to that rule; though the point need not be laboured. Typically, divination is called for in cases of illness and death, and in other life-crises; in the corroboration of a marriage-choice and in individual or collective moves involving some change in social alignments or, perhaps, economic condition; and in situations of loss, calamity, or unresolved conflict, whether on a personal or a much larger scale. For each society in which divination is practised there is, to be sure, a proper list of its occasions; and such a list may say much about the sources of strain in that society—the Chinese diviner in Singapore (Elliott 1955: 159 seq.) does not receive the same pattern of cases as does the Zulu; nor has European contact failed to change (by enlargement) the scope of the institution among the Plateau Tonga (Colson 1958: 79–80). Divination is associated with the sense of danger, and often seems to relieve it. But those who have regarded the diviner only as a sort of primitive therapist, relieving his client of doubt and indecision, or explaining away such phenomena as convulsions, may surely be accused of understating the case. For it is generally true that where convention calls for divination, its omission might have genuinely difficult consequences for the person or group who acted without it. Divination normally provides more than the 'psychological release that comes from the conviction that subsequent action is in tune with the wishes of supernatural forces' (Herskovits 1938, II:217); the association of divination with situations of problematical action is best explained, after all, by the fact that it lends to a client's subsequent act a peculiar but effective type of legitimation.

What I propose is, put most simply, that a 'sociological' interpretation of divination will be found more general, and more satisfactory, than the 'psychological' analysis which is so much more readily suggested by the usual circumstances of actual observation in the field. The ethnographer to-day seldom observes divination in conjunction with what Durkheim called 'collective representations'; far more often it is a mere matter of individual purpose—irrelevant, almost, to anything so grand as the collective welfare. A Yoruba employs Ifa divination, for example, in the selection of a house site. Stripped of its social context, and taken only from the immediate point of view of the actor, divination for such a purpose would seem to have doubtful value. On the one hand, as Bascom (1941: 45) observes, 'the elimination of fruitless hesitation and indecision would seem to enable the individual to concentrate his entire energy, without distraction, upon the task at hand'. But against this one must weigh a heavy material cost and all the added 'distractions' which, among the Yoruba, that is likely to entail. Yet the choice of a house site by a Yoruba has, in fact, a special gravity readily apparent from the point of view of social-structural analysis, although perhaps unlikely to be intelligibly conceived by the actor himself. Where one builds must decide where a particular family is to be placed in social space. Thus the inclusive lineage splits whenever a member establishes a compound in a separate town; while within the town the assortment of households into small, tightly localized, lineage units (*omole*) is similarly dependent upon voluntary choice of residence. Overcrowding and quarrelling within the *omole* leads to the formation of a secedent group which co-operates over an extended period in establishing a new compound, and hence a new *omole*. A 'first chamber' is established for the leader, who is helped and will gradually be followed by 'any other men of the *omole* who may care to join him' (Bascom 1944: 11–16).

On the testimony of the ethnographer himself, then, the choice of a house site is scarcely to be regarded as a decision affecting the principal actor alone. The *omole* is defined by agnatic descent *and* by common residence in a given compound. In building a house one must either desert or remain with that nuclear kinship unit of which one has been a part; one must join or fail to join a particular party of secession; whatever choice one adopts must be comparatively permanent. I suggest that the custom of prescribing divination in such a context is eminently understandable on the ground of social function. For it is the peculiar property of the diviner's role that he is able, in the public conscience, to remove the agency and responsibility for a decision from the actor himself, casting it upon the heavens where it lies beyond cavil and beyond reproach. In the Yoruba case which has been cited, the diviner in effect provides a legitimating sanction upon a process of structural realignment which, depending as it does upon a voluntary act, would be difficult indeed to sanction in any remarkably different manner.

Nor is the Yoruba case exceptional, unless in the fact that one is able to reconstruct, from the ethnographer's material, the social context of a procedure which too often is presented simply as an isolated bit of magic, of no social consequence.[1] In other societies where a similar insight is to be gained, divination appears to play a similar 'structural' role, sanctioning by depersonalizing the various types of action which may normally be required in the process of sorting and resorting local living arrangements. Often the diviner plays a part in the cleavage of groups through conflict. By means of divination, a groundless and merely personal or private accusation may be given publicity as an apparent fact, shorn of the obvious bias of its original sponsor. Thus among the

[1] The reader acquainted with some of the older published sources cited in this paper will appreciate the difficulty of reconstructing, from materials organized only as description and in keeping with a layman's interests, the effective social context of 'sorcery' and its allied arts. I have been led, however, to make use of accounts from before or only shortly after authoritative European contact; for divination was then more importantly concerned with social control than now. Junod (1927, II:571) was prepared to rate the art of 'astragalomancy' very highly indeed: 'All the elements of Native life are represented. . . . It is a resumé of their whole social order, of all their institutions.' But he went on to deplore its use, as a bulwark of backwardness; and I think few later observers have been in a position to note so high a development of the art.

Yao a large measure of voluntarism is involved in the process by which, in a matrilineal and largely uxorilocal society, a headman comes to command a village or hamlet mainly composed, on the male side, of a congeries of individuals tied to him only by marriage. There are strains toward virilocal marriage which are countered by the stress laid upon matrifiliation, which increases, the more successful a woman may be in producing children (Mitchell 1956: 144). Again, succession within the matrilineage to the position of headman or chief is competitive and often transitory; it depends upon political ability and upon that peculiar social talent by which a leader is able to avoid serious accusation of such acts as sorcery (Mitchell 1956: 158), incest for the sake of maleficent power (Mitchell 1956: 146, 180), or lack of diligence in protecting the interests of the lineage women who hold the balance of power in the village. Inevitably, the cycle of alignment, succession, and secession is moved by accusation and counter-accusation; and in virtually every new initiative the diviner plays a part. But Yao divination differs in form and degree of 'objectivity' from the Ifa divination of the Yoruba; and this characteristic difference accords with the more nearly transitory and, apparently, more 'emotional' character of Yao social relationships.

Ifa divination has been carefully described (Bascom 1941; 1942; Ogunbiyi 1940; Clarke 1939) and perhaps needs no special recounting here. The questions asked of the oracle are often kept secret, in the precise form asked, even from the diviner himself; the diviner repeats set verses, corresponding to the throw of a chance device; recognition of the applicability of a verse by the client is the chief means by which subjective selection is allowed to enter the procedure. Mitchell describes Yao divination as follows:

'The type of divining is usually by gourd and object (*ndumba*). The diviner first of all establishes the reason for the visit, i.e. death, illness, theft, or whatever it is. He then consults his gourd and throws into his hand a variety of symbolic objects. He builds a story round these objects, and finally pronounces that he sees some person whom he vaguely defines. The consultor is then asked to mention who this could be. Though sorcery is supposed to be practised mainly in order to get human flesh for ghoulish feasts, it is not believed to act haphazard. In other words, a sorcerer is supposed to select his victims for revenge as well as for meat. The selective processes at work, therefore, when the consultor seeks to reconcile the diviner's findings with his own suspicions, are that he should select someone who is obviously evil, i.e. from his own point of view, one with whom he has been quarrelling, and he should appraise the possible motivation for sorcery. After he has made the selection the name is tested by the diviner and the consultor may later submit a chicken to the poison ordeal to test the diviner's findings' (Mitchell 1956: 153 n.).

It is notable that the form of divination, as described here, allows a degree of flexibility and publicity to which an accused might reasonably object; nor in the cases which Mitchell presents is there any hint that determinations of this sort are normally un-challenged by the accused. On the contrary, an inconvenient divination is often doubted and belittled; and it may be tried again elsewhere. In the end, it is not so much the choice of the divining instrument but that of the public, reflecting the alignment of interpersonal loyalties, which decides whose divination will prevail, and how far.

II

It may be objected that in a system like that of the Yao, since divination is ultimately overridden by opinion, the diviner can play no functionally significant part. But public credence goes by degrees; it is not absolute. Moreover, divination is not simply a weapon to be taken in hand by any who wishes to increase his in-fluence; the call upon the diviner requires a particular sort of oc-casion, and the diviner must look to his own rules and to his own need for professional independence. An important aspect of divina-tion as institutionalized procedure is just this—that it provides 'resistance' in its own right to any client's proposal.

An interesting but, I think, not all-important source of such 'resistance' lies in the employment of chance or chance-like mech-anisms in the rendering of decisions. In Moore's brief but sug-gestive analysis of scapulimancy among the Naskapi of Labrador (Moore 1957) the point was made that the chance elements in divination may sometimes have a very practical effect in dispersing hunting activities, and the like, so as to prevent over-use of a favourite resort. The emphasis was here upon the practical consequences of the use of a randomizing device in the selection of certain critical courses of action. One is led to conceive of the diviner as a sort of spinner of a wheel of fate, which is wiser than any human judge.

But there are objections to what may be called the 'probability theory' of divination, even when full justice be done to it. One is that it puts an incongruous emphasis upon the actual 'objectivity' of the divining process, an emphasis very hard to justify on ethnographic testimony. A related objection is the obvious one that the theorist must dig very hard amongst the descriptive materials to find only a few examples where a random device, by scattering choices, might have some use; while he is surrounded by unplausible cases. (Is it useful or not to scatter accusations of witchcraft?) Finally, divination in many societies thrives in the face of the fact that it possesses no truly 'objective' forms at all. Among the Dinka, chance devices are evidently mere imports with no firm standing and uncontrolled by the safeguard of known and respected rules; the diviner of repute is 'one who is thought to have an important Power, a free-divinity, in his body' and who divines by uncontrolled possession (Lienhardt 1961: 68 seq., 71). If we are to identify a generic function in divination, then, it must be one of more general applicability.

We have considered the point that the Yao override the decisions of their diviners in many cases, and yet that the practitioner thrives among them. The Azande, who refer major questions to a procedurally guarded poison oracle for which the probability of a given outcome in response to a given query is subject to mathematical calculation, certainly possess a more 'objective' procedure; and they honour its objectivity frankly, by relegating other important oracles to lesser places. But complementary to their respect for the major oracles is their disinclination to take seriously others, which none the less persist in use. Such is the *makama,* which, though it is only used to indicate a witch, 'is regarded lightly by every one and rather in the nature of a joke' (Evans-Pritchard 1937: 376). If we now ask why Yao divination persists in the face of obvious scepticism, the answer may perhaps be phrased analogously to the drama of *makama* divination among the Azande. The instrument is a cone of wood, inserted in a tight-fitting sheath which is held by the witch-doctor at a séance. No one supposes that the witch-doctor cannot, by the way he inserts the conical peg, decide whether or not the man he hands it to is likely to be able to pull it out. Yet when one who has taken the peg is unable to tug it away, the force of the demonstration upon the audience is clear enough. The *makama* has been told to stick tight if the man is a witch 'and has come to spoil divination'; and behold, tug as he may, that man cannot dislodge the peg from the sheath held by the diviner. In this way (I think we may suppose) the witch-doctor who chooses to manipulate his audience may gain its effective consent in barring a certain person from the séance. And so in a great variety of other and less artificial situations may an act of divination become the occasion for the emergence of consensus where before there was none. That all shall agree, the previous commitments of some must meet resistance in a moment of unanimity.

My point is that divinatory procedure, whether 'objective' in quality or merely inter-subjective, constitutes a technique for establishing an effective consensus upon a rather particular project. If that project be conceived in its entirety by the client prior to his seeking the corroboration and quasi-religious sanction of the diviner, the requirement to divine yet proves an obstacle to him. By deflecting his plan, divination may tame it. But more often, I judge, a client's 'project' is but vaguely formed; he has a grievance or cause for acute anxiety but no clear path before him. Then divination may act as a decision-making mechanism by taking the matter, as it were, out of the client's hands. Here a random device, for which intelligent alternative proposals must be framed, is most appropriate. Such was Moore's case among the Naskapi. A band must hunt together or its essential unity would be lost; yet in the context of Naskapi culture the band had no permanent structure. Scapulimancy was much used by the Naskapi in connexion with the broadest imaginable range of purposes, and seems to have permitted of fairly free interpretation. As an instrument for achieving a collective decision on the direction of hunting it was probably not particularly 'random'; but it was suited by its apparent impartiality and its association with prescience to the task of rendering a decision with exceptional authority (Speck, 1935: 139 seq.).

By contrast to the Naskapi, differently situated migratory groups may make no use at all of divination in determining routes, which may be determined by politically established rules of precedence or on economic grounds; for the little-structured organization of the Naskapi is not universal. The appropriateness or inappropriateness of divination *per se* is thus one question; and the appropriateness of a truly random device is another. Both questions require analysis of the context of social structure and conventional thought as well as of the immediate situation of divining. External or 'objective' divination may be called for where the status of the diviner is relatively low; but 'objective' divination which is also truly random may have very limited uses. Azande *makama* divination has its own proper context, as does, in great measure, each separate oracle used in that society. Divination by 'objective' oracle characterizes the Azande social system as clearly as prophetic divination characterizes the Dinka. In both societies divination is rather clearly stratified, in the sense that there is greater attribution of reliability to pronouncements from one source than to those from another. On the other hand, the Yao know no such universal stratification. For better reliability one has no fairer alternative than to take the trouble of going farther away from home, where the atmosphere of contention may be less heavy. The consequence of such egalitarianism is one of a general tentativeness in all social arrangements predicated on moral allegations which were legitimated by divination; and that, indeed, would seem as essential to the operation of the Yao social system as is formal procedure to the Azande or depth of faith to the Dinka.

III

I have attempted to place divination among the important institutions of the primitive world by comparing its operation in several different social contexts, and suggesting that in each case divinatory procedure has the effect of stamping with a mark of special legitimacy a particular decision or a particular kind of response to crisis. Paradoxically, divination appears to have a derandomizing function; establishing consensus, it renders action more predictable and regular. We have thus come to the point of regarding divination as a practice closely related to the problem of controlling and channelling public opinion and belief; and thus we come close to the more general subject of ritual and its sociological meaning.

Ritual occasions presuppose an underlying consensus; and by demonstrating that consensus in a dramatic fashion they strengthen it. The 'field' of ritual in time and space is indefinitely extended to the borders of the social world known to its congregation. By contrast, the 'field' of the diviner's séance is restricted, centring upon an immediate problem, and dissipating as distance and time rob the problem of reality. Yet divination and ritual interplay; nor is the scale of divination always so small as the situation of the 'séance' suggests. Ritual is employed to solemnize attitudes toward the diviner and toward his paraphernalia amongst his public, and even to solemnize his own attitudes toward his professional role. Thus an Ovimbundu divining-basket is to be 'put to bed' each night by a procedure suggesting the 'ritual' of psycho-analytic literature. The basket is further set apart from ordinary things by containing the skull of a poisoned child, bits of the corpse of a famed diviner, and durable remains from animals who appeared in portentous circumstances (Tucker 1940). The conceived 'power' of such a basket, it would seem, must be equal to the dramatic effect required of it in use.

The same theme of solemnization may be remarked in the close association of divination with sacrifice. The consultant diviner may invariably prescribe sacrifice, as among the Yoruba; in priestly divination omens are sought through solemn ritual. The context within which a class of priestly diviners might intervene in affairs of state has been suggested by Sidney Smith in an essay, 'The Practice of Kingship in Early Semitic Kingdoms' (1958: 31):

> 'The subjection of the individual actions of the king to a procedure —the framing of a question capable of only a positive or negative response, the examination of the liver or the flight of birds or the like, the decision as to how the many omens were to be interpreted to procure a majority of favourable or unfavourable results—shows that no king acted according to his own judgment alone, without the possibility of interference by others. They were themselves well instructed in the devices of divination. . . . But they cannot always have forced measures through, if the diviners were in opposition.'

The suggestion of a check-and-balance system, stabilized by a qualitative division of role, is supported by what is known of the importance attributed to divination by the Assyrian kings themselves, and by records of the severe ritual constraints to which the king, at the hands of the priest, was subject. The point upon which I would insist, however, is that of the necessary relationship inhering between omen and public attitude in a society which so exalts the diviner. The war-lord who disregards published omens cannot but prejudice victory and, in the case of reversal, invite disaster: such is the plot of many an ancient tale.

It is perhaps then a little less important to know how such a system actually worked than to understand how, of necessity, it must have been supposed to work. The stability of ritual and structure over centuries, which for ancient Mesopotamia is subject to careful documentation, bespeaks a rootedness in universally shared conventional understandings. The favour of the gods was regularly tested in public by the king himself; and the procedures were patently such as to lie convincingly beyond public suspicion—they possessed a genuine drama. If the effect of that drama was, directly, only to enhance the verity of myth, yet the resulting sacredness of myth and ritual—as being the whole basis for the legitimacy of the system of authority itself—was such as to provide a terrible safeguard of due procedure against the depredations of expedience. It is most unlikely, I suggest, that a critical military decision ever was thrown up to mere chance; or that chance ill-omens ever were allowed in fact to shake the legitimacy of a king's rule. Such possibilities are no more likely than that the Naskapi of Labrador ever went off in a completely wrong direction as the result of an odd crack in a scapula. The function of the ritual precautions, then, was precisely indicated by their manifest purpose of colloquy with the gods. No enterprise of state could proceed without the drama of suspense by which the eventual approval of the gods was made known, and the fact of the direction of such enterprise by beings higher yet than the king was demonstrated to all.

The verity and the power of the myth are thus of greater importance to us than the genuineness of the chance or inspirational devices employed, which need have only dramatic truth. If we would correctly understand Yoruba precautions against contamination of the 'objectivity' of their oracles, or Zande downgrading of devices which they believe may sometimes be rigged, we should think of such precautions as protective of the essential credibility possessed by their more solemn procedures of divination—procedures which, having ceased to be convincing, cease to have value. For while in one social context the requisites of compelling drama may be music, dancing, and shouting, and the appearance of sudden 'possession' in an immoderately decorated diviner, in a quite different context a drama of markedly different quality may be the only appropriate one. For the canons of popular drama are not everywhere the same.

We began with the point that divination must 'resist' in order to produce conviction; and we have been brought to the point of conceiving that resistance in dramatic terms. Where it is used, the genuine randomizing mechanism effects a set of baffles to direct movement toward a goal, and the drama is that of a maze; but it is functionally equivalent to the merely ritual or emotive dramatization found in other contexts. If the types of divination should be named, then, I would call them mechanical, ritual, and emotive; although the three types easily shade into one another in many systems of divinatory practice. Thus the drama of 'possession' is not necessarily a frightening one; it may merely serve, like a mechanical device, to establish the apparent presence of otherwise invisible beings. Clairvoyance and mediumship or ventriloquism are in different contexts the functional equivalents of the induced convulsion of the body. Divining bones and similar collections of paired and named objects, even though they be cast out in public view or cast by the client himself, and even though they be interpreted by a wholly exoteric calculus, as Junod (1927, II:564) made it quite clear that they might be, only dramatically resist nice application to the case in hand— they do not refuse but parry, reverse, and redirect the questioning until it finally culminates in a meaningful resolution, a denouement which, ideally, suddenly reveals the hidden clue to the turns of the drama, like the verb in Virgilian verse. Among the Sotho by 1935 (Ashton 1952: 296–300) the element of chance, or fate, or direct communication by spirits was merely asserted in the formal act of casting the bones; the emphasis lay not there but in the skill with which the diviner was able to achieve insight into the problems of his client and to bring what was usually a protracted séance to an impressive conclusion. Thus the great work of the Sotho diviner was not in the cure or charm which he finally sold to the client, but in the artificial task of discovering what the client had come about—by skilful diagnosis he must establish his own extraordinary powers as a practitioner; and that would give to his cures their value.

So among the Buye it was the lesser diviners who employed the more random and emotionally less impressive devices; the *kilumbu* diviner, upon whose word a man might be seized for a witch and submitted to the poison ordeal, was in his body but in strange voice the medium of communication from a spirit world. The finding of a witch was through a culminative process. It began with an 'objective' séance; and sorcery could only be divined when, after spirits and ancestors all alike had been tried and refused, it was necessary to hint at living persons. There followed an impressive séance with the *kilumbu* diviner, whose mechanical devices only supplemented and coloured his own charismatic aura. Beyond, there was a sort of 'high oracle' of final recourse, or the poison ordeal (Colle 1913, I:381–92; II:469 f.). It is my suggestion that these various forms of trial should be conceived as ranging along a gradient of increasing unimpeachability; and that each item of procedure should be understood as essentially contributing toward that end—the dramatic establishment of an ostensibly irrevocable judgment.

IV

There is perhaps a certain lack of logic in a cumulative system of trials, each of which is ritually exalted to the pitch of infallibility, but any one of which may contradict the proceeding. But there is no lack of drama here; nor does the same characteristic in the developed court system in the urban society prevent the lower courts from pronouncing final judgments. Instead, there is an enhancement of the sense that truth, eventually, must always be found out. A hierarchical system of guilt-divination parallels, in the logical frame of its organization, a system of courts. The drama and seriousness of procedure increases, as only the 'guilty' pass on to a further trial; suspense holds, for each succeeding test offers a chance of exoneration; only no person or body present is invested with apparent responsibility for the critical judgment. At the bottom of the system is the lowly consultant diviner; at the top, perhaps, the ordeal, divination by invisible diviner—that *ne plus ultra,* as it has so often been pictured, of human irrationality.

But ordeals in many societies are interchangeable with other forms of guilt-divination. Bourgeois (1956: 260 seq.) reports from Rwanda and Burundi[2] techniques of guilt-determination ranging from accusation by a jumping grasshopper to a series of ordeals, some of which could manifestly operate only on a 'psychological' basis, and others which as clearly are insensitive to the psychic state of the accused. Here the social context of the ordeal as a trial for sorcery is perhaps epitomized in the fact that torture must be used to extract confession where the signs indicated guilt but the accused denied; and by the further fact that the drama might even then turn: for a stout submission to torture could result in pardon by the highest authority.

The analytical problem, I suggest, which such facts present is essentially one of showing a constant relation between a divining procedure, insusceptible to any but a procedural criterion of validity, and the public conception of right. As the Yoruba, moving in social space, legitimates his move by submitting alternative plans to divination, so a movement of witch-killing, whatever its true determining conditions, must have legitimation. Moreover, as in the political theory of legitimacy, we must distinguish between formal and substantive manifestations: it is in the necessity of achieving more than formal grounds for public execution that the puzzle of the mortal ordeal may be understood. At the moment of action, I would argue, it is substantive legitimacy which is most essential; the act which is predicated upon the decision of divinatory proceedings must be the one which, as all concerned now concede, ultimate wisdom would find true. But there is the further fact that, in the long run, the emotional consensus created by the divining session will fade; so that the legitimacy of the

---

[2] The precise ethnographic reference of the materials reported by Bourgeois is rarely explicit, whether as to place, ethnic group, or time level. For this reason only the immediate context of the system of torture he describes is clear; and the same would apply to all the rich catalogue of divinatory practices contained in his work.

action, in retrospect, will rest upon formal considerations. Both conditions, the formal and the substantive, must therefore be met; the latter to prevent immediate disorder, the former to preserve the chartering myth of constituted authority—its claim of embodying transcendent justice.

The immediate importance of substantive legitimation is well illustrated in the materials reported by Bourgeois, Weeks, and Colle. Where a confession is required before execution, it is evident that the formal indication of guilt is felt to have insufficient weight. We must imagine, I think, that in a segmentary society no accused is without his kin, disposed to support him if the matter is not handled well; and that it is their acquiescence above all which must be publicly demonstrated before an exacted death will become an act of the greater collectivity and quite distinct from action by a vengeance group. But public torture can, in certain contexts, bring about a revolution in group sentiment. One way of handling that emergency would be to reserve the possibility of a pardon; another, I think, is to be found where procedure relies more fully on the logic of the mortal ordeal.

A comparison of Buye and Kongo ordeals is instructive. The importance of the state of public sentiment, and an indication of the logic in the ordeal, emerge from the Kongo materials of Weeks (1914: 263–64). A duly accused witch is given bark poison and may exonerate himself by vomiting it in four successive trials. Normally, on succeeding in this way, he is fêted with great enthusiasm; no taint of the earlier indictment remains against him. Yet in some cases there is no immediate reversion of public sentiment. A person 'very obnoxious to the people generally' (a person deserted even by his kin?) is subjected to a further procedure, a sort of intellectual torture or ordeal. Dazed from the effects of the poison, he must none the less show normally quick powers of discrimination, identifying the species of twig thrown to him, or the type of ant, butterfly, or bird pointed out; and a single miss legitimates execution on the spot. The poison ordeal is intended, as it were, not so much to determine guilt as to demonstrate it. Where opinion is divided, it may demonstrate either guilt or innocence. But where opinion is one, and the poison yet fail to demonstrate its truth, a more certain ordeal may be added, whose form is tinsel but whose decision will validate the popular man-

date. The same bark poison which, in four administrations,
should kill a witch is employed in a single dose in a lesser case;
yet the value of the poison is here reversed. Innocence is demonstrated by retaining the poison unharmed; and vomiting demonstrates guilt, whose punishment is short of death. Yet there is a
consistency of logic, when the ordeal is perceived as demonstration and not merely trial: if the poison is to demonstrate guilt in
a capital offence, it cannot fail to kill; if poison is to demonstrate
innocence in a less-than-capital offence, it must be retained without killing. Here is divination by 'objective' sign.

The procedures of Buye (Colle 1913) law in connexion with
the poison ordeal suggest a rather different social context, in
which the poison in fact operates as legitimating divination, of
the highest order, in what is not a public execution but a public
vengeance-murder. If the accused failed quickly to vomit the poison upon the first trial, he was set upon by the waiting relatives
of his supposed victim, who cut off head and limbs and threw
them into 'un grand brasier', probably then to be bought from the
group by an anthropophage, whose secret society would obtain
from such a body the sense of increased supernatural power. The
ceremonial ordeal here recounted was administered, away from
the village of the deceased, by a ritual specialist of official standing; but it might be duplicated on a less imposing, though equally
mortal, scale in private vengeance trials administered wholly by
the vengeance group itself (ii:813 seq.; 469 seq.). The interplay of formal procedure and direct, vengeful aggression indicates
the immediate translation of formal legitimation into substantive
right. Presumably, the divinatory system could be said to have
reduced bloodshed as against a putative vengeance system requiring a death for a death. Since Colle remarks (p. 814) that the
ceremonial ordeal would be imposed in a given case by the *kilumbu* diviner himself, we may suppose that he was not unaware
of the relation inhering between the social situation of achieving
formal legitimation and the certainty with which it may be expected to resolve the problem of substantive right. Divination
without the diviner is peculiarly suited to such a context of con-
troversy. As a public demonstration of guilt, or equally of innocence, the mortal ordeal could possess a dramatic quality
unequalled by the other techniques we have examined. The mere

publicity of the event as a mortal trial, with its apparent acceptance as such by a great crowd suffering it to proceed, appears to rule out the possibility that, in the public conception, the actual result might have been predetermined by the official mixer of what the modern reader must regard as a merely chemical poison. It was not so regarded by the Buye.

There are, I think, two major puzzles in connexion with the ordeal. One, however, is simply an artifact of the meeting between believer and sceptical observer; it evaporates when attention is shifted from the superficial plausibility of the beliefs which support divinatory practice to the problem of understanding how such beliefs in fact become established and reinforced in collective experience. The other puzzle is the technical one of understanding the peculiar properties of the ordeal which have made it a widespread phenomenon in various parts of the world at various times. I have suggested in this paper that the poison ordeal has in several societies functioned as the apical procedure in a system of guilt-determination; and it is in those terms that I have offered a functional analysis of the custom. The ordeal, like other forms of divination, has been presented as an instrument by which, in concrete situations calling for action, a particular construction may be put upon a problem, and a particular resolution socially established as the right one. In the context of guilt-divination, the consequence is legitimation of demands for punishment or restitution. The ordeal is characteristic of societies in which the right to demand punishment has not been successfully pre-empted by constituted authority, or where that authority requires the drama of human sacrifice to penetrate the public conscience.

v

Divination is typical of the folk, and not of the contemporary urban, form of the social life; its distribution is also uneven within the folk world. 'Divination', wrote Lowie (1935: 255), 'is rightly considered atypical for American Indians.' His perspective was that of the Plains Indians, possessed of a social life in which loss, theft, illness, and death were met in a manner wholly different to that which has characterized most of the African societies considered in this paper. As the individualistic quest-religion of the Plains differed diametrically from a congregational religion centred in the regard for common ancestry, so was the relation of man to man amongst such groups as the Crow or Cheyenne distinct, whether in war, in hunting, in marriage, or in the ceremonial solemnification of those peculiar values which characterize a tribe's commitment to the life it has known. If one were to set oneself the task of discovering what particular cluster of human sentiments might most probably be found in constant association with a developed system of divination, the contrast between Plains Indian and Bantu African responses to physical helplessness, loss by death, characterological deviance, and mortal danger would offer a starting-point of obvious merit. Nor can such a task, I think, ultimately be avoided if we are to understand the ethnographic distribution of divination, and thence to establish a scientific comprehension of its nature.

It has been the tendency of this paper to suggest that divination is regularly associated, in a comprehensible manner, with certain types of social situation; and it is perhaps unnecessary to insist that, with due regard to the operational fictions of 'pure structuralism' in anthropolitical analysis, equivalent social situations cannot occur in two widely different cultures. That is because actual human situations arise as much out of actor-perception and actor-definition as they do out of such events as death or cattle-theft. If divination is to be known as an important institution of the folk world, and not as a mere example of what unscientific thought can uncork, I have suggested that it must be appreciated in its context of private sentiment and public opinion as these are found in variously structured societies. Guilt-divination among the Buye culminated in a public vengeance-murder and cannibalism; among the Azande (Evans-Pritchard 1960) neither cannibalism nor the mortal ordeal had any such firm place; rather, by historical times, the very sentiments which were celebrated in the Buye practice had been subjected among the Azande to firm and formalistic control:

> 'It is apparent that when a witch is exposed by the oracles a situation fraught with danger is created, since the injured man and his kinsmen are angry at an affront to their dignity and an attack on their welfare by a neighbour. No one accepts lightly that another

shall ruin his hunting or undermine his health out of spite and jealousy, and Azande would certainly assault witches who are proved to be injuring them if their resentment were not directed into customary channels backed by political authority' (Evans-Pritchard 1937: 85).

The active role of witch is all but wholly imaginary amongst the Azande; yet persons identified as witches abound and are neither cut off from most normal social ties nor usually killed. The witch is identified by formal and 'objective' systems of corroborative divination, which accept and reject proposals at random; and the act by which a witch recalls and cancels his psychic aggression is equally formal. Public opinion is little roused; substantive legitimacy is not a problem but follows from general acceptance of the correctness of those formal procedures of divination which are supposed to have been followed. When substantive legitimacy does, rarely, prove a matter of some concern, the case may be put to a test; although normally not until the accused dies a natural death, when public examination of entrails again puts to proof, by corroborative divination, the proposal that in life he was indeed a witch. A particular belief, moreover, would appear specifically to discourage the relatives of a deceased from insisting upon such a test—witchcraft is thought to be inherited, and the taint, in the case of a damaging finding, then falls upon the living. It would be only an already embattled group of kinsmen who would stand to gain from raising the issue; in general, the Azande are content with formal and undramatic procedure, so that public feeling fairly readily subsides, excuses, and forgets. While all may agree that the witches about them are many, there is no general agreement as to who they may be (Evans-Pritchard 1937: 23 seq., *et passim*).

The social system of the Azande, I submit, is very different from that of the Buye; nor is there any obvious need that we should trace the reason for this general difference to a source, as it were, in one of its parts. The differences of political and social organization are manifestly important; but so are the differences of ecological setting; nor would an analysis betraying preference for 'psychological' causes be barren of pertinent evidence. The concern of this paper is with systems of divination, and it seems evident to the author that these, also, have some explanatory value. It should be clear that Zande divination is suited to the character of Zande life, as Buye divination is suited to another; but divination, I have insisted, has a logic of its own and is not an inconsequential institution. We may as reasonably propose, then, that Zande ideas about witchcraft follow from Zande divinatory practices, as we may put the case the other way round. And in similar fashion we may insist that the drama of Buye divination was not merely a fierce sort of entertainment, but was an instrument by which the prevailing social appetites, fears, and ideas, as reported for the Buye at the beginning of this century, had been shaped. It is in this light, I think, that we may best perceive the affinity between ordeal and crucifixion, or between the poisoning and the burning of witches.

As a legitimating procedure, divination in the folk world has much in common with what we may call the 'licensing and certifying complex' in the contemporary urban world, which is similarly concerned with such matters as birth, marriage, and death, and which functions in connexion with movement over social boundaries and the infringement of property rights, as well as with crime and dangerous or irksome insanity. Yet a world which is cleansed and ordered by a vast hierarchy of licensing bureaux has a quality lacking in the world which must resort to supernatural ratification of all its minor changes of status. In peasant China, as exemplified in West Town (Hsu 1948: 85 seq.), there was no ritual intervention in marriage, of the sort which requires a solemn commitment to the choice by the two individuals or families concerned. There was, however, at a preliminary stage in the betrothal, a quiet procedure of submitting the 'eight characters' of a son and prospective daughter-in-law to divination, which should expose an unsuitable match before the start of a long and eventful schedule of gift-giving and negotiation essential to the establishment of the match as a duly acknowledged contract. The social context was that of a seclusionist society, in which publicity had a peculiarly symbolic and putative quality, centring in notions of family dignity and honour, which required objective expression from time to time in the form of elaborately ceremonial feasts, processions, and gifts to the living and the dead. The submission of a marriage-choice to divination was felt to be genuine, even though a negative result was not necessarily final: if one diviner found the 'characters' incompatible, the father of the boy might, on consideration, simply go to another. Divination then provided no more than a formalistic ratification of the choice; yet in its context it had function and meaning. The negotiation during betrothal was pre-eminently a test of the status of the boy's family; and as such it strained the family's economic resources to the utmost. Divination here preceded and legitimated the launching of a peculiar, ceremonial splurge by which the family must pair itself in the public eye with another and unrelated family, demonstrating its own means in the negotiated size of its gifts in money and kind, only a portion of which would probably be returned as dowry.

More usually, divination in West Town had an even more routine character—it was employed only to hold and check ceremonial proceedings at each point until the auspicious hour was met. Yet even in this form divination betrays, on analysis, its peculiar usefulness; for the longer, in West Town, one might stretch a ceremony, the greater was one's demonstrable importance. That proposition illuminates particularly, I think, the use of divination in burial. Predetermining and saving for the cost of an old man's death could become a major preoccupation for his family, which recognized an impending test of its public and heavenly standing (Hsu 1948: 133). The extent of mourning, feasting, and economic outlay for a procession must be wisely decided. In the event itself, much depended upon the length of the dead man's stay, as a corpse, with his family; for this was a sign, not only of the family's regard for the man, but also of its regard for the house whose fortune he had guided in life. Thus it was, I suggest, that divination must determine 'the hour when the coffin lid will be nailed on the coffin, the hour when the coffin will be removed from the house, and the day when the coffin will be lowered into the pit for burial' (Hsu 1948: 156). But the system of divination was not here one which left the matter to chance. Poor families divined only the hour, not the date; while an important burial amongst the well-to-do might be delayed for one or two months. The diviner who set the worth of a family by thus timing its funeral shared the universal exemption from reproach of a peculiar institution: he was the midwife of decision, knowing not its author.

I have attempted to sketch the meaning which divination might have had in the context of Chinese family institutions because it has usually been treated only as a minor part of an intellectual or criteriological system and because I have found it illustrative of the manner in which divinatory legitimation may parallel and supplement in its working the most formal ritual sanction. Legitimation is a process whereby a particular act, event, or establishment is declared to be an example of a class already defined in the presupposed norms of a society; and where formal legitimation only is concerned the movement is simply, as in a lower court of law, from 'norm' to 'case'. But as in a higher court the movement has a tendency to reverse, and the 'case' from providing precedent comes to modify the 'norm', so I think we should regard divination as a two-edged instrument of social control. Earlier anthropologists were not sufficiently impressed, perhaps, with the airiness of 'norms' in the preliterate society: Sumner's *mores* were forces in themselves, as real as Durkheim's mechanically-conceived Society or as the Church to earlier unsympathetic historians of mediaeval life. Yet Durkheim had the insight to perceive that Society is the creation of ceremony, and to stress the importance of emotional interaction in the ceremonial gathering; later anthropologists have come to see that the *mores* do not live on of themselves but must be recreated by ritual, ceremony, and the act of constituted authority in the experience of each individual; and history has perceived that the ordeals of witches and the torture of heretics may have been more than the mere application of secure 'norms' to 'cases'—that such cruel and dramatic phenomena reveal to us a crisis in the security of the norms themselves.

14 WITCHCRAFT AND CLANSHIP IN COCHITI THERAPY

J. Robin Fox

INTRODUCTION

ILLNESS, both "mental" and "physical," though based on universal psychobiological factors, is in its expression highly culturally patterned. One becomes "sick" or "crazy" in a well defined, culturally delimited way (Kiev 1961). What is defined as illness differs from culture to culture. Behavior labeled as "sickness" in one culture may count as religious ecstasy in another. The sociocultural system of which the individual is a member provides the stresses that cause the illness; the medium of expression of the illness; a theory of disease (spirit possession, soul loss, witchcraft, or attack of gods, ghosts, or germs); the basis for mobilization of help for the patient; a cure; and, in varying degrees, insurance that the cure will be permanent, that is, that there will be no relapse. In many primitive societies, fine balances have been achieved among these factors. Personality traits, cultural traditions, and social groupings combine both to cause and to cure disease. In many societies, however, there are considerable hiatuses among these factors. The society provides the stress but fails to find a cure, or, if it finds a cure, it fails to provide continuous reinforcement. Our own culture sharply dichotomizes the "hospital" and the "society," and, in the case of mental illness, the society is often directly or indirectly hostile to the patient and the hospital. Primitive societies and religious healing groups often have the edge on hospitals in that they more often incor-

Reprinted from Ari Kiev (editor), *Magic, Faith, and Healing: Studies in Primitive Psychiatry Today* (The Free Press of Glencoe, 1964), 174–200, by permission of the author and Dr. Ari Kiev.

porate the sick person into the society and indeed often *utilize* the sickness in some cultural sphere.

Kilton Stewart gives a detailed account of one type of hypnotherapy, practiced by the *negritos* in northern Luzon (Philippines) (Stewart 1954). Here the shaman induces a trance in the patient and instructs him to fight and overcome the "demon" that is attacking him and causing the complaint. Having mastered the demon, the patient demands from him a dance and a song. The shaman then ends the trance, and the patient is told to perform the dance and sing the song just learned—while the whole band witnesses the performance. The important thing about this type of cure is that all the aesthetic life of the band is derived from it. That is, all the songs and dances of the *negritos* are originally learned in such therapeutic trance conditions. These songs and dances are then regularly performed before the whole band, each person doing a dance-drama, in which he illustrates how he overcame his illness (the demon), and receiving the support and applause of the band. He in turn appreciates and applauds the dance-dramas of his fellows. The likeness to certain types of group therapy is striking, but with the difference that, among the *negritos,* a large slice of the total culture—the aesthetic and recreational—is involved, indeed is derived, from the therapy. Reinforcement is built into a continuing cultural process in which all participate. The group therapy involves the whole social group acting in a whole cultural area; it is not divided between clinic and "outside."

In the American Southwest, the home of the Cochiti, the Navaho Indians have an ethnographic reputation as curers *par excellence.*[1] Their "nine night sings," involving complex rituals and the assembly of thousands of Navaho, have a Durkheimian grandeur. Certainly such a huge effort to achieve a curing suc-

[1] The research on which this paper is based was carried out mainly in the Pueblo of Cochiti, New Mexico, 1958–59, and was made possible by the Social Science Research Council and the Laboratory of Social Relations, Harvard University. A grant from the British Academy assisted in writing up the material. The help of Charles H. Lange, Evon Z. Vogt, Dell H. Hymes, John W. M. Whiting, and the late Clyde Kluckhohn is acknowledged. A portion of this material appeared previously (J. R. Fox, "Therapeutic Rituals and Social Structure in Cochiti Pueblo," *Human Relations,* 13 [1960], No. 4, 291–303), and acknowledgment is made to the editors of *Human Relations* for permission to incorporate it into this report.

cess is bound to have a supportive influence on the patient and therefore helps to effect a cure (Leighton and Leighton 1941). But the cure does not necessarily last. When the guests have packed up and gone home, the cure is over. Cochiti cures are less spectacular but are, I think, more subtly successful, especially in reinforcement.

Before describing them in detail I shall offer a brief résumé of Cochiti culture and society.

CULTURE AND SOCIETY OF THE COCHITI

The Cochiti Pueblo (population approximately 300 in 1958) is one of the Eastern Keresan group of Pueblo (village dwelling) Indians in New Mexico (Lange 1959, Goldfrank 1927). These villages lie near the Rio Grande between Santa Fe and Albuquerque and take water from the river by means of elaborate irrigation ditches. The villages were traditionally compact but, of late, have spread out. The houses, often of two stories and closely packed together, are built of adobe (sun-dried mud and straw) and plastered with mud. Agriculture is the basis of the economy, but recently work for wages has become important.

Cochiti is one of the more acculturated and "liberal" of the Keresan villages, which are notorious for their conservatism and secrecy, but it retains a major part of the traditional culture. As in all the pueblos, this culture is largely concerned with ceremonialism. The indigenous religion was polytheistic and animistic, with the sun, the earth-mother, and a pair of hero twins as its major deities. There were many cults, and the "work" involved in them was divided among various social groups and roles. The main aim of the religion was to achieve fertility of persons, crops, and animals and harmony in society. This entire aim was expressed by saying that "the ceremonies were for rain" (Benedict 1934: ch. 4). Rain in fact symbolized goodness, health, fertility, happiness, and so forth. It came from the clouds, which were identified with the souls of the dead and with certain of the deities, the *shiwana*. The major cult, that of the *katsinas*, was concerned with these deities. There were numerous *katsinas*, and in the rituals men especially chosen from among initiates into the cult performed masked dances in imitation of the *katsinas*. During the dances, the dancer was in fact the embodiment, the essence of the god he represented. Other cult groups performed rituals concerned with hunting, war, and the curing of disease. Most important aspects of Cochiti life had their ritual counterparts.

The tribe was divided into moieties, called *kivas* (*chitya*) after the semiunderground circular chambers used for ceremonies. These *kivas* also had charge of rituals, primarily the public rituals. The most famous is the "corn" or "rain" dance—one of the few ever seen by non-Indians—in which each group dances in turn throughout the day (Lawrence 1927, Lange 1957). Two "clown" groups, the *koshare* and the *kwirena,* are important in "managing" the ceremonies. The former represent the dead and the winter season, while the latter represent life and the spring and harvest (Bandelier 1890).

The government of Cochiti was essentially theocratic. The *cacique* (the "chief" of the tribe) and the main medicine men constituted a ruling elite, but their positions were not hereditary, and a show of reluctance was required of those chosen for office. The *cacique* was concerned with the spiritual welfare of the tribe, and his complement was the war captain (priest or chief), who was responsible for discipline. He and his assistant are named after the two war gods, Masewi and Oyoyewi, mythical hero twins.

The coming of the Spanish (c. 1542) and their final firm establishment after the Pueblo revolt (1680) changed much of the outward way of life (Dozier 1961, Aberle 1948). A new form of government was imposed, including the office of "Governor," but the new officials were in fact the nominees and puppets of the old priestly hierarchy. Catholicism was accepted but not incorporated into the old religion. The two were allowed to run side by side, with a few minor calendrical adjustments. Economic life changed with the introduction of ploughs, horses, and sheep. The coming of the Americans (c. 1830) changed few of these arrangements, and the pace of change has rapidly accelerated only since World War II.

Cochiti society is characterized by a great complexity of groupings. Like all the Rio Grande pueblo societies, it has the dual-division (moiety) system. In Cochiti, there are two *kiva* groups, Pumpkin and Turquoise. Membership in the *kivas* is patrilineal for males, and women join the *kivas* of their husbands. The *kiva* groups are not exogamous, and roughly 50% of the women marry men of their fathers' *kivas*. The *kivas* are ceremonial corporations, complementing each others' functions and providing dance teams for the big public ceremonials. Each has a head and a group of officials, all male, and an all-male drum cult. The role of women in *kiva* affairs is limited to maintenance work on the structure and the provision of food and dancing partners at the ceremonies. It is possible for a man (but not a woman) to change *kiva* voluntarily, but it is a serious and rare step. Patrilineal membership for males and the enormous amount of time spent in *kiva* affairs means that the father-son-grandson bond is quite strong in this ceremonial context. A small group of consanguineally related males and their wives constitutes a kind of informal subgroup of the *kiva*.

The next most important group in the formal structure is the matrilineal clan (*hanuch*). Exogamous, nontotemic (but named) dispersed clans number about thirteen (it was impossible to obtain complete clan rosters). Some are large, (like the Oak, with more than 100 members); others are near extinction. Their place in the social structure has puzzled investigators, who see their functions now largely in terms of exogamy. Previously they also served as economic units of a kind, co-operating in harvesting, for example (Goldfrank). The eldest male was *nawa* or headman and, together with the eldest female, exercised some authority over members but not much. The clans apparently had no governmental functions and little ritual apart from curing. These characteristics set them off from the clans in the "western" pueblos (in Eggan's sense) (Eggan 1950) which play a larger part in social life, but this difference should not lead us to think too readily in terms of the "decline" of the Cochiti clans. They have remained stubbornly in evidence in Cochiti social organization throughout the period of investigation, even though in 1890 Bandalier thought them a "mere survival." They are simply one way of organizing kin for particular purposes, tending in large part to lie dormant in the structure and coming to the fore on certain occasions—marriage, baptism, and curing.

The clans are in theory not internally segmented, and no wide span of segmentation is recognized. Indeed, the Cochiti show little interest in genealogy, and it is rare for relatives to be remembered for more than four generations. The place of the father in pro-creation is not denied; it is simply not regarded as very relevant. The "unit" of the clan is thus not very apparent. Yet clanspeople think of themselves as "closed" relatives, and the clan of the father is regarded as important.

The larger clans are, of course, internally divided *de facto*. The largest, Oak, has at least five distinct lineages. If lineages could be traced back far enough, no doubt most of them would be found to be related, but several may have originated in "foreign" women who intermarried from other pueblos. Each of these lineages has some of the unity that the clan as a whole lacks. In fact, any unity the clan has is derived from the unity of its lineages—each of which is internally strong—linked in a loose federation. The line-age is the unit of most significant interaction in the field of mat-rilineal relationships. As opposed to the basic alliance of the *kivas* (fathers and sons), it is based on the alliance of mothers and daughters. Two or three old sisters, their married daughters, and their granddaughters form the typical grouping. The males of the group are the "brothers" of these women but are now be-coming detached. Indeed, this detachment would constitute the most important change in the social structure of any matrilineal society. In Cochiti, it may be a situation of long standing, dating from the move into the Rio Grande area (Wittfogal and Gold-frank 1943; Reed 1949; Dozier 1961). As long as the males were firmly attached to the core of women in the lineage, then the lineage was strong. When they became relatively detached, it was bound to lose its cohesion and wane as a major social group.

This detachment has to be seen in terms of the twin influences of household as a classical matriuxorilocal setup. The female core of the lineage resided together, and the males regarded this resi-dence as "home" and were but loosely attached to their wives' households. This system has now completely collapsed (if it was ever predominant) and has been replaced by neolocal residence—very often in a house built by the husband. This change and the Catholic prohibition on divorce have strengthened the bonds of marriage. The lack of a specific "house" to return to on divorce or separation has made the man more willing to stick to his wife and home. As the woman is still firmly attached to her sisters and mother, the man becomes attached to this group as well. A maternal extended family group is thus becoming the "domestic" unit in Cochiti, as the paternal extended family group is to some extent a "ritual" unit—both within the field of kinship. In terms of role relations, the husband-wife relationship has been strengthened at the expense of the brother-sister relationship. The lineage, while still existing conceptually, lies dormant most of the time, but its core and strength, the group of women, remains active.

Since Cochiti is a small pueblo, everyone is ultimately related to everyone else by ties of consanguinity, affinity, and ceremonial kinship. A "web of kinship" therefore exists, and from it two groupings emerge that are concentrations of families linked in various ways. The division between these two groups is not sharp. It is rather that the clustering of important bonds is more intensive in two areas of the total network. The two networks are the basis of recruitment to the baseball teams, which are deadly rivals (Fox 1961a). Kroeber, who stresses the dichotomy between "kinship" and "clanship" in Zuni, and Forde, in his study of Hopi land tenure, see the importance of this "bilateral" web of ties (Kroeber 1917; Forde 1939). Eggan tends to overstress the importance of the lineage and clan, two elements better regarded as part of the "formal" organization of the pueblo life (Eggan 1950). In terms of the existence of actual decision-making groups, other principles than those of matrilineal descent can be important or even predominant.

The "medicine" and "managing" societies are associations of which membership is voluntary. The former are sometimes related to the latter in terms of membership and complementary functions. Two managing societies, Koshare and Kwirena, are linked to the two *kivas* respectively and help to arrange and supervise ceremonies. A third, the Shrutzi society, manages the Katsina cult. The medicine societies have both curing and governmental functions, in that they nominate the "secular" officers of the village. Membership in all these groups is falling off, and some are near extinction.

The secular officers ostensibly form the most powerful group in the pueblo. The governor and his assistant and the war captain and his assistant are the most powerful men in secular and ceremonial affairs respectively—although it is often hard to separate the two functions. The religious head of the tribe, the *cacique,* has very little real power but a good deal of influence. Together with the council of *principales*—past officials—these men govern the pueblo.

Among informal groupings, the factions are probably the most important, although the virulence of factionalism is abating in Cochiti. The "progressive" faction favors changes, while the "conservatives" stick to the "old ways." The ex-servicemen in the pueblo are doing much to pull these two together in a constructive way (Fox 1961b).

This breakdown by no means exhausts the groupings in the pueblo (one important group, for example, is the Katsina cult), but it presents some of the most important and gives some idea of the structural and organizational complexity of the village. The society can be seen as based on the double division of the two *kivas* cut across by the clans, extended families, medicine societies, and so forth—although this point of view is not the only one possible. There is considerable overlapping of group membership as a result of the large number of groups and the small population, and this overlapping in turn helps to provide internal unity despite a high degree of conflict.

COCHITI THERAPY

Typology of Disease and Cure

The distinctions in Cochiti thought between various types of disease and their appropriate cures are not always easy to see. My own data were not collected with this question in mind and therefore show annoying gaps. It seems, however, that there are three main types. First and simplest are "natural" diseases (burns, fractures, and so forth), which are largely curable by natural means—herbal treatments, elementary first aid and sometimes treatment by the United States Indian Service doctors. Then come illnesses caused by witches, which are treated either by a member of a medicine society or, in severe cases, by an entire society. Each society specializes in certain types of cure. The various diseases treated in this way are characterized by some

informants as "sharp" (*tsiati*): They are generally sudden illnesses that "seize" patients and are always considered the result
of witchcraft. These illnesses are contrasted with "dull" illnesses
(*tsatsi tsiati,* literally "not sharp")—those that, in the words of an
informant, "just go on and on and don't seem to get better."
For these illnesses, the society cures are considered too drastic
and "clan cures" are employed. While not able to verbalize the
distinction between these two types of disease very clearly, the
Cochiti "know" one kind from another and can demonstrate details. In practice, the drawn-out "dull" diseases are not treated as
though they had been caused by witchcraft, although it is impossible to pin the Cochiti down to a coherent theory of the causation
of disease.

Curing Societies and Witchcraft

There are in the literature many details of curing ceremonies
gleaned from informants, but no observer seems to have attended
a cure. Some of the societies and their methods are common to
all the Keresan pueblos. I shall concentrate on Cochiti, but much
of this material is true for all the Keresans.

There are societies proper and "degrees" within societies. In
the important Flint society, its two degrees of Snake and Fire
are now inextricably merged. This society is powerful because of
its associations with the Koshare managing society and because
the *cacique* is chosen from it. It also nominates the war captain
and his assistant. The Giant society is next in importance, and its
head is first assistant to the *cacique*. This society, which nominates the governor and his assistant, is also closely associated
with the Shrutzi society and the management of the Katsina cult.
The Shikame society is loosely associated with the Kwirena and
nominates the *fiscale* and his assistant. The medicine societies
are thus intimately bound up with the ritual and political life of
the tribe, and form a theocratic hierarchy of government as well
as an agency of medical and spiritual well-being.

Recruitment to the societies is voluntary, by "trapping," or by
cure: One can join as a result of vocation, of being "trapped"
through entering a forbidden area during a ceremonial, or of a
desire to perpetuate a cure. There is an elaborate initiation, often

lasting many years and involving abstentions, fastings, and retreats.

There are three primary functions of the societies: curing, rainmaking, and government. The last is largely delegated to the "secular" officials, and the medicine men concentrate on the first two. In general, they are the guardians of tribal well-being, ensuring its continuing fertility and health, although they function only in a context of immense communal effort in this direction. While sacrifice and prayer, mainly through dance and ritual, are required of all Cochiti, the medicine men are, in Bandalier's words, the "chief penitents of the tribe." They continually fast and pray on behalf of the Cochiti and indeed of all Pueblo Indians. Most of their time, however, is spent in curing. There is evidence of some division of labor among the societies. The Flint society was "considered primarily as doctors, curing illnesses, setting fractures and helping the people combat witchcraft" (Lange 1959). They were called on to preside at births and deaths and were particularly proficient at curing wounds. The Snake society cured snake and other bites, while the Fire society specialized in burns and fevers. The Giant society also treated fevers and was perhaps preferred for births. The societies collectively led communal fasts and purifications.

In their general role as "penitents," members of societies fast, pray, and make "prayer sticks" in seclusion, thus gaining the good will of the tribal deities and ensuring rain, fertility, and good health. To understand their specific curing methods, one must understand the nature of witchcraft and its place in the theory of disease. Some diseases are to the Cochiti obviously "natural." The medicine men have considerable knowledge of first-aid measures and herbal cures for these illnesses. Others are not so obviously due to natural causes and are attributed to the supernatural malevolence of witches. In Cochiti thinking, witches are almost exclusively concerned with causing disease. In Pueblo cosmology, there is an uneasy balance of forces in the universe. The forces of good—the *shiwana* and the various other deities and spirits—are only precariously in control. Even they have to be compelled by elaborate rituals into producing rain and health. The witches represent a vast conspiracy of ill defined but definitely malignant beings that seek to destroy Pueblo civilization by attacking the health of its members (Simmons 1942). They are of various types, appearing as humans, animals, and birds (especially owls) or as fireballs. Living humans can be witches by being born with two hearts, one good and one bad. Practically everyone is suspected by someone at some time of being a witch or of practicing sorcery. This distinction is not made in ethnographic writings or in Pueblo thinking, but a person actually practicing sorcery (as opposed simply to "being" a witch) is by definition himself a witch or "two-heart." Persons found indulging in sorcery would, in the old days, have been clubbed to death by the war captains after a trial before the pueblo leaders. Such evidence would be required as the proofs of possession of owl feathers or other sorcerer's devices. Witchcraft mythology is riddled with inconsistencies, and it is often difficult to know whether an accused person is simply a "passive" witch, an active sorcerer, or an ordinary human in league with the witches. Witchcraft accusations are rarely specific as to the nature of the witchcraft or the identities of the victims. The accusation is simply that "he is a witch." Such an accusation can only gain sympathetic hearing if feeling generally is roused against the accused on some issue. Accusations have to be made with care because the strong notions of matrilineal heredity make them, by implication, indictments of the accused's matrilineal kin.

It is against this terrible conspiracy of evil that the people, helpless in their lack of ritual knowledge, seek aid from the medicine societies. The societies possess the knowledge, paraphernalia, and courage to combat the witches—the sources of their great power in the pueblos.

The witches cause illness by two basic methods. They either steal the heart of the victim, or they shoot objects into his body. To cure him, the medicine societies must suck the objects from the body or recover the heart by fighting the witches. To understand the nature and effectiveness of this curing process, one must enter sympathetically into the Cochiti imagination. For most of the time, they feel that there is an uneasy balance in the universe. The enormous ritual efforts of the tribe and the vigilance of the medicine men are keeping the universe on an even keel and the witches at bay. But threat is always present. When someone falls very ill or behaves oddly, violently, or erratically, it means that the witches have broken through, in the same way that a drought means that the *Shiwana* have withdrawn—usually because of faulty ritual, which can itself be the result of witchcraft. The terror of mind produced by the feeling that one is in the grip of the witches—that is by being ill—is profound and real and is accentuated by the fear of those around. It is equivalent perhaps to the real medieval terror at feeling irredeemably damned. The fact that this conspiracy of evil has allies in the pueblo and even among one's own relatives is doubly terrifying. Even the doctors can be suspected, and the Katsinas themselves are not above suspicion. Sometimes people fear that they may be unconsciously guilty of witchcraft, for example when their "bad thoughts" about someone seem to result in his death or illness. The over-all atmosphere in the face of sickness or violence or anything completely untoward is one of real, helpless fright. Into this situation step the medicine men. Their curing method consists of accentuating the terror almost to breaking point and then, by triumphing over the witches in a fight, recapturing and returning the heart or removing the objects from the body. Here is White's matter-of-fact summary of the process (White 1928):

> When a person is ill he may ask to be treated by a medicine man or by a society. If the illness is not severe, one medicine man only will come. But if the patient is very ill, or wishes to become a member of the curing society, the whole society will come. The father of the patient summons the doctor (or society) by taking a handful of meal to the doctor selected or to the head man of the society.
>
> When one doctor only comes to treat the patient, the procedure is simple. He smokes, sings, mixes medicine in a bowl of water, puts ashes on his hands and massages the patient's body, and sucks out any objects that he locates. But when a whole society comes, there is an elaborate ceremony in which considerable paraphernalia is used. Usually a society spends four days in its house in preparations before visiting the patient. Then when they go to his house, the medicine men smoke, sing, and pray over the sick one for three nights, and on the fourth have their final curing ritual. But if the condition of the patient is critical, they will perform the curing ritual at once. . . . A meal painting is made and paraphernalia laid out. The chief item of paraphernalia is the *iarriko*, the corn-ear fetish. Each doctor receives one at initiation. It is returned to the head man at death.

It is the badge *par excellence* of the medicine man. Stone figures of *Masewi, Oyoyewi, Paí yatyamo, K'oBictaiya,* and of lions, bears, and badgers, etc. are laid out on the meal painting. The medicine men do not possess power to cure disease in and of themselves; they receive it from animal spirit doctors (the bear is the chief one, others are mountain lion, badger, eagle, etc.). Meal lines are drawn on the floor from the door to these stone figures; when the songs and prayers are begun, the spirits of the animal medicine men come in, pass over the "roads" of meal, and invest the stone images. Medicine bowls, skins of the forelegs of bears, flints, eagle plumes, rattles, etc. are used. A rock crystal (*ma cai'yoyo* or *ma coitca'ni*) is used to obtain second sight.

The medicine men wear only a breechcloth. Their faces are painted red and black, and they wear a line of white bird-down over the head from ear to ear; songs are sung, the headman tells the people present to believe in the medicine men that they are doing their best, etc.; water is poured into the medicine bowl from the six directions, each doctor puts some herb medicines into the bowl. The doctors rub their hands with ashes, and massage the patient. When they find some foreign object they suck it out and spit it into a bowl. The rock crystal is used to locate objects in the body and to "see witches." Witches gather about a house during a curing ceremony; they wish to harm the patient further or to injure the doctors. They have been heard to rap on the door (at Cochiti) and call to the doctors, defying them. The War Captains and their assistants always stand guard outside the door during a curing ritual. They are armed with bows and arrows since rifles would not hurt a witch.

Frequently the doctors decide that the heart has been stolen by the witches. Then it is necessary to find it and bring it back. This almost always means fighting with the witches. They go out armed with flint knives; they wear a bear paw on the left forearm, a bear claw necklace, and a whistle of bear bone. The War Chief's guards try to accompany the medicine men when they leave the curing chamber, but the doctors travel so fast it is impossible; sometimes the medicine men leave the ground entirely and fly through the air.

These combats with the witches are occasions of great moment. Cries and thuds can be heard in the darkness. The witches sometimes tie the queues of two or three doctors together and leave them in a tangled mass on the ground. Or, a medicine man might be found lying on the ground bound with baling wire, his knees under his chin. The witches try to overpower the doctors by blowing their breath, the odour of which is unbearable, into their faces. Sometimes the doctors have to seek refuge in the church, when the witches "get too bad."

But sometimes the medicine men capture a witch. He is usually man-like in shape and about a foot and a half long (although he may be as large as a man, or he may be in the form of some animal). Often he looks like a Koshare. He squeals when they bring him in. They place him before the fireplace and then call the War Chief in to shoot him with a bow and arrow. The medicine men frequently return smeared with blood or "black" after a fight with witches. Often, too, they fall into a spasm or lose consciousness upon their return.

The medicine men come home with the heart (*wí nock*). This is a ball of rags with a grain (or four) of corn in the center. The patient is given this to swallow.

When the ceremony is over and everyone has been given medicine to drink, food is brought out (stew, bread, and coffee). The medicine men eat first, then the people. Baskets of cornmeal and flour are given to the medicine men in payment for their services. They gather up their paraphernalia and go home.

This account seems to fit pretty well the experience of both doctors and patients in Cochiti. The sequence of a full-scale cure is interesting. The doctors spend four nights preparing, and it is a pretty exhausting preparation. They do not eat or sleep during this time, and they smoke a lot. They can be heard chanting in the society house. Witch phenomena (fireballs, owls, and so forth) increase during this time, and everyone gets keyed up. Then the doctors go to the house where the patient has been waiting—an agonizing wait—and repeat the performance. They manipulate the paraphernalia, invoke their spirits, smoke, chant, and build up more tension. By the fourth night of this ceremony (the eighth in total), the tension is almost unbearable. The witches are gathering to thwart the efforts of the doctors. The doctors maintain that they can only do their best and that the issue is still very much in doubt. Then a final supreme effort must be made. The monotonous rise and fall of the chant, the near-darkness with the flickering fire, the hideous make-up, the cries in the night and rappings at the door and windows, the elaborate precautions—all these elements build up until the doctors, worked into a controlled frenzy, dash from the house to do battle. Patients describe how they have been nearly mad with fear by this time, unable to move or to cry out and convinced that they are to die. Then comes the terrible battle in the darkness. The doctors claim that, although of course they do a lot of the "business" themselves, it is the witches who get "inside them" and make them do it. They do indeed roll in convulsions and lacerate themselves. One explained, "We are more scared than they are [those in the house]. The witches are out to get us. They get inside us and make us do these things until we don't know what we're doing. We run to the church sometimes." Finally, exhausted, they return. Those in the house are by now at screaming point. "Sometimes we think the witches have got them [the doctors] and that they will come for us." The doctors reappear and enact the ultimate horror. They come in the semidarkness, huddled together fighting with something in their midst that screams horribly. It is the witch who stole the heart. Then, by the firelight, the war chief shoots it, and it disappears. The effect on the patient can be imagined. The incredible relief and tears of joy and gratitude leave him "feeling like all the badness has gone out." The "heart" is returned to the patient. Then, almost nonchalantly, the doctors and people eat stew and drink coffee. Life returns to normal; the universe is on an even keel again.

There is no doubt that much Cochiti illness is psychosomatic. They do not distinguish formally between physical and mental illness. All "illness" is abnormal. Belief in witches provides a cultural medium through which illness can be "expressed." Also, in many cases, a pathological fear of witches can itself bring on illness. Any Cochiti who suffers from certain illnesses will believe himself bewitched, but not all Cochiti are so afraid of witches that the fear drives them to sickness. In the more markedly paranoid individuals, intense fear of others is expressed, indeed felt, as witch fear. The paranoiac traits and the cultural beliefs in witches obviously reinforce each other. When a person feels ill, he suspects witchcraft, which in turn accentuates the illness. But the society has, in the medicine man, a cultural mechanism to deal with the situation. Terror of witchcraft is utilized to provide a kind of shock therapy. The patient is put through a terrifying experience, "saved," and his "heart" restored. His relief is so great that, in many psychosomatic cases, this ceremony suffices as a cure. He does not have to join the society that cured him, but he may do so out of gratitude or to help perpetuate the cure.

Cures of this type have usually been of illness among men.

The complaints are various but mostly seem to be abdominal pains, rheumatism, and respiratory troubles, as well as anxiety and erratic behavior, insomnia and vomiting. At least two men described as having recurrent "fevers" appeared to be mentally abnormal, and the "fevers" (rises in temperature) were accompanied by violence and hallucinations of such ferocity that they had to be restrained and were shaking and sweating with fear. The hallucinations were, of course, mostly about witch phenomena. The witch theory accounts neatly for all symptoms.

Clan Cures

The other type of cure involves the clan rather than the society as curing agent. The question arises, how is it decided whether a clan or society cure should be employed? This point has never been pursued by other writers, and again data are scarce, but several striking facts emerge. The most obvious is that, in cases where a clan cure is selected, no mention of witchcraft is ever heard as the cause of the sickness, and it is not called upon to effect the cure.

The clan cure is a variation of the clan adoption ceremony. Clan adoptions are performed, for example, for anyone coming to live in the village who does not have a clan. His head is washed by a woman who becomes his clan "mother," and from then on he is a member of her clan. He is given a new name, and feasting takes place among his new-found clansfolk. Tewa wives are usually treated in this way, in order that their children may have clans, the Tewa being bilateral. A man can be adopted, but it is not so important that he should be. Since the clan organization is matrilineal, it is necessary that the woman should have a clan to pass on to her children. For a man, membership in one of the moieties is more important.

The whole notion of adoption in Cochiti is interesting because it too is bound up with the preoccupation with health. A child is often adopted into a clan or clans other than his own as a kind of insurance policy. The child may be perfectly healthy, but it is thought good for his future health that he should acquire some "extra" clans. He does not become a full member of these clans (for example, a girl does not pass on membership in her adopted clan to her children), but he does stand in a very special relation to their members. They "care for" him in a spiritual sense. Clanless immigrants are believed to enjoy better health as a result of being adopted. One does not have to be ill in order to benefit from adoption, but such benefit can help those who are suffering from certain illnesses. I was able to trace the case histories of some of the patients cured by this method, of one in particular. I shall outline this case, reserving further general discussion until later.

Case History

The patient, whom I met in 1958, was a woman of forty years. Her immediate family at that time consisted of her father, a man of seventy-five years who had gone blind in about 1945; her sister, three years younger than herself; and her illegitimate son aged sixteen. Her life history revealed that her mother had died in about 1930, when the patient was twelve. Her father then remarried. (His second wife was a Cochiti woman who had married a man from Zia Pueblo. After her husband's death, she had returned to Cochiti, bringing her son, who married a Cochiti girl.) Neither the patient nor her sister was considered attractive by the men of the village, and neither ever married. The patient, however, had borne a son in 1942. Three years later, her father began to go blind. Her sister then got into trouble with the pueblo council for giving information to outsiders on some ceremonial matters. Her father was totally blind by 1948, and the cure took place in 1951. Shortly after the cure, the stepmother died following a long period of declining health.

EARLY LIFE. The patient's early family life had been overtly secure and happy. The mother had been a beautiful, energetic woman and the father an important ceremonial official. The patient, while of below normal intelligence, was a serious and conscientious girl who looked after her younger sister with her mother's help. Then, when the patient was about eleven or twelve, her mother died. The running of the household and the care of her sister were thrust upon her. She evidently took the death of her mother very hard. Her relatives say it was useless to console her. Her father's remarriage did not help. While it is difficult to ascertain the relations between the patient and her stepmother, they were evidently strained and distant. This state of affairs was attributed to the patient's "queer" behavior, which began shortly after her mother's death.

SYMPTOMS. The first symptom was apparently insomnia. She would wander about at night and complain constantly that she could not sleep. Then during the day, she was too tired to do anything, and simply sat around. She was censured for this behavior at first, but then it became worse. Her sister describes the symptoms, "She used to put on her best clothes in the morning and just sit on the step combing her hair. Then she put on her jewelry, all of it, and sat there all the rest of the day. She'd cry and moan and she was always sick around the place. She had pains in her stomach and couldn't eat anything. She sat and talked to herself all the time, crying and talking." She had vague fears, but "not about anything in particular"; she simply "acted scared" all the time. Fear of relative strangers and inability to recognize people were also in evidence. The pains and vomiting became acute, and she was taken to the Indian hospital. She was better for a while but was discharged without being fully cured. "Them doctors couldn't do anything for her, she was sick in her mind."

The content of her "talk" consisted almost entirely of complaints about her lack of a home. Her father's rapidly failing sight made him utterly dependent on his daughters and relatives. Under the old matrilocal system of residence, a man was always dependent on his wife's mother for a house. This man had never had a house of his own but had always lived in a house supplied by his affinal relatives. At the time of the onset of his daughter's serious symptoms, he was living in a house owned by the son of his second wife, his stepson. This house had been built by the stepson for his mother on her return to the village, and it was legally his. As the stepson was himself living in a borrowed house at the time, the two sisters and their father were under threat of a possible eviction. This threat was not so great as long as the stepmother was alive, but she was a fragile woman whose health was progressively failing throughout the period. Under the matrilineal system of inheritance and the institution of female house ownership, the two sisters should have received their mother's house at her decease. But in this case, as in many others, rules and practice did not coincide. Houses are not infinitely divisible, and the house that could have come to the patient in the female line in fact went to the children of her mother's mother's sister. As the recent Pueblo preference for neolocal residence has grown stronger, it has become less common for sisters to share houses, each preferring a house of her own. The onus of providing a house thus in most instances falls on the husband, unless his wife is senior of a group of sisters and inherits her mother's house. The father of our patient was unfortunately caught between the two systems, and his sight began to fail before he could adapt himself to the newer system of male house-ownership.

The result of this potential housing problem was to create actual insecurity for the patient, who was already subject to emotional insecurity. The situation was by no means tragic, for it is doubtful that the stepson would ever have turned them out (in fact, evidence suggests the contrary), but the patient seized upon the uncertainty of the housing situation and used it to express the deep feelings of abandonment and insecurity consequent upon her mother's death. The house that she fretted over should have come to her from her mother, and that it had not done so was a reinforcement of her anxieties over the discontinuance of the mother's love.

There is some evidence that, for all its outward calm, the early life of the patient may have contributed to these feelings. Her sister, three years younger than herself, took her place as the spoiled "baby" of the family, and there was some resentment on the patient's part at having to play nurse to her younger sibling. During the mother's illness immediately prior to her death, the patient had both to look after the unruly child and attend the sick woman. It was during this period that she first became sullen and withdrawn. To understand the patient's fright at the thought of her mother's death, we must appreciate the nature of the mother's continuing relationship with her daughters. This relationship lasts as long as the mother lives. All advice and help in personal and family matters that a woman may need are obtained from her mother. Particularly in the matter of marriage and childbirth and the rearing of children, the mother plays a crucial part, being constantly at her daughter's side. Even today, when there are very few matrilocal households left in Cochiti, this bond remains as firm as ever. Mothers will trudge miles and ford the river in order to help daughters and *vice versa*. It is not simply a matter of practical help but of emotional dependence of an intense nature. With initiation, the boy is to some degree weaned of this dependence, but the girl remains at home with her mother all her life— in feeling if not in fact. Bearing this relationship in mind, we can appreciate the acute anxiety that the sickness and death of her mother must have aroused in the patient. All informants agreed that the "spells" became worse during her own pregnancy and after the birth of her child. She was assisted in childbirth by her mother's mother's sister's daughters—one of whom owned the disputed house. The fear of going through the first birth without the help and emotional support of the mother has been noted in a number of other instances. It is one of the reasons why girls refuse to go to hospital for the delivery. (This prejudice is breaking down in the present generation.) Shortly after the birth of her son, the patient's father began to go seriously blind, although his sight had been bad for some time. At this point, the patient was taken to the hospital as previously described. Since she was essentially a dependent person, the responsibilities of a blind father, a sickly stepmother, an irresponsible younger sister, and a "fatherless" baby, coupled with the lack of a home of her own, were too much, and she broke down completely. She failed to give milk properly just before leaving for the hospital, and this function was handed over to a female relative, as is the Cochiti custom.

MOBILIZATION OF HELP. The situation was growing progressively worse, and after her dismissal from the hospital the girl's relatives decided to take some more positive action. To understand what was done, we must examine the network of extended family and clan relationships surrounding the patient (Fig. 1). The relatives are indicated with the patient (P) as reference point. In Generation 1, there are two sisters who own a house. In Generation 2, two brothers married the daughters of these two sisters, one brother being the father of the patient. The house went to the wife of the other brother, as she was the elder of the two cousins and married first. Finally, it went to the patient's second cousin (her mother's mother's sister's daughter's son), who was also her father's brother's son. The patient's mother died, and her father married a woman from the patient's own clan— Oak. The patient's father's sister's daughter married the patient's stepbrother. It was this stepbrother who had built the house for his mother in which the patient, her father, stepmother, sister, and son were living.

The surviving relatives who could be considered to have some responsibility for the fate of the patient and her family were her maternal second cousin (who was also her father's brother's son); her father's sister's daughter; and the latter's husband, who was also the patient's stepbrother. The first move was made by the cousin who had the house that was ostensibly the cause of the trouble. He made a deal with his father's brother, the father of the patient. The latter owned some land that was suitable for house-building, and the cousin agreed to trade the house for the land. The patient and the other members of her household were thus able to move into a house that was indisputably theirs; they had a home. This solution, however, was not in itself a cure. A fuller cure was arranged by the patient's stepbrother. It had to be a clan cure as, according to my informants, that was the only type that would fit the circumstances. Meanwhile the cousin's own stepmother had provided him with a house until such time as he could build his own.

To arrange for the clan cure, the stepbrother had to take several factors into account. He had first to find someone who would

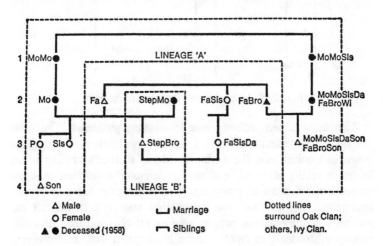

Fig. 1. The Patient's Extended Family and Clan Relationships.

be willing to bear some of the expense, and it had to be someone who knew the cure. Ironically enough, the person best qualified to do the cure—the one who knew the ritual best—was the patient's own father. But it was impossible for him to carry out the cure on his own daughter. Central to the idea of the clan cure is the acquisition of new relatives, so that it is obviously a disadvantage to use as curer someone as closely related as a father. The Cochiti did not rationalize it in this way, however—they simply said that it would be "unthinkable" for a patient to be cured by her own father or mother. A complete outsider to the network of relatives would probably be unwilling, however. In these circumstances, the stepbrother turned to his mother's brother for help. This man was under no obligation to undertake the cure, but he nevertheless agreed that he and his wife should do so. The relation of curers to the patient is outlined in Fig. 2.

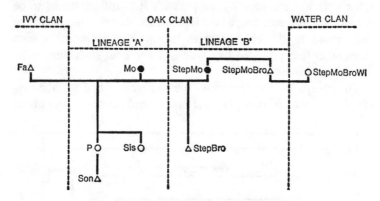

Fig. 2. Relationship of Patient and Curers.

This arrangement raises some interesting problems. The clan system as an effective form of social organization is breaking down in Cochiti, and the authority of the mother's brother is no longer a reality. But when a matter demands a solution that involves the old basis of grouping, the old patterns seem to repeat themselves. In this case, the stepbrother was right to consult his mother's brother as the proper adviser on clan matters, and the mother's brother was right to help his nephew out. If, however, the central part of the cure is the adoption of the patient into two other clans than her own (the clans of the curer and his wife), then half this advantage of the cure was consciously being foregone in this instance. This compromise has occurred in other Cochiti cures and is largely due to diminishing willingness to undertake the cure. People have to look more and more to an immediate circle of relatives and also to the numerical dominance of the Oak clan over the others. There is no indication that the patient's father deliberately chose his second wife from the Oak clan, but as this clan is very large the chances of his drawing a wife from it were quite high. The problem arises, however, of how the cure will proceed if one of the curers is of the same clan as the patient. How can the patient be adopted into her own clan? Informants say that, "You just go ahead with the ceremony anyway, like she wasn't an Oak." I think the clue to this apparent anomaly lies again in the gap between theory and practice. Although in Cochiti, there are many people with the title of *ha'panyi* (Oak) and although they are members of the same clan and so theoretically related, the actual relationship is in many cases either very tenuous or nonexistent. More cases of endogamy occur within the Oak clan than within any other, and there is apparently little censure of such marriages. One other clan cure known to me involved an Oak patient and a curer of the same clan. It seems then that, with regard to Oak participation, it is accepted that there may be overlap in membership and that, as long as the curer is of a *lineage* that is not related to the lineage of the patient, the common clan is overlooked. There was in this case no known relationship between the stepmother's lineage and that of the patient. This kind of compromise has to be effected on many occasions in a small community carrying the burden of an archaic social structure intended for a much larger community. The other clan involved in the cure, that of the stepmother's brother's wife, was the Water clan. Initiation into this clan was especially beneficial for the patient, for it contained important medicine men.

THE CURE. The stage was thus set for the cure. It took place at the home of the sponsor (the patient's stepmother's brother). An announcement was made four days before, properly relayed with a pinch of cornmeal to all the clan members concerned (Oak and Water). The Water clan and the members of the Oak lineage B were present. The patient's lineage gathered at her home, along with members of her father's clan, Ivy; everyone feasted, and then the patient was conducted to the curer's house where all present joined in washing her head with *amole* suds, the traditional method of sanctifying adoptions. (It is also the method used to indicate and sanctify any significant change in status, such as that undergone at initiation.) All the others brought presents for the patient, including food like melons, rabbits, and corn. Then the patient was given new names, and returned to her people at her own house. The curer's wife and her sisters and all the women of her clan would be henceforth "mothers" of the patient. Similarly, the women of the stepmother's lineage (B) would be "mothers" and would be addressed as such by the patient. One of Lange's informants describes the status of a patient after such a cure: "If an Ivy is cured by Sage and Oak, he is still Ivy but also he is a little Sage and a little Oak. Later if a Pumpkin asks the Sage or Oak to be cured, then the Ivy who is a little Sage or Oak goes along to help out" (Lange 1959). The cure is unlike an adoption, however, in that the patient's children will not inherit her "little" clans.

This cure took place in 1951, and shortly afterward the patient and family moved into the house that had been given up to them. Since then, the patient has never had a "spell," shows no organic symptoms, and behaves normally. Before the cure, I was told, she was "wasted away to nothing" and "she was pretty near dead sometimes." There may be a tendency to exaggerate in such a case, but opinions were sampled and, as far as independence of opinion could be assured, they were agreed on the symptoms.

We can see how the institution of clanship is utilized to effect a cure and to help maintain it. Our patient is now a member of the Water clan and a different lineage of the Oak clan—she is a "little" Water and is dependent on continuing membership in the Water clan for her continued good health. By becoming a member of this clan she is cured, and by continued membership she stays cured. She acquires a relationship of dependence with a previously unrelated set of people. What is more, her faith in the efficacy of the cure is reinforced when she goes along to participate herself in cures conducted by the Water people. Clan, or rather lineage, membership is also of practical importance in mobilizing help for the patient. The clan system is thus an anchor on to which therapy can fasten and by which continuous reinforcement of treatment can be assured.

I have no other case recorded in such detail, but in three of the other cases (all involving women), the data do suggest a striking similarity in the total syndrome: a hiatus in the mother-daughter relationship leading to considerable anxiety and consequent illness. In all cases, the physical symptoms were vague and the traits of insomnia, erratic behavior, withdrawal, and amnesia were predominant. In other cases, the data were sparse or showed no conclusive evidence of mother-child problems. But it should be remembered that the adoption-cure is thought to be generally effective in ensuring health and is not specifically confined to the type of illness based on problems of maternal deprivation.

INTERPRETATION

We have then an interesting problem. There are two kinds of cure for two types of illness. In one type, an illness thought to have been caused by witches is cured by an elaborate shock therapy. In the other type, an illness not associated with witchcraft is cured by adoption into a social group.

Interpretation is bound to be speculative, for we have no proper clinical data for these people, but some conclusions, however tentative, may aid in sorting out the problem.

Witch Illness

We have suggested that paranoia may be at the root of the witch illness complex. This analysis excludes, of course, the purely "physical" illnesses, to the degree that there are such things. In any case, even if the primary cause of the illness is "physical," the fear of witches engendered by it produces secondary "mental" symptoms that serve to intensify it. An individual is either to some degree paranoid, with stress inducing physical illness, or he is physically ill, which induces a state of acute paranoia. In either case, the paranoia must be dealt with, and the witch theory offers a medium for the expression of the illness, an explanation of its cause, and, through the societies, a means for its cure. Elaborate shock treatment attacks the "cause" of the disease and, by conclusively eliminating it, restores the patient, even if only temporarily. There is no provision in Pueblo cosmology for the final overthrow of the witches.

The sources of paranoia in the culture are hard to trace without clinical data. In a sense, the elaborate witch fears are a kind of "customary" paranoia. But we cannot imagine them persisting unless a good many individuals were motivated by exaggerated fear of others and the world generally, independent of the cultural beliefs about spirits, witches, and so forth. As we have suggested, the two are mutually reinforcing. Various theories of paranoia suggest that its cause may lie in homosexual tensions (Freud 1924, 3:387–470), general sex anxiety, or projection of hostility as a result of socialization anxiety over aggression (Whiting and Child 1953). We find some of these factors present in Cochiti to some degree. I have little evidence regarding homosexuality, but certainly aggression problems are rife. The child is indulged initially by a body of female socializers and later is partially rejected in favor of a younger sibling. Even without this rejection, it would be impossible for the degree of indulgence the child receives initially to be sustained, and a perception of rejection is inevitable. Overindulgence has given him no training in self-control, and he is ill prepared to restrain his aggressions later. Restrain them, however, he must. Aggression is the cardinal sin in Pueblo eyes. At times, the society seems to be geared entirely to reducing, controlling, and repressing it. Pueblo institutions stress co-operation and friendliness, but this stress is a counter to aggressive tendencies, rather than a channel for acting out of harmonious ones (Fox 1961a). Individuals driven too hard by this child-rearing system will probably develop real paranoia, but most individuals will have a streak of it. This deep motivational aspect of paranoia is reinforced by the stories and experiences of witchcraft with which the child is fed and frightened as a disciplinary technique (Goldfrank 1945; D. Eggan 1943). Conscious and unconscious learning develop in harness.

Here, unless we are wildly wrong, is the basis provided by the society for its "typical" illness. The witch illness complex illustrates the whole cycle of the society, providing the strain that causes or aggravates the illness, giving it a culturally approved and patterned mode of expression, and using this mode of expression as the basis for a cure by a social group—the medicine society, which, we may note, the patient can then join.

Clan Cure

The clan cure and its associated types of illness should be seen against the background of the adoption system and its ideology and the ideology and sentiments respecting the clan or, more particularly, matrilineal descent. Why does it seem sensible and successful to the Cochiti to adopt a child into a clan for the sake of its future health or an adult to restore its lost health? For the former, the Cochiti have the readier explanation. The most terrible thing that can happen to a child, they say, is to lose its mothers —its own mother and her female matrilineal relatives. The adoption gives it a set of reserve mothers in the case of the loss of its own, and in any case one cannot have too many mothers. The clan is matrilineal, which means that, for any individual, its pivot is his mother, through whom he acquires his clan relatives. The clan is strongly identified in the Cochiti mind with the mother herself and therefore with nurture and security. When the loss of a mother is feared, or actually occurs (through death, estrangement, or remarriage), the breach is healed by adopting the patient into another clan—by giving him or her new "mothers," who perform such symbolic acts of nurture as washing the head, giving food, and renaming. All these acts are associated with a ritual of change in status (initiation) and symbolize the shedding of an undesirable personality and the acquisition of a new and "healthier" one. At initiation, it is the status of "child" that is shed; at the clan cure, it is the status of "motherless person."

The Cochiti do not verbalize it in this way, but they do express sentiments that are revealing. "We get our clans, like ourselves, from our mothers." "Our clans come from our mothers like all good things." "Why do we have clans? Because we have mothers." "My clan is my mother's name." The idea of uterine kinship is the most popular in explaining the notion of clanship. Clansmen ultimately come from the body of the same woman. If we couple this sentiment with the already mentioned extreme dependence on the mother herself—especially in women—we can begin to see both the sources of the nonwitch disease and the basis of its cure.

As in the case of the witch disease, the society provided the strain
—the mother-child (particularly daughter) relationship and its
imminent breakdown; the ideology—of matrilineal descent and the
sentiments associated with it; the mobilization of help—the clan
and lineage; and the means of cure—adoption into a clan and the
acquisition of "mothers" and maternal nurture. Even in cases
where the source of the disease is not the same as the source of
the cure (mother-child relations), maternal nurture is still thought
to be effective. We must note that the acquired clans do not "do"
anything material for the patient. The whole process is symbolic.
What they "do" is spiritual. They restore lost security by accepting the patient as one of themselves.

The whole complex of "mother" symbolism is interesting. What
Eggan says of Acoma is in general true of Cochiti (D. Eggan
1943):

> One important pattern at Acoma, which is characteristic of
> Keresan villages generally, and which contrasts with the Hopi and
> Zuni to a considerable extent, is the emphasis on the concept of
> "mother." In the Origin Myth we have seen that the central figure
> is Isatiku, who is the "mother" of the people whom she created and
> whom she receives at death. The corn-ear fetishes represent her and
> have her power; the cacique is her representative and is referred to
> as her "husband" in the mythology. In the kinship system the term
> "mother" is widely extended, and recent changes have extended
> it still further. In ritual relations the wife of the "ceremonial father"
> performs many of the ritual functions performed by the ceremonial
> father's sister among the Hopi and Zuni. In the Scalp Dance it is
> the mother of the twins who dances rather than their sister or aunts.

In Cochiti, the *cacique* is in fact referred to as "mother," as
are the medicine-society heads. The fetishes of the medicine men
are also their "mothers," and in the ritual addresses both to them
and by them the concept is elaborated at length (Dumarest
1919). Although the sentiment and symbolism are more elaborate
among the Keresans than in Hopi or Zuni, I suspect that a strong
element of maternal identification is present in all these societies.
Whiting has suggested that identification occurs with the sex-
typed role of the parent who mediates the major resources in the
child's life, a resource being anything the child wants (Whiting
1959). Undoubtedly among the Keresans and in the western
Pueblos, this person is the mother. The child thus grows up with

a strong female-maternal identification (this fact may, of course, be a source of homosexual tensions). In boys, initiation may well serve to sever this identification to some extent, but in girls it persists. It is noticeable that among the Keresans, where the mother sentiment is so pervasive, the initiation ceremonies are neither so universal nor so fierce as in Hopi and Zuni (Whiting, Kluckhohn and Anthony 1958).

It may well be that the strength of the identification or sentiment is a reason for the persistence of the clan ideology and some associated practices (exogamy, curing) even after the economic and social bases of clan organization have disappeared. In other words, when it ceases to have any other *raison d'être,* the clan may continue to survive because it serves to reduce the identity-dependency drives—especially in its role as healer.

What is striking in this role of the clan is the unconscious cultural insight that "sees" that the motivations involved in the clans' persistence and those involved in much nonwitch illness are the same. The neurosis of our patient was based on a breakdown of those sentiments and social relationships on which the clan system depends in large measure for its effective persistence. The breakdown was repaired by restoring the disrupted relationships (by adoption) and so reinforcing the shaken sentiments. Durkheim and Radcliffe-Brown have argued that ritual serves to emphasize and reinforce those sentiments on which the social structure depends for its continuation (Durkheim 1912; Radcliffe-Brown 1952), and here we have an example of the truth of this assertion. The cure is "built into" the social structure.

CONCLUSION

Cochiti culture provides the sources of its people's illnesses; it provides the media of expression for them; it mobilizes help for the patients; it effects the cure, and it ensures reinforcement. It distinguishes the illnesses that require dramatic shock treatment from those that require more peaceful nurture treatment, and in each case it utilizes the motivational source of the illness as a means of cure. This system is not the result of individual insight but rather of the slow working-out of cultural patterns over the centuries and the achievement of a kind of adjustment that, given the cultural premises, is very successful.

Already, however, these patterns are changing. The medicine societies are becoming extinct, and American education does not encourage confidence in "witch doctors." The clans are ceasing to function effectively even in their limited spheres, and changes in household composition are complete. All these forces affect the efficacy of curing techniques. They affect the causation of illness more slowly. The Cochiti therefore face the prospect of a persistence of traditional illnesses without the benefits of traditional cures—a situation that necessarily faces many primitive societies in transition. Those concerned with health and sickness in these societies would do well to take some hard looks at the relations among sentiments, culture, and social relations before doing anything to upset their often delicate balance. In many cases, the hospital and the physician are but indifferent substitutes for the society and the shaman on which the patient has learned, and is moved, to depend.

15 GROUP THERAPY AND SOCIAL STATUS IN THE ZAR CULT OF ETHIOPIA

Simon D. Messing

INTRODUCTION: HEALING OF THE SPIRIT IN ABYSSINIAN CULTURE

IN A NUMBER of diverse parts of the globe, observers have noted that healing cults often require the active cooperation of the patient. Even when patients have not previously been initiated in the mysteries of the cult, information has usually trickled down to them during normal enculturation and the patient thus knows something of the performance expected of him when he "falls ill." Indeed, his first task in the new role of patient is often to demonstrate his sickness, e.g., spirit-possession, so that society in general will accept him in this role.

An elaborate process of this kind is found in the "zar" cult of northern Ethiopia. The center of the cult is in the town of Gondar, on the highland plateau. There the major zar doctors have their headquarters and their societies of chronic patients (devotees).

Symptoms of possession by the zar spirits include proneness to accidents, sterility, convulsive seizures, and extreme apathy. The healer is himself zar-possessed, but has "come to terms" with the spirit. His first task is to diagnose what specific spirit or syndrome of spirits ail the patient.

Everyone in the culture knows the procedure that follows: The patient will be "interrogated" in the house of the doctor. There the doctor will lure his own zar into possessing him in a trance, and through his intercession try to lure the unknown zar of the patient ("his horse") into public possession. Then the spirit will be led to reveal his identity by means of adroit cajolery, promises,

Reprinted from *The American Anthropologist* 60 (6), 1958: 1120–26, by permission of the author and the American Anthropological Association.

and threats. The demands of the zar will be negotiated through a lengthy process of financial dickering. Finally, the patient will be enrolled, for the rest of his life, in the "zar society" of fellow-sufferers, renting, as it were, his temporary freedom from relapse through regular donations and by means of participation in the worship of the spirit.

The patient knows this, too, and responds to the doctor's questions, though often only after a considerable show of resistance. The latter is attributed to the activity of certain mischievous minor spirits, whose only power is to create confusion. The zar's identity is revealed by the patient's "individual" zar dance ("gurri"), which the spirit obliges his human "horse" to perform publicly while the doctor watches and directs.

The chronic patient finds many benefits as a member of the zar society. He calls attention to himself as an individual and may rise in social status in the family or community. Most patients are married women who feel neglected in a man's world in which they serve as hewers of wood and haulers of water, and where even the Coptic Abyssinian Church discriminates against females by closing the church building to them. Married women in the predominantly rural culture are often lonely for the warmth of kinship relations, for typical residence is in an exogamous patri-local hamlet. Members of the lower classes, such as the Muslim (mostly Sudanese) minority, find social contact across religious barriers in the zar cult. Ex-slaves, many of them descended from alien African tribes ("Shanqalla"), are also admitted to full membership in the zar cult. Finally, occupational and economic benefits are dispensed by the zar doctor, who also functions as treasurer of the society but does not render any financial accounting. Thus he has the opportunity, rare on the simple material level of traditional Abyssinia, to accumulate capital which he invests in economic enterprises (e.g., brewing honey-wine) and which further enhances the reputation of his special powers.

Active opposition to the cult comes from husbands who fear the sexual and economic emancipation of the wife. Although there are no orgies of the kind assumed and suspected by outsiders, membership in the zar cult does give opportunity for liaisons. Passive resistance comes from priests of the Coptic Abyssinian Church, who profess to condemn the zar cult but do little to counteract it. This may be because many priests secretly believe in the cosmology of zar themselves, particularly in spirits that are regarded as Coptic Christian (others are "muslim" or "pagan").

In the Abyssinian calendar, the most active period for zar activity is the 9-month dry season, beginning when the spirits escape from the confinement of cold rains and the landscape blossoms forth. The major zar celebration occurs just before the "little rains" which coincide with the onset of the Coptic Lent.

INDIVIDUAL VULNERABILITY AND ZAR COSMOLOGY

Every human being is considered potentially vulnerable to being possessed by a zar spirit or spirits. But humans differ considerably in degree of vulnerability, and certain situations are considered particularly inviting to the zars. Most of these situations are points of psychological or social stress.

Heredity, usually mother to daughter (paralleling the dominant patrilineal principle in Abyssinian culture) predisposes some victims. Some mothers even promote this transfer deliberately, if the individual zar has been turned into a powerfully "protective spirit" ("weqabi"); they do this by promising continued devotion.

A sort of psychic predestination is responsible in other cases. Persons are "chosen" by the zar for their melancholy natures or weak personalities (e.g., alcoholics). In some cases the illness plays the role of a religious revelation, which "calls" the chosen into the zar cult.

In this connection it is interesting to note that not only weaknesses create points of stress that attract a zar. Some zar spirits choose their victim for unusually attractive qualities, e.g., the beauty of a woman or the enchanting voice of a chorister ("däbtära").

Natural situations which attract a zar include geographical spots, especially the bush where the spirits have their abode. There they ride wild beasts, milk them as "cattle," and protect them from hunters.

Human situations which attract certain zars feature elements of cross-sexual persecution. In many cases the spirit is regarded as having sexual intercourse with his human victim of the opposite sex. A woman who sleeps alone renders herself vulnerable to a male zar. A man who sleeps alone and has a seminal emission blames it on a female zar. The convulsive seizures of a male patient are commonly regarded as evidence that a female zar is experiencing sexual climax with him. Similarly, when a woman patient cannot readily be coaxed out of her state of apathy, it is thought she is sleeping with a male zar.

The Abyssinian myth of the origin of the zar spirits is probably a superimposed rationalization. They are regarded as having originated in the Garden of Eden, where Eve had given birth to thirty children. One day the Creator came to visit and began to count the children. In apprehension, Eve hid the fifteen most beautiful and intelligent ones; as punishment, they were condemned to remain always hidden, nighttime creatures. Consequently, they envy their uglier and weaker human siblings who are children of the light.

The world of these hidden zar spirits mirrors Abyssinian feudal and ethnocentric society. Some zars are powerful lords, others serve them as retainers. Some zars are classified as "rich man's zar," others as "poor man's zar." Coptic Christian spirits are regarded as superior in social standing and education to Muslim or "pagan" spirits. Those who have their abode on the highland plateau of Abyssinia, home of an ancient literate culture, are regarded as superior to zars whose home is among the lowland, Sudanese, and ex-slave tribes.

One intellectual zar is credited with having taught mankind the use of fire and cooking, by lending from his own flame atop a rock that juts out from the Red Sea. He and some other benevolent zars can be persuaded to teach healing medicines.

THE PRACTITIONER

Such potential benevolence is utilized by the zar doctor. Once a patient himself, he has learned to control the situation and has turned it into a profession, but both he and ordinary possessed are referred to by the same term ("balä zar").

To become a recognized doctor, he must have certain talents. One is the ability to cultivate a stare that can calm cases of hysteria. Another is linguistic ability, for he often speaks in "zar language" which Abyssinians regard as a completely different, esoteric language, but which is actually an argot composed of deformed Amharic (the major of the three main Abyssinian languages), paraphrases, and foreign loanwords. Before he begins practice, the zar doctor identifies himself more and more with the most powerful of the spirits possessing him, so that he can use this power against the lesser, mischievous ones. In his name he opens a "coffee-tray" ("gända") in his own house, symbolizing the altar of the cult.

Female zar doctors almost always claim professional sanction through transfer of power and knowledge from their mothers. This is paraphrased as "transferring the monkey." In order to compensate for the lack of inheritance, male zar doctors often substitute a myth of contagion. They may claim that they had been kidnapped by zar spirits during childhood and released in adolescence, and they make arrogant and extravagant claims more often than do female doctors. Confronted with the technological superiority of the "European," the male doctor may try to reduce the effect by claiming that only the night before he had magically visited the stranger's homeland and is familiar with all his gadgets. Male doctors often dress like old-time Abyssinian warriors, and like them anoint the hair so that it stands up stiffly. By contrast, female zar doctors, often regarded as superior to male ones, rarely show arrogance. When not in a violent trance, they usually assume the phlegmatic composure of the Abyssinian noblewoman. This was the usual poise of Woyzäro (Lady) Sälämtew, chief zar doctor at Gondar in 1953–54, although she was of low-class descent.

Thus, in the traditional form of the zar cult, it was mainly the doctor who improved his social status. Gondar itself has only about a dozen powerful doctors, mostly female, but there are hundreds in the surrounding rural areas, lesser doctors who are usually male.

DIAGNOSIS THROUGH DEMONSTRATION

First aid may be given a patient by relatives. Sudden extreme apathy is regarded as dangerous, for the zar may "ride his horse to death." The patient is therefore surrounded by sympathetic kinfolk, entertained with song and dance, and promises are made to fulfill any desires. In cases of hysterical possession, which typically takes the form of wanting to run into the bush at night and mingle with the hyenas, relatives may restrain the patient with ropes. In either case, he is never left alone.

At nightfall the patient is conducted to the house of the zar doctor. The scene inside is warm with illumination, burning incense, and the assembled membership of devotees, all chronic cases themselves. A relative hands an entry gift, called "incense money," to a disciple who passes it quietly to the doctor behind a screened platform. The doctor ignores the new arrival until the spirit has taken full possession. Only then does the doctor emerge, her eyes bright and curious, her gestures commanding, for the spirit is now using the doctor as a medium. She greets her flock and orders drinks for everyone. The male reader-composer of liturgy of the zar cult intones old or new hymns of praise to the zar, accompanied by the rhythmic handclapping of the worshippers. This ritual recharges the interrogation whenever it becomes difficult.

The zar doctor pretends that she has guessed the identity of the spirit who plagues the patient, but this spirit must be made to confess publicly so that negotiations can be conducted. The patient is asked leading questions, beginning with his recent activities. If answers are not satisfactory, the patient (i.e., the zar speaking through him) is accused of lying. Gradually the answers become more satisfactory. The doctor alternately lauds and threatens the spirit, giving the patient no rest. The latter is made to confess shortcomings such as neglect of family, of kinfolk, sometimes even of the church, and of course of the zar himself, who may have been insulted unintentionally. Finally the patient dances the individual whirl ("gurri") of his particular zar, thus identifying him through minor variations in the rapid movement which ends in temporary exhaustion. Still later the patient learns to intone the proper war-chant ("fukkara") of his spirit. Sometimes several nights are needed to achieve this final expression.

TREATMENT AND SOCIAL STATUS WITHIN THE ZAR SOCIETY

The doctor does not usually proclaim the final diagnosis until he has studied the social and economic status of the patient, for an important part of the doctor's function is to match the social class of zar with the socioeconomic class of patient. The zar of poor and low-class members usually belongs to the class of "pages serving great zars" ("wureza"). Such poor patients may work off their dues by "serving the tray." When a doctor regrets his earlier overestimate of a patient's financial position, he may "transfer" his expensive zar to another devotee better able to bear the offerings demanded.

Much of the treatment consists of negotiations with the irritating zar in order to transform him into an attitude of benevolence as "protective zar" ("weqabi"). This is done by asking him, through the mouth of the patient, what he will demand in order to reduce the frequency and severity of the patient's sufferings. Some zars have simple demands such as ornaments, new clothing, or sandals. Many zars have symbolic requests. Thus a zar whose symbol is the lion may demand that a tawny-colored goat be sacrificed at regular times.

Most zars are never exorcised. This is done only rarely, particularly in the case of female zars (whose "contracts" are regarded as unreliable) who cannot be made protective. Such exorcism is accomplished by transferring the spirit to a place near a path in the bush where he can pounce on some unsuspecting stranger. The doctor then assigns his patient another zar as a protective spirit from among the zars who are currently available in the house of the zar society and without "horses" to serve them.

THE CHANGING ZAR CULT AND SOCIAL MOBILITY

While the zar cult continues in full force in Abyssinian culture in Gondar, certain significant changes can be traced from the early 1930's when a French expedition observed it there, to the time I studied it in 1953–54.

For one thing, attempts are now made to conceal its existence from the rare foreign visitor, and in Addis Ababa the cult has been entirely suppressed.

More significant is the change in the membership, leadership, and location of the cult, even in Gondar, and the increased use made of it by low-class members to achieve upward social mobility.

In 1932 the center of the zar cult and house of the chief zar doctor was located in the "respectable" Coptic sector ("Bäata"), on top of the truncated hill that forms the geographical center of the town. The chief practitioner was an Amhara (dominant ethnic class of Abyssinia) woman in good standing with the Coptic Church.

In 1953–54 the cult was centered in the old Muslim suburb (Addis Aläm) at the bottom of the hill, now a slum even by local standards. It is inhabited largely by poor Amhara, half-Sudanese Muslims, and ex-slaves, who constitute most of the members of the zar cult. The social benefits of the zar cult continue for them, for at dusk Amhara patients still descend the hill to participate or consult the chief practitioner on matters of business. This chief doctor is herself part-Sudanese, but has learned to speak the upper-class Amharic language well. Just as twenty years ago, the doctor is a middle-aged woman and her devotees are largely females. She has a reputation for considerable achievement both in her spiritual and business activities.

CONCLUSION

(1) The "zar" is a catch-all for many psychological disturbances, ranging from frustrated status ambition to actual mental illness.

(2) Healing is in the context of a culture which is socially more highly organized than commonly found under the "shaman" type. The zar cult thus reveals many aspects of social structure (feudalism, position of women, and so forth).

(3) Since no patient is ever discharged as cured, the zar cult functions as a form of group therapy. Chronic patients become devotees who form a close-knit social group in which they find security and recognition.

(4) The zar cult is not a deviant cult; its significance in maintaining the status quo in society has traditionally been greater than improvement of social status. By matching the social status of patient and spirit, the doctor inadvertently functions to maintain the social structure of old Abyssinia. Moreover, the patient must confess neglect not only of the zar but of his other social duties as well. Once his demands have been met, the zar spirit

helps the patient to carry on his normal role in the community.

(5) The motivation is now shifting toward desire for upward social mobility. Even in the past a neglected wife could punish her husband by having her zar extort economic sacrifices from him on threat of relapse. But now ex-slave and low-class patients are increasingly being "chosen" by the zar. The epidemiology of possession starts a chain of events that enables them to escape from their social confinements.

16 SPIRIT POSSESSION AS ILLNESS IN A NORTH INDIAN VILLAGE[1]

Stanley A. and *Ruth S. Freed*

T HE POSSESSION of a person by a ghost or godling which results in somatic or psychological illness is widespread in
India. This paper discusses spirit possession as illness in Shanti
Nagar, a north Indian village near Delhi, and briefly compares
spirit possession in Shanti Nagar and other parts of northern
India. First we describe in detail the case for which we have the
fullest data: that of a young bride named Daya. During a two-
week period in which Daya suffered a series of possessions, we
interviewed her several times in an attempt to gain some indication of why she should become possessed. We report Daya's
testimony at length after the description of her possession and
treatment by shamans. Second, we describe several other cases
of spirit possession in Shanti Nagar. Third, we analyze spirit
possession in Shanti Nagar as a psychological and cultural phenomenon. The behavior of persons possessed by spirits closely
resembles hysteria. Daya's testimony and the social circumstances of Daya and others suffering from possession suggest

Reprinted from *Ethnology* 3 (2), 1964: 152–71 by permission of the authors
and the editor, *Ethnology*.

[1] This paper is based on field work in the village of Shanti Nagar (a
pseudonym) from November, 1957, to July, 1959. We thank the Social
Science Research Council and the National Science Foundation for the post-
doctoral fellowships which supported the field work, and the University of
North Carolina for a faculty research grant to help with secretarial expenses. We also thank Margaret Mead and John J. Honigmann, who
carefully read and criticized the manuscript. We thank Edward Harper
who supplied us with a copy of his paper on spirit possession in southern
India before it was readily available. We received it too late for inclusion in
the body of our paper but have referred to it in footnotes. The names of
individuals used in this paper are pseudonyms.

that spirit possession, like hysteria, has two conditions: a basic condition due to the individual's intra-psychic tension and a precipitating condition due to an event or situation involving unusual stress or emotion. The basic condition of spirit possession is psychological. The precipitating conditions are cultural events or situations which exhibit two general characteristics: (1) the victim of spirit possession is involved in difficulties with relatives within the nuclear or joint family, and (2) he is often in a situation where his expectations of aid and support are low. Finally, we analyze spirit possession in Shanti Nagar as compared with eastern Uttar Pradesh and Calcutta. The comparison indicates that spirit possession as illness is a basically uniform pattern in northern India, although regional variations do occur.

DAYA'S POSSESSION

Daya was fifteen, married, and a member of the Chamar caste, who are leatherworkers and laborers ranking close to the bottom of the caste hierarchy of Shanti Nagar. On the day we observed her possession we visited her family for another purpose and paid no particular attention to the girl, who was quietly sewing on a machine which was part of her dowry. Young brides are expected to be inconspicuous. Daya's mother-in-law, husband's older brother, husband's sister, and several other Chamar men, women, and children were present.

The conversation immediately preceding the possession seems, in the light of later analysis, to have some significance, for Daya could interpret some of the comments and behavior as subtle and indirect reflections on her good character. The husband's older brother was teasing Daya. He told us he could do this because he was the older brother of the husband. (The relationship is fictive; see Freed 1963 for a discussion of fictive kinship in Shanti Nagar.) We replied that we thought it was the husband's younger brother who could tease the bride and not the husband's older brother. (Ideally, the relationship of the husband's older brother and the younger brother's wife is one of respect. The wife covers her face before him and does not address him. The husband's younger brother and the older brother's wife have a warm, joking relationship.) The Chamars avoided answering directly and pointed to another man and said, "He's also a husband's older brother and never says anything."

Then the husband's older brother who had been teasing Daya said, "Say what you will, this business of tailoring is suitable only for men." We asked, "Why shouldn't a woman do it if she has the skill?" A woman said, "He's just ignorant and can't do anything." The husband's older brother replied that the woman's family was ignorant. He said that if a man is a tailor, he can get anyone's measurements, but a woman can't do this. For a woman to sew clothes for members of her family or lineage has recently been accepted in Shanti Nagar, and a sewing machine as part of a dowry carries considerable prestige. Daya was the first low-caste girl to bring a sewing machine. Although Daya's activities were perfectly proper, the aggressive teasing of her husband's older brother, from which she could not defend herself, and the fact that this was a breach of the traditional relationship could have disturbed her.

Abruptly the mother-in-law changed the subject and began telling us about an illness that was plaguing the new bride. Apparently Daya emitted subtle cues before her possessions, and the mother-in-law was aware of the impending possession a few minutes before we noticed anything amiss. The first really noticeable symptoms of spirit possession were when Daya complained of feeling cold and began to shiver. She was moaning slightly and breathing hard. The mother-in-law and one of her daughters helped Daya lie down and piled about six quilts on her. She moaned and talked under the quilts; then she lost consciousness. The ghost had come.

The husband's older brother brought some burning cow dung. The mother-in-law, husband's sister, and husband's older brother helped Daya sit up and wafted some dung smoke into her face. All at once she started to jerk violently. The three relatives grabbed Daya to restrain her. They shouted, "Who are you? Are you going?" The ghost, speaking in normal Hindi through the girl, said, "Yes, I am going." Then the three relatives released Daya and she remained sitting. Suddenly she fell backward unconscious; the ghost had returned. This time the relatives revived her by putting some water from a hookah in her eyes while pulling her braids. When she began to return to semi-consciousness, she made a high wailing sound which seemed to announce the presence of the ghost. The three relatives again had the girl sit up. The mother-in-law asked, "Who are you?" The ghost replied, "No one." The relatives repeated the question, and then the ghost said, "I am Chand Kor." They asked the ghost what it wanted. The ghost said it would not leave until it had taken Daya with it.

Daya sat for a time and then once more fell unconscious. This time she was brought back to a semi-conscious trance state by putting rock salt between her fingers and squeezing them together. She again emitted the high-pitched wailing, and the ghost was ready to talk. By this time several other Chamar women had gathered and began conversing with the ghost. The ghost complained that it had been promised noodles (a delicacy eaten in summer) that morning but that the mother-in-law had given it none. A woman then said that she would give the ghost cow dung to eat. The ghost said, "In the morning the girl was fed noodles, but I wasn't given any." The woman repeated that she would give the ghost cow dung. The ghost said to the woman, "You stop talking rot." The woman said, "You mother-in-law [an insult], you eat cow dung." The ghost said, "You eat cow dung." The woman retorted, "You mother-in-law, you bastard, you eat cow dung."

Daya sat quietly for a while, and it seemed as if the ghost had gone; but it returned, and Daya once more lost consciousness. Again they put salt between her fingers, but the ghost said that it was leaving before they had a chance to squeeze the fingers together. Daya, however, asserted that she could see the ghost standing in the next room. Her mother-in-law and the other women tried to convince her that there was nothing in the next room but a trunk. Then Daya fell back again and lay still. This time no effort was made to revive her, and the spectators drifted away. Daya remained unconscious for several hours until a shaman was summoned who revived her.

Although the mother-in-law was quite distressed during the possession and on one occasion cried, none of the others present gave the impression that they thought the possession was strange or unusual. They all seemed to know just what to do. During the lulls in the possession, they speculated as to the ghost's identity and discussed ways of driving off the ghost. Much of the conversation with the ghost, beside the insults, was to determine the ghost's identity. The ghost said its name was Chand Kor, who was a woman from Daya's mother's brother's village. Daya had lived with her mother's brother for some time, and she and Chand Kor had become close friends. Chand Kor drowned in a well and, having died an untimely and violent death, became a ghost. The ghosts of women who die in this fashion do not keep their promises. On previous occasions when the ghost possessed the girl, it promised not to return. One of the women present during the possession kept repeating that the ghost was a "widow [an insult] who did not keep her promises." In the last conversation between the ghost and the women, the ghost changed its name saying, "You can never get hold of me." The women decided that the ghost had been lying about its earlier identity but were not convinced that the new name was correct.

Among the remedies suggested for driving off the ghost were putting hookah water in the girl's eyes or squeezing rock salt between her fingers while pulling her braids, the smoke of burning cow dung or pig's excreta, a copper coin, a shaman, and beating the girl. The daughter struck Daya once; but a man of the Jat caste (farmers) who came in about midway during the possession protested, saying that the girl had some ailment and that no ghost was present. Most of the methods used by the villagers to exorcise ghosts involve shock (beating, pulling, and squeezing) and/or unpleasantness (e.g., burning pig's excreta and verbal insults). Certain substances such as salt and cow dung are inimical to evil spirits (see Crooke 1894: 147–48, 194, 198, 201; Lewis 1958: 295–99).

CURES BY SHAMANS

Daya's frequently repeated possessions indicated that a permanent cure was beyond the powers of the villagers; consequently shamans were summoned from outside of Shanti Nagar. Several treatments by different shamans took place before the ghost was banished, and no one could be really sure that the ghost would not again return. On at least one occasion, two shamans treated

Daya together. We never saw any of the shamans at work, but we interviewed one the day after he treated the girl.

This shaman told us he had stayed in Shanti Nagar a night and a day, apparently waiting in vain for Daya to be possessed. Then he spent a day in Delhi, and upon his return he found the villagers waiting for him at the bus stop with the news that the girl was possessed. The shaman claims he has considerable power. His major source of power is Hanuman, a popular Hindu deity, who the shaman claims is his *guru* (spiritual teacher). He also has power from the "conjurer (*jadugar*) of Dacca [in Bengal]," from Sayyid Pir (a Muslim saint), from a spirit called Barwari who lives at a fruit (*ber*) tree, and from the goddess Kalka of the cremation ground. The ghost identified itself as Prem, a girl from Daya's village, and said it wanted to take Daya. The shaman asked why, and the ghost replied, "I just do." The shaman then inquired, "Is there anything else you want in place of her?" The ghost answered in the negative. The shaman said: "You still have a chance. I haven't called my powers yet, and you can choose something else. If I call my powers you won't be able to go even one step." The ghost still refused.

Then the shaman called one of his minor powers, the minister of Hanuman. He thought of Hanuman, said some words in his heart, and asked the minister to catch the ghost. The minister then caught the ghost, which kept trying to escape. The shaman held Daya's braids so that the ghost could not escape and made the ghost promise to leave the girl alone. However, the shaman told the ghost that its promises were worthless and threatened to call his *guru*. The ghost said, "No, no; let me go, and I won't come again." The shaman asked the ghost when it was going, and the ghost said it would leave Shanti Nagar in the company of the shaman. The shaman replied that he had people at home and could not take the ghost with him, but the ghost insisted that it wanted to go with the shaman. According to the shaman, all this talking is a joke and superficial; the real process of catching the ghost goes on in the heart.

The ghost then asked for several presents which the shaman felt were too expensive. The shaman and the ghost finally settled on an offering of Rs. 1.25 (26 cents), a length of red cloth, and a coconut to be taken to Kalka temple in Chirag Delhi near Delhi.

The shaman asked the ghost who would make the offering, and the ghost said it would. When the shaman pointed out that only a man could make the offering, the ghost instructed the shaman to do it. But the shaman said he could not because his *guru* would become angry. So the shaman and the ghost decided that someone from Daya's family should make the offering at a fair which is held twice a year at the temple. As a parting threat, the shaman told the ghost that if it came again he would summon his *guru*, Hanuman. The shaman claimed that the ghost departed and Daya was cured. However, six days later she was again possessed, and her family called two shamans. (For a similar shamanistic cure see Lewis 1958: 297–98.)

Other remedies used by various shamans were the following: to recite sacred verses (mantras) and tie a blue band around the girl's neck; to cut some of her hair and throw it in a fire; to cut a little of her hair, tie it in a cloth, and carry it away; and to make an offering of sweets. Shamanistic cures seem to emphasize spells, offerings, and the transference of the ghost from the victim to something or someone else, not infrequently the shaman. The remedies involving physical shock used by the villagers are not prominent in shamanistic curing. Both styles of curing involve considerable conversation, during which the ghost can complain and insult to its heart's content. This might have a therapeutic effect upon the one suffering the possession.

INTERVIEWS WITH DAYA

Daya's testimony is presented in the following order: her symptoms and mood, recent history, comparison of her parents' and husband's houses, relations with her affinal relatives, relations with her husband, and who the ghosts were and what had been her relationships to them. These were obvious areas to investigate. Since Daya had never been possessed before arriving in Shanti Nagar, her comments about life in Shanti Nagar and in her parents' house seemed essential in exploring the reasons for her possession. Because Daya and one of the girls whose ghost possessed her had been as close as sisters, we thought that some features of this girl's life or personality or some aspect of the relationship of the two girls might be relevant. Two themes dominated the interviews: Daya's expressed fear of sexual relations with her husband, and her interest in the illicit sexual adventures of her girl friends.

Ruth Freed, through an interpreter, interviewed Daya because we felt that the girl would talk more freely with a woman. The interpreter was a man, but he did an excellent job of effacing himself. At the beginning of the interview, Daya addressed a few remarks to the interpreter, but she soon was looking at the interviewer and talking directly to her. The interpreter was reduced to a mouthpiece, and he played this difficult role perfectly. Daya was encouraged to talk freely with a minimum of stimulus through direct questions. The interviews were unusually easy. The girl obviously identified with the interviewer (she said she was used to schoolteacher types) and was eager to talk to someone congenial. Daya was cheerful and co-operative, spoke freely, and impressed the interviewer as quite intelligent. Daya's mother-in-law was very helpful in being willing to leave the interviewer alone with Daya, for she knew that Daya could not talk freely in her presence. The mother-in-law gave the impression that she thought the attention Daya was getting and the opportunity for her to talk would be good for her. The interviewer recorded Daya's remarks in a notebook during the interviews. Regarding her physical and mental symptoms, Daya said:

> My legs, arms, and whole body ache. Sometimes I feel giddy as though I were going to fall, and sometimes I feel sick to my stomach. I sleep too much. Sometimes when I am just lying on a cot, I fall asleep, even when I don't want to. Sometimes I think I hear someone calling, "Daya, sleep, sleep." I feel very hot, even at night, yet I don't perspire.[2] Then I have the feeling that I am being suffocated, that weights are pressing on my body, legs, feet, and chest. When I'm sitting I have difficulty breathing, and I feel a queer sensation in my stomach as if it is becoming larger and larger. I don't feel like working, only like sleeping; yet I was quite active and did all sorts of work in my parents' house. [Daya frequently dreams that she is passing through the village and that all the boys are quarreling with her.]

Four or five days before the observed possession, Daya arrived in Shanti Nagar for a stay with her husband's family. This

---

[2] We did not take her temperature but doubt that she had a fever, for the villagers never regarded her ailment as a fever. However, Majumdar (1958: 236) reports spirit possession accompanied by a high fever.

was her third visit to her husband. The first, during which the bride and groom traditionally have no sexual intercourse, took place at the time of the marriage ceremony. The second occurred a few months later, and, as is customary, Daya and her husband had their first mating. The first two visits are always brief, but the third is usually an extended stay. Because Daya had reached her menarche a few months before her marriage, her second and third visits to her husband followed soon after the marriage ceremony. This sequence of events is normal for villages in the Delhi region. Villages are exogamous, and women move to their husbands' villages, but the shift of residence takes place gradually. In the early years of marriage, women frequently return to their parents' villages for considerable periods and usually spend more time with their parents than with their husbands. The Chamars generally send brides to their husbands for the second time within six months of marriage if the girl has reached the menarche. In the few days following the beginning of Daya's third visit to Shanti Nagar, she was possessed three times.

Daya emphasized the prestige her family enjoys in their own village. Her father is in military service, and one uncle is a bus conductor. Among the Chamars any steady job carries some prestige, and military service is considered a desirable occupation by many people of all castes. In addition, Daya's family owns two or three acres of land, a matter of considerable pride among the predominantly landless Chamars. This contrasts with her husband's family, who are landless, have only one wage earner in a low-paying factory job, and live primarily as agricultural laborers. With regard to her new life in Shanti Nagar, Daya said:

> I feel lonesome and restricted here. In my parents' village, I was free and could do as I liked. In Shanti Nagar I must cover my face from older men and not leave the house unaccompanied. I don't feel at ease with my face covered. Sometimes I forget, and then people remind me. I have no one to talk to, and so I stitch clothes or just sleep when I finish my work.

Daya's relationships with her relatives by marriage and her feelings about them are the normal ones for young brides. She says that for a day or two she disliked all of her affines but realized that she would have to get used to them. Her husband's younger brothers, who are young boys, tease her. She feels at home with them. This is the traditional, warm joking relationship between the husband's younger brother and the older brother's wife. She is afraid of her father-in-law because she must tell him if anyone talks or jokes with her. The relationship of the father-in-law and daughter-in-law is one of respect and avoidance on the part of the daughter-in-law and of authority and avoidance on the father-in-law's part. Daya and her mother-in-law like each other. This relationship is traditionally one of tension and antagonism, but these feelings often develop after the daughter-in-law is older and has sons of her own. When the daughter-in-law first comes to her husband's family she is quite young, and in the early years the relationship with the mother-in-law can be warm. Daya says that her mother-in-law goes everywhere with her and protects her. If the mother-in-law is not available, a small female child accompanies her. She complains that the boys of the village joke with her. She did not mention her husband's older brother's wife except to note that this woman told her what to do when her husband visited her at night. This was the wife of her husband's real brother, not the husband's brother who had been teasing her. The husband's older brother's wife is often the one to tell newly married people how to have sexual intercourse. She did not discuss her husband's sisters or older brother.

Daya says that she is terrified of her husband when he comes in the night, but that he is quite gentle and tells her not to be afraid. He says he will do whatever she likes; he won't even touch her. She has become less frightened than she was at first. Her mother-in-law and the wife of her husband's older brother are no help to her when she is afraid. She says she learned about sexual relations from listening to her older married friends, that is, girls from her village who had married and returned home for a visit. They told her what would happen to her and that she would become annoyed and start crying. When she came to her husband's house, her husband's older brother's wife explained sexual relations to her. She says that she was afraid and told her husband's older brother's wife that she would sleep only with her. The husband's older brother's wife merely said that, when her husband joined her, she must be quiet and not scream—that it is only natural and is how her mother and father had children. Nevertheless, she slept with her husband's older brother's wife, who, however, moved away during the night; when Daya awoke in the morning, she found her husband had joined her. When she came for her most recent visit, she slept with her husband three or four days and had sexual intercourse. Then she was visited by the ghost and did not sleep with her husband for two weeks. When her husband again asked her to sleep with him, she said she was too weak. However, when she awoke in the night she found him there. He said he was staying with her only because she was alone; they did not have sexual relations.

Daya discussed in some detail the sexual adventures and subsequent misfortunes of two girls she had known. Both died violently a few years before Daya's possession, and one, Chand Kor, became a ghost and possessed her. According to Daya, Chand Kor was forced to commit suicide by her family because of a premarital pregnancy. Chand Kor was pregnant when she was sent to her husband's family, who therefore rejected her and returned her to her parents. Her father was very angry. Chand Kor begged forgiveness, but her father replied: "I won't keep you. Go jump in a well." Chand Kor's parents continued to abuse her for several days, telling her to commit suicide by jumping in a well. So one day when Chand Kor was playing with a group of girl friends, she excused herself and ran and jumped in a well.

The events which befell Chand Kor are typical of the way premarital pregnancies are handled in Shanti Nagar and nearby villages. A pregnant, unmarried girl or a married girl who has not had sexual intercourse with her husband is such a grievous blow to a family's prestige that she will not be allowed to live. If such a girl is married, she will be sent to her husband's family, for she belongs to that family and her natal family can take no action until the husband's relatives have indicated their wishes. Moreover, the girl's parents hope against hope that the husband's family will be gentle and forgiving people and will keep the girl. However, we never heard of a case where this happened; the girl is always returned to her parents, which means she is not wanted. The fact that the girl was sent to the husband and then returned readies village opinion for what is to follow. The villagers feel that the girl's father has done everything possible to save her life and that he cannot avoid the next step. The father and other relatives may either force the girl to commit suicide, or the father may simply kill her. Village opinion will solidly support the family which takes this drastic step. The death will be reported to the police as an accident, suicide, or result of illness. When Daya told us the story of Chand Kor, she began by saying that the fall into the well was an accident but quickly switched to the story of suicide. Villagers like to pass off the deaths of women in wells as accidents; but all such events are suspect, and they more often are suicides.

Girls are well aware of the risks they run through premarital sexual intercourse. Daya knew that Chand Kor was having relations with a man and warned her that, if her father or husband found out, they would not let her live. Daya also told Chand Kor that she could not be too friendly any longer. Gossip starts so quickly in Indian villages that Daya may have thought her character could be destroyed if she continued her close association with Chand Kor. When we witnessed Daya's possession, the ghost of Chand Kor seemed to be the principal one involved although there was some switching of names toward the end. In a later possession, a shaman identified the ghost of Prem.

Daya had another friend whose premarital sexual activities resulted in her death. Daya mentioned this girl, named Santara, while discussing her schooling. Daya attended school for only five grades. Her parents refused to let her go further because Santara, one of her classmates, was molested by one of the male teachers. Villagers are reluctant to send older girls to study with male teachers. Considerable unfavorable gossip about the character of local school teachers is current in Shanti Nagar and presumably in other villages; and, while most such gossip is undoubtedly groundless, parents nonetheless usually insist upon female teachers for older girls. Daya says that one of the teachers had sexual relations with Santara. One day a boy saw the teacher touch Santara's breast, and the news spread quickly. Santara's father was furious. According to Daya, the father took Santara into the fields a few nights later, had sexual relations with her, cut her throat, and threw her into a well. The father said that Santara was his daughter and he had every right to do with her as he liked. He was never punished, although Daya said he had to give the police a bribe so that the murder would not be investigated. Daya's account of this case departs from the usual procedure only in the statement that the father had sexual relations with his daughter.

The ghost of Santara did not come to trouble Daya. Prem, the other ghost which possessed Daya, was a girl from Daya's village who died of illness and about whom Daya had little to say. We believe that the ghost of Chand Kor was uppermost in Daya's mind and that Prem served principally to confuse the identification. Deception and confusion about the ghost's identity hold the interest of spectators and prolong the curing procedure through several sessions. Thus the person possessed gains additional attention and has greater opportunity for expressing himself through the ghost.

OTHER CASES OF SPIRIT POSSESSION

Four other villagers had attacks of spirit possession or were suffering its aftereffects while we were in Shanti Nagar. These cases add to our knowledge in showing that (1) spirit possession affects both men and women of varying ages;[3] (2) it is related to difficulties and tension with close relatives; (3) it often affects persons whose expectations of aid and support are low; and (4) while the victim usually recovers, the condition can develop into a different and apparently permanent psychological affliction. Much of our data about the possessions of these four villagers come from interviews with their relatives and other persons. We briefly interviewed three of the four and observed one of the attacks.

Bhim Singh, a Brahmin man in his fifties, suffered a series of ghost possessions lasting about ten days. He was possessed by the ghost of a sweeper (Chuhra) who had died in Shanti Nagar during an epidemic. The sweeper was born in another village and was moving from place to place. Because he died an untimely death, he became a ghost. He is one of the three ghosts permanently resident in Shanti Nagar and is considered the strongest of

[3] Among the Havik Brahmins of southern India, spirit possession affects only women—with few exceptions those who are married but do not have grown children. Harper (1963) suggests that this is due to the authority system of the Havik Brahmins.

the three, being credited with causing a death about twenty years ago.

The cure followed the usual method of determining the ghost's identity and then driving it out. Identifying the ghost was no problem, for it kept shouting its name and asking for sweet things to eat. The ghost of the sweeper was known to have a fondness for sweets. The ghost also asked for a hookah to smoke and, when offered a Brahmin's hookah, refused it, insisting on a sweeper's hookah. Then the villagers were certain of the ghost's identity. (In general, each caste smokes the hookah only with others of the same caste.) Exorcising the ghost was relatively simple: the villagers went to a neighboring village and procured a liquid which, when thrown in a fire, produces a smoke which banishes ghosts. Some villagers said the liquid was put in Bhim Singh's nostrils and eyes.

Bhim Singh is a widower and has no children. He lives in a joint family with his two brothers and their descendants. He has a history of spirit possession. One informant told us that Bhim Singh was possessed some twenty years ago because an elderly woman of the family died over some dispute. The informant was not sure of the details of the woman's death but implied it was murder or suicide. Bhim Singh's family has more than the normal share of troubles. One man in the family has only one good eye, and one-eyed men are considered inauspicious. This one-eyed man married a widow, thereby causing a great scandal since Brahmin widows are not supposed to remarry. The scandal is still alive in village gossip even though the couple live away from Shanti Nagar. The family is relatively poor for a high-caste family, having only three acres of land for eleven people, and the family's sole wage earner recently lost his job. The sons and daughters-in-law of Bhim Singh's brothers have been suggesting that the joint family separate into three nuclear families. The separation of a joint family is a serious step and may involve considerable tension.

We believe that Bhim Singh's latest possession was precipitated by family problems, especially the possibility of a division of the joint family which would isolate Bhim Singh and place him in a difficult situation. Because he has no wife or sons, he would have no woman to cook for him and no relatives to help in his

agricultural work. One informant said that Bhim Singh's possession was because he asked his younger brother's wife to have
sexual intercourse with him and she refused. This opinion was
based on no more than the generally appreciated fact that men
without wives have almost no opportunities for sexual relations
with women and are therefore likely to be frustrated. Most villagers, in discussing Bhim Singh's possession, generally dealt
with its most superficial features. They said Bhim Singh became
possessed because he ate sweet food, for which the ghost has a
fondness, and then walked through the area frequented by the
ghost.

Santosh, a woman of the beggar (Bairagi) caste in her middle
forties, was possessed by the ghost of her older brother. She said
she had gone to a garden to get some fruit. On the way she
jumped across a ditch. She thinks that this was when the ghost
caught her, for her knees began to behave badly and she came
home. She lost consciousness. Her two sons, one of whom lives
in a separate family, tried to banish the ghost. One son held her
hair and asked, "Who are you?" The ghost replied that it was
Santosh's older brother. This brother had been close to Santosh
and had always helped her. The son asked the ghost why it had
come, and the ghost answered, "Why does my brother-in-law hurt
my sister?" The son told the ghost to go away and not hurt his
mother; he promised that in the future Santosh's husband would
not trouble her. The next day a second spirit possessed Santosh,
and the village shaman was called. Apparently he cured Santosh,
for her possessions ceased.

Because of the remarks of the ghost, we believe that Santosh's
possession was related to difficulties with her husband. We are
not certain as to what the trouble was, although we knew Santosh
and her husband well. The husband was a very mild mannered
person and at least fifteen years older than she, his second wife.
We noticed no particular tension between them. However, we
suspect that Santosh was having a sexual affair with a powerful
Jat landlord who is a widower. If this were true, it would certainly have led to trouble between Santosh and her husband. A
noteworthy feature of Santosh's possession is that it was by an
older brother, a relative with whom a sister has very warm ties
and from whom she expects gifts, sympathy, and support. The

possession indicates that Santosh may have felt a lack of such support.

One day early in our residence in Shanti Nagar we were called to aid a Brahmin woman, named Chameli, who had lost consciousness. We arrived to find her lying on a cot, completely limp, with her eyes closed. Her jaws were together, but her lips were slack. Her mother-in-law, one son, and one daughter were present. We gingerly shook her by the shoulder, but this failed to revive her or to have any effect whatsoever. Chameli's son and mother-in-law seemed entirely unconcerned. Her daughter, who had summoned us, was mildly disturbed. We could think of no way to help and, as nothing was being done to aid Chameli, we left. We learned later that Chameli remained unconscious for about 45 minutes. Chameli later told us that just before she lost consciousness she had seen the ghosts of one of her husband's father's brother's sons and his wife, who said, "Come with us." The next time Chameli had an attack, a swami (who was a curer) was called from a neighboring village. This man was not a shaman, but apparently he treated her successfully, for she had no more attacks while we were in Shanti Nagar.

Chameli was 42 years of age and had seven living children, two boys and five girls, all unmarried except one daughter. We knew her very well, for we lived only a few steps from her house. Chameli's health was not good, and she was going through the menopause. Her relations with her husband and mother-in-law were very unsatisfactory. Chameli and her husband had not engaged in sexual relations for several months. The principal reason was probably the desire on the part of the husband and his mother to avoid the birth of another daughter, for she would be an added economic liability due to marriage and other ceremonial expenses. Chameli desired normal relations with her husband, and when he occasionally did not come home at night because of business or visits to relatives, she accused him of having other women. The mother-in-law, who as senior woman in the house controlled the stores of food, refused to give Chameli ghee (clarified butter) for her bread. Chameli said that her mother-in-law wanted her to die. Dramatic quarrels between Chameli on the one hand and her husband and mother-in-law on the other frequently broke out. Chameli and her mother-in-law traded insults. The husband complained that Chameli was killing him (by creating extreme tension in the household) and told her that she would have to live at the feet of her mother-in-law. For two months he refused to accept food or water from her hands.

Except for her oldest daughter, who occasionally sided with her, none of Chameli's children supported her in her quarrels with her husband and mother-in-law. Moreover, she constantly fought with her sister, who lived next door and was married to her husband's brother (i.e., her husband's father's brother's son); even in these disputes she could not always count on the support of her family. She complained bitterly about this, saying that she was fighting her family's battles alone.

Chameli's attack of spirit possession seems clearly related to the tense relations with her husband and mother-in-law. It is particularly noteworthy because of the response of the other members of the family; they made no effort to induce the state of trance in which the ghost can be identified and persuaded to leave. Nevertheless, Chameli's illness was not entirely ignored, for a curer was summoned after the next attack. A few months after Chameli's possession she and her husband resumed sexual relations and tension in the house subsided considerably.

The fourth case of spirit possession differs from the others because of its psychological aftermath: the woman never recovered and apparently developed a permanent psychological illness. She was Bhagwani, a sweeper (Chuhra) in her forties. Her possessions began about three years before our visit. Her early attacks were similar to other spirit possessions: she saw the ghost and would point it out to the spectators. However, the ghost was apparently absent from her later attacks, which featured abuse of relatives, even her husband, and destructiveness.

Bhagwani's appearance and behavior differ from the others who suffered spirit possession. During our interview she crooned, muttered, moaned, and acted as if she were falling asleep. She was withdrawn and sullen or hostile. She showed almost no physical energy. She sat in a semi-reclining position and occasionally plucked at things. She seemed irritated by noises, conversation, and at having to do anything. Whenever the conversation turned to her husband or sons, she flared up in an irritable manner. Her eyes were inattentive and never seemed to focus.

Bhagwani told us she feels depressed and often cries. She says that she can never be cured and that this knowledge makes her irritable. She wants to commit suicide and says that everyone watches her so that she will not kill herself. When she lies down, she sees animals and insects moving before her eyes. When this happens, she is terrified; she cannot close her eyes and sleep; she yawns, shrieks, and feels that she will die. Bhagwani said that her illness was because someone put something in her food and that she would kill the person if she could find him.

According to Bhagwani's relatives, her possession involved difficulties with one of her daughters-in-law named Sita. We think that this is probably accurate as far as it goes but that Bhagwani's changed relationships with her son and possibly her husband due to Sita's arrival also entered into the possession. Sita's husband gave us the following account. Bhagwani and Sita do not get along well, although when Sita first came to Shanti Nagar the two were very affectionate. One would not take her meals without the other. Sita had two children, the second about three years ago. After the birth of each, Sita suffered attacks of spirit possession. Her husband says that these attacks occurred two to five times a day for about a month. Bhagwani's husband is a shaman and attempted, unsuccessfully, to cure Sita. While he was attempting the cure, he became involved in a dispute with Sita. She spoke to him, which she should not have done as a daughter-in-law, and he abused her, apparently making uncomplimentary remarks about her mother. (Something occurred between Sita and her father-in-law, but we doubt that this is exactly what happened.) Because Bhagwani's husband could not affect a cure, Sita returned to her parents' village. Her father had been a shaman, and, although he was dead, his disciple was active and possessed considerable power. The disciple cured Sita. While in her parents' village, Sita mentioned that she had been insulted by her father-in-law. She stayed in her parents' village for about three years and returned to Shanti Nagar only quite recently. Shortly after Sita left Shanti Nagar, Bhagwani suffered a possession. Sita's husband said that the disciple had sent spirits to possess her, and this opinion was shared by all with whom we talked. Sita's husband said that his mother's attacks were the reason Sita stayed in her parents' village so long.

PSYCHOLOGICAL AND CULTURAL ANALYSIS

Almost all who have written on spirit possession regard it as a form of hysteria. A concise and exhaustive definition of hysteria is not possible, for a large number of symptoms and etiological factors have been ascribed to this condition. Abse (1959: 274) states that the possible symptoms are so numerous that a discussion of all of them would assume encyclopedic proportions. Parker (1962: 93, n. 2) uses the term hysteria "to cover such phenomena as temporary states in which there is a loss or clouding of consciousness, manifestations of convulsive, hyperexcitable, or 'freezing' behavior, and which involves no progressive psychic deterioration such as is often associated with schizophrenia." Abse (1959: 274) says the typical clinical features are: (1) "physical symptoms without an ascertainable structural lesion"; (2) complacency in the presence of physical disability; and (3) episodic disturbances in which "an ego-alien homogeneous constellation of ideas and emotions occupies the field of consciousness." Pain is the most common complaint (Abse 1959: 279). Dramatic somatic symptoms include convulsions and other conversion reactions such as deafness, dumbness, and blindness. Globus hystericus, "a sensation of contraction of throat or a globular mass rising from the stomach into the esophagus" (Warren 1934: 116), is a noteworthy symptom. Dizziness may occur. Abse (1959: 276) notes that attacks of convulsive hysteria occur only in the presence of spectators and that the victim does not fall in a dangerous situation.

In his survey of the literature on hysteria, Abse (1959: 274, 276, 283, 285) frequently notes sexual disturbances, among which are guilt feelings arising from infantile incestuous attachments, as conditions of hysteria. "When traced to its roots," says Abse (1959: 283), "hysteria in all its forms is predominantly related to the climax of infantile sexuality, the oedipus situation, with its struggle to surmount incestuous genital-sexual and hostile strivings." Chodoff and Lyons (1958: 735), in discussing characteristics of the hysterical personality, mention, among other things, sexual frigidity, intense fear of sexuality, and sexual apprehensiveness. FitzGerald (1948: 710) also notes the sexual frigidity of hysterics. The dependency cravings and strong need for love and approval which Parker (1962: 80) mentions as being frequently ascribed to hysterics seem to be derived from emotional attachments to the parents which the hysteric is unable to replace with a normal adult sexual relationship (Abse 1959: 285–86; FitzGerald 1948: 710–14). Tension due to intraphysic conflict can be thought of as the basic condition of hysteria.

Events or situations involving unusual stress or strong emotions precede hysterical attacks (Abse 1959: 276–77; Yap 1960: 121–22; FitzGerald 1948: 702; Parker 1962: 78). These events are the precipitating conditions of hysteria. The stresses of war, dangerous situations encountered while hunting, and difficulties with parents and employers are examples of situations which can precipitate hysterical attacks. Such events can also precipitate other forms of psychiatric disturbance. Opler (1958) lists a number of precipitating events for possessions in a rural area of eastern Uttar Pradesh: the murder of a husband in a feud, difficulties involving urban employment, quarrels over land, the problems of young brides, and others.

Abse (1959: 283–84) distinguishes primary and secondary gains for the individual's psyche from an hysterical attack. He describes the primary gain as follows: "The symptoms consist of an autoplastic attempt to discharge the tension created by intrapsychic conflict, and express drive and defense simultaneously, short-circuiting conscious perception of conflict related to the oedipus complex." The secondary gain, the importance of which Abse believes is often underestimated, involves the individual's use of his symptoms to attract attention, gain sympathy, and manipulate other people and his current life situation. Other studies mention these secondary gains (e.g., Yap 1960: 130–32; Parker 1962: 80). It is not difficult to see a close connection between the secondary gains of hysteria and the crisis which precipitated the condition. Opler's (1958) discussion of spirit possession in Indian villages emphasizes precipitating conditions and secondary gains.

The possession of Daya was clearly a case of hysteria, as defined by Abse and Parker. Her attack involved loss of consciousness, shivering, and convulsions. It occurred before an audience.

She fell unconscious in surroundings presenting no physical dangers. She complained of physical symptoms: pains in her body, dizziness, and a sensation as if her stomach were swelling (possible globus hystericus). However, she seemed quite cheerful and unconcerned about her condition. She recently moved from the warm, supporting environment of her parents' house to her husband's house, where she lived under considerable tension and could count on little support from her affines. She experienced no spirit possession before coming to Shanti Nagar. Her testimony stressed fear of sexuality and a concern with sexual episodes involving incest between father and daughter and/or severe punishment by the family, especially the father.[4] Daya's remarks indicated that, in accord with Abse's analysis of hysteria, tension and conflict related to the oedipus complex were the underlying condition of her possession. The precipitating condition was her new role as a wife.

Daya achieved substantial secondary gains through her possessions. She became a center of attention. She aroused sympathy and concern among all her affines. Her husband reduced his sexual demands. Daya's parents and other consanguineal relatives rallied to her support. Her father came to see her and, thinking she might be weak, brought some vitamins and arranged for a series of vitamin injections. Even unsophisticated villagers have considerable faith in injections, and the girl's father, who was in military service, no doubt favored modern medicine. Daya is the only daughter in her nuclear family, and therefore many of her relatives, including all of her male relatives, came to see if she were all right. They spoke of arranging a marriage between Daya's younger sister, of whom she is quite fond (actually the daughter of her father's younger brother who lives in a joint family with Daya's father), and her husband's younger brother.

Although the other cases of spirit possession in Shanti Nagar contribute little to our knowledge of its symptoms and psychic conditions, they do aid in better understanding the precipitating events and secondary gains; and one of them, the case of Bhagwani, is especially important in showing the possibility of a transi-

[4] One of the cases described by Harper (1963: 168) is of a bride who suffered an attack of spirit possession a few minutes after entering the nuptial chamber.

tion from hysterical spirit possession to a psychological condition which resembles schizophrenia.[5] In the case of Bhim Singh, the precipitating event was most likely tension in his joint family, especially over whether or not to separate. In the event of a separation, Bhim Singh would be all alone in a separate family. One villager, a bit of a gossip, suggested a sexual rebuff from his brother's wife as a precipitating factor. While this can not be substantiated, sexual frustration should not be overlooked in Bhim Singh's case. The precipitating condition in Santosh's case was probably tension with her husband, possibly regarding a sexual relationship with a powerful Jat landlord. Her possession brought her sons to her aid, saying they would not permit their father to trouble their mother. Chameli's attack was clearly brought on by considerable tension with her husband and mother-in-law. Although Chameli had many children and a sister living next door, she received little support in her troubles. The three latter victims recovered.

The possession of Bhagwani involved difficulties with her daughter-in-law and probably also with her son and husband. At first Bhagwani's possession conformed to the normal pattern. However, she failed to recover, and gradually her behavior changed. Her later attacks featured abuse of relatives and destructiveness instead of spirit possession with its loss of consciousness, trance, and conversion symptoms. Delusions of persecution were present: she believed that her condition was caused by someone's putting something in her food and said that she would kill the person if she found him. She had hallucinations, seeing animals and insects moving before her eyes. Her attention was impaired. Talking to her was somewhat difficult because of her muttering and seeming to be on the verge of falling asleep. Bhagwani's symptoms resemble an early stage of schizophrenia of the paranoid type as described by Arieti (1959: 459–61, 466–67). Abse (1959: 275, 284) notes that transitions between hysteria and schizophrenia occur. In discussing Bhagwani, one astute villager said, "Formerly she was possessed by a ghost and behaved like Daya [the Chamar girl] pointing and saying the ghost is there and there; but now she is mad."

---

[5] One of the cases described by Harper (1963: 167–68) resembles schizophrenia.

One tentative inference from the Shanti Nagar data is that events precipitating spirit possession are likely to be difficulties involving relatives of the nuclear or joint family and that the victim is often in a position where he can expect little support. These conditions pertain much more frequently to married women than to males or unmarried girls, and this is reflected in the preponderance of married women among those suffering possession. Spirit possession may be thought of as a means of controlling relatives. Other common situations of stress do not seem to call forth hysteria: for example, the considerable tension surrounding the statewide examinations for college and high school degrees, loss of employment, disputes with people of other families or castes, disputes or lawsuits over land, and financial reverses such as crop failure, theft, and the death of valuable animals.

SPIRIT POSSESSION AS ILLNESS ELSEWHERE IN NORTHERN INDIA

Spirit possession as illness appears basically uniform from Punjab to Calcutta (Temple 1884–86: ii, 164; iii, 202–3; Lewis 1958: 295–99; Majumdar 1958: 234–36; Opler 1958). The general elements of the pattern are as follows. A person begins to act in an odd manner or contracts an illness which does not respond to ordinary remedies. Often events involving unusual stress precede the attacks. Spectators or a shaman suspect spirit possession and use a variety of methods to force the spirit to reveal itself. The spirit is most often the ghost of a person who has died an untimely death. The patient is cured by exorcising the ghost, which can be done in a variety of ways: ritual offerings, transferring the ghost to another person or thing, and various measures designed to make the ghost uncomfortable such as beating, cursing, and smoking with burning dung. Complete recovery seems to be the rule.

Within the basic pattern, the particular details of the precipitating events, behavior during the attack, diagnosis, and treatment show considerable variety. Three broad features of this variation appear noteworthy with regard to possible regional differences. The first concerns the typical behavior during an attack; the second involves spirit possession as a mechanism of controlling others; and the third pertains to differences in the readiness with which people attribute a wide variety of illnesses and misfortunes to spirit possession.

The typical attack in Shanti Nagar involves loss of consciousness, trance, and conversion symptoms. In eastern Uttar Pradesh and Calcutta, attacks are characterized by aggression and threatened or actual physical violence. Loss of consciousness does not always occur or may occur only after the shaman has begun the cure. Opler (1958: 554–56, 559, 563) briefly describes several cases of spirit possession in eastern Uttar Pradesh in which aggression and threatened physical violence seem to dominate the attack. A woman "suddenly began to curse and snap at those around her, shouting that she would bite and eat them"; a young man "became violent and abusive and was constantly in trouble"; a young man had "violent attacks . . . during which he spoke abusively to those around him and sought to strike them"; a boy "would disobey his parents, curse them, and remain away from home for long periods"; and a woman "who is well-known for her moody nature and uncertain temper was found by another woman trying to hang herself." Temple (1884–86: iii, 202–3) reports a case from Calcutta in which a woman attacked her husband and tried to strangle him. He escaped and gave the alarm to his family. This made the woman furious and she screamed nearly all night.

These descriptions indicate that the features of spirit possession typical of Shanti Nagar are not necessarily typical elsewhere. In Shanti Nagar, the victim shivers, moans, or feels weak, loses consciousness, goes into a state of trance, and eventually recovers. In eastern Uttar Pradesh and Calcutta, the victim suddenly lashes out at those around him; then a shaman induces a trance, the ghost is exorcised, and recovery follows. Although we have only a few cases, many of which are described very briefly, the apparent contrast between aggressive possessions in Uttar Pradesh and non-aggressive possessions in Shanti Nagar may be significant.

As a means of social control, spirit possession in Shanti Nagar and in eastern Uttar Pradesh shows two noteworthy differences. When the precipitating condition of spirit possession is tense interpersonal relations, the people involved, in Shanti Nagar, are always close relatives, whereas in eastern Uttar Pradesh they may frequently be nonrelatives (Opler 1958: 554–55, 557, 562); consequently, spirit possession in eastern Uttar Pradesh is a more general form of social control than in Shanti Nagar. Second, spirit possession in Shanti Nagar does not typically involve accusations of witchcraft, whereas in eastern Uttar Pradesh such accusations are common (Opler 1958: 556–57, 562–63). The witchcraft accusations and the typically aggressive behavior of spirit possession in eastern Uttar Pradesh and their lack in Shanti Nagar seem to indicate that spirit possession is a generally more aggressive behavior pattern in the former area.

The third regional difference is the tendency of the villagers of eastern Uttar Pradesh, especially women, to attribute a considerable variety of illnesses and misfortunes to spirit possession, whereas the people of Shanti Nagar are much less inclined to do so. This difference may partly be due, we believe, to the greater influence of the Arya Samaj reform movement in the Shanti Nagar region. Followers of Arya Samaj are hostile to the belief in and worship of ghosts and godlings. Opler mentions eight women who suspected ghosts and sought the aid of a shaman because of menstrual pain, death of children, barrenness, miscarriage, and other ailments. Opler does not say whether these women merely suspected ghosts or whether they actually experienced attacks of spirit possession before going to a shaman. In one case, a shaman induced a possession in order to identify and exorcise the ghost, but in the other cases, while the shaman confirmed the attribution of the difficulty to a ghost, it is not clear whether or not he induced a possession. In cases of this kind, where there is no attack of spirit possession or where possession is induced by the activities of a shaman, the basic intrapsychic conditions associated with spirit possession may be minimal or lacking. Spirit possession of various kinds so permeates Indian culture that many people can become possessed, especially when aided by a skillful shaman or priest. Cases in which spontaneous attacks are lacking are probably best analyzed entirely from the point of view of precipitating events and secondary gains. Barren women, for example, can possibly convert the condemnation of relatives into sympathy by attributing their barrenness to ghosts.

SUMMARY AND CONCLUSIONS

This paper has described and analyzed several cases of spirit possession which occurred in Shanti Nagar, a village in northern India near Delhi. These were all cases of spirit possession which were regarded as illness. Psychologically, spirit possession seems to fit contemporary descriptions of hysteria. Spirit possession is best analyzed as having two conditions: a basic condition due to the individual's intrapsychic tension, and a precipitating condition due to an event or situation involving unusual stress or emotion. Precipitating conditions have two general characteristics: (1) the victim of spirit possession is involved in difficulties with relatives of the nuclear or joint family, and (2) he is often in a situation where his expectations of mutual aid and support are low. The primary gain of an attack of spirit possession is to relieve the individual's intrapsychic tension; secondary gains include attention, sympathy, influencing relatives, and other manipulation of the individual's current situation. Sometimes spirit possession can develop into schizophrenia. Precipitating events may precede schizophrenia as well as hysteria. Spirit possession appears to assume a basically uniform pattern in northern India, although regional variation may occur in the behavior during an attack, whether nonrelatives as well as close relatives are involved in the tense situation preceding the attack, the frequency with which accusations of witchcraft occur, and the readiness of people to attribute a wide variety of illness and misfortune to spirit possession.

BIBLIOGRAPHY

Aberle, D.
1948   *The Pueblo Indians of New Mexico: their land, economy and civil organization* (Memoirs of the American Anthropological Association 70).
Abse, D. W.
1959   "Hysteria," in: Arieti, S. (editor), *American Handbook of Psychiatry* Vol. I. New York.
Arieti, S.
1959   "Schizophrenia: the manifest symptomatology, the psychodynamic and formal mechanisms," in: Arieti, S. (editor), *American Handbook of Psychiatry* Vol. I. New York.
Ashton, H.
1952   *The Basuto.* London.
Balikci, A.
1961   "Suicidal behavior among the Netsilik Eskimos," in: Boishen, B. (editor), *Canadian Society: Sociological Perspectives.* Glencoe.
1962   *Development of Basic Socio-Economic Units in Two Eskimo Communities.* Ph.D. dissertation, Columbia University.
Bandalier, A.
1890   *The Delight Makers.* New York.
Barnes, J. A.
1949   "Measures of divorce frequency in simple societies," *Journal of the Royal Anthropological Institute* 79.
Bascom, W. R.
1941   "The sanctions of Ifa divination," *Journal of the Royal Anthropological Institute* 71.
1942   "Ifa divination," *Man* 1942.
1944   "The sociological role of the Yoruba cult-group," *American Anthropologist* 46 (1, pt. 2).
Beattie, J. H. M.
1957   "Initiation into the Chwezi spirit possession cult in Bunyoro," *African Studies* 16 (3).
1960   *Bunyoro: an African kingdom.* New York.
1961   "Group aspects of the Nyoro spirit mediumship cult," *Rhodes-Livingstone Journal* 30.

1963 "Sorcery in Bunyoro," in: Middleton, J., and E. Winter (editors), *Witchcraft and Sorcery in East Africa*. London.
1964 "The ghost cult in Bunyoro," *Ethnology* 3 (2).
Benedict, R.
1934 *Patterns of Culture*. Boston.
Boas, F.
1930 *The Religion of the Kwakiutl*. New York.
Bourgeois, R.
1956 *Banyarwanda et Barundi*. Brussels.
Brasseur de Bourbourg, C. E.
1859 *Histoire des nations civilisées du Mexique et de l'Amérique*, Vol. 4. Paris.
Brinton, D. G.
1894 "Nagualism: a study in native American folk-lore and history," *Proceedings of the American Philosophical Society* 33.
Bunzel, R.
1952 *Chichicastenango: a Guatemalan village* (Publication of the American Ethnological Society 22).
Cannon, W. B.
1942 "'Voodoo' death," *American Anthropologist* 44.
Caudill, W.
1958 *The Psychiatric Hospital as a Small Society*. Cambridge, Mass.
Central African Statistical Office.
1952 *Report on the Demographic Sample Survey of the African Population of Northern Rhodesia*. Salisbury.
Chodoff, P., and H. Lyons.
1958 "Hysteria, the hysterical personality and 'hysterical' conversion," *American Journal of Psychiatry* 114.
Clarke, J. D.
1939 "Ifa divination," *Journal of the Royal Anthropological Institute* 69.
Colle, P.
1913 *Les Baluba*. Brussels.
Colson, E.
1958 *Marriage and Family among the Plateau Tonga*. Manchester.
Coser, L. A.
1955 *The Functions of Social Conflict*. Glencoe.
Crazzolara, J. P.
1950 *The Lwoo*. Verona.
Crooke, W.
1894 *An Introduction to the Popular Religion and Folklore of Northern India*. Allahabad, London (1926).
Davis, M. B.
1938 *A Lunyoro-Lunyankole-English and English-Lunyoro-Lunyankole Dictionary*. Kampala.
Devereux, G., and E. M. Loeb.
1943 "Antagonistic acculturation," *American Sociological Review* 8.
Dozier, E.
1961 "Rio Grande Pueblos," in: E. H. Spicer (editor), *Perspectives in American Indian Culture Change*. Chicago.

Dumarest, Father N.
1919 *Notes on Cochiti, New Mexico* (Memoirs of the American Anthropological Association 6).
Durkheim, E.
1912 *Les formes élémentaires de la vie religieuse.* Paris.
Eggan, D.
1943 "The general problem of Hopi adjustment," *American Anthropologist* 45.
Eggan, F.
1950 *The Social Organization of the Western Pueblos.* Chicago.
Elliott, A. J. A.
1955 *Chinese Spirit-Medium Cults in Singapore.* London.
Evans-Pritchard, E. E.
1937 *Witchcraft, Oracles and Magic among the Azande.* Oxford.
1960 "Zande cannibalism," *Journal of the Royal Anthropological Institute* 90.
Fenton, W. N.
1936 "An outline of Seneca ceremonies at Coldspring longhouse," *Yale University Publications in Anthropology* 9.
1953 *The Iroquois Eagle Dance: an offshoot of the Calumet ceremony* (Bureau of American Ethnology Bulletin 156). Washington.
Field, M. J.
1937 *Religion and Medicine of the Ga People.*
Firth, R. W.
1929 *Primitive Economics of the New Zealand Maori.* London.
1955 "Some principles of social organization," *Journal of the Royal Anthropological Institute* 85 (1).
Fisher, A. B.
1911 *Twilight Tales of the Black Baganda.* London.
Fisher, R. A.
1935 *The Design of Experiments.* Edinburgh.
FitzGerald, O. W. F.
1948 "Love Deprivation and the Hysterical Personality," *Journal of Mental Science* 94.
Forde, D.
1939 "Hopi agriculture and land ownership," *Journal of the Royal Anthropological Institute* 61.
Fortes, M.
1945 *The Dynamics of Clanship among the Tallensi.* London.
1949 *The Web of Kinship among the Tallensi.* London.
Foster, G.
1944 "Nagualism in Mexico and Guatemala," *Acta Americana* 2.
Fox, J. R.
1961a "Pueblo baseball: a new use for old witchcraft," *Journal of American Folklore* 74.
1961b "Veterans and factions in Pueblo society," *Man* 61.
Freed, S. A.
1963 "Fictive kinship in a North Indian village," *Ethnology* 2.
Freud, S.
1924 *Collected Papers.* London.

Gamitto, A. C. P.
1854 *O muata Cazembe*. Lisbon. Translated by I. Cunnison, *King Kazembe*, Lisbon.
Gluckman, M.
1954 *Rituals of Rebellion in Southeast Africa*. Manchester.
1955 *The Judicial Process among the Barotse of Northern Rhodesia*. Manchester.
Goldenweiser, A.
1921 *Early Civilization*. New York.
Goldfrank, E. S.
1927 *The Social and Ceremonial Organization of Cochiti* (Memoirs of the American Anthropological Association 33).
1945 "Socialization, personality, and the structure of Pueblo society," *American Anthropologist* 47.
Goode, W.
1951 *Religion among the Primitives*. Glencoe.
Griaule, M.
1933 "Mission Dakar-Djibouti, 1931–1933," *Minotaure* 2.
Halliday, W. R.
1913 *Greek Divination*. London.
Harper E. B.
1963 "Spirit possession and social structure," in: Ratnam, B. (editor), *Anthropology on the March*. Madras.
Harris, G.
1955 *The Ritual System of the WaTaita*. Unpublished Ph.D. thesis, University of Cambridge.
Herskovits, M. J.
1938 *Dahomey*. 2 vols. New York.
Holland, W.
1961 "Tonalismo y nagualismo entre los Indios Tzotziles de Larraonzar, Chiapas, México," *Estudios de Cultura Maya* 1.
Hsu, F. L. K.
1948 *Under the Ancestors' Shadow*. New York.
Hunter, M.
1936 *Reaction to Conquest*. London.
Jackson, H.
1830 *Sketch of the Manners, Customs, Religion and Government of the Seneca Indians in 1800*. Philadelphia.
Junod, H. A.
1927 *The Life of a South African Tribe*. London.
Kaplan, L. H.
1956 "Tonal and Nagual in Costal Oaxaca, Mexico," *Journal of American Folklore* 69.
Karubanga, H. K.
1949 *Bukya Nibwira*. Kampala.
Kenton, E. (editor).
1927 *The Indians of North America*, 2 vols. New York.
Kiev, A.
1961 "Spirit possession in Haiti," *American Journal of Psychiatry* 118 (2).
Kluckhohn, C.
1944 *Navaho Witchcraft*. Papers of the Peabody Museum 24 (2).

Kroeber, A. L.
1917 "Zuni kin and clan," *Anthropological Papers of The American Museum of Natural History* 18 (2).
La Farge, O.
1947 *Santa Eulalia: the religion of a Cuchumatan Indian town.* Chicago.
—— and D. Byers.
1931 "The year bearer's people," *Middle American Research Series* 3.
Landtmann, G.
1927 *Kiwai Papuans.*
Lange, C. H.
1957 "Tablita, or corn, dances of the Rio Grande Pueblo Indians," *Texas Journal of Science* 9.
1959 *Cochiti: a New Mexico Pueblo past and present.* Austin.
Lawrence, D. H.
1927 "The dance of the sprouting corn," *Mornings in Mexico,* London.
Lee, D. D.
1941 "Some Indian texts dealing with the supernatural," *Review of Religion,* May 1941.
Lee, S. G.
1951 "Some Zulu concepts of psychogenic disorder," *South African Journal for Social Research,* 1951.
Leighton, A. H., and D. C. Leighton.
1941 "Elements of psychotherapy in Navajo religion," *Psychiatry* 4.
Leiris, M.
1933 "Le taureau de Seyfou Tchenger (Zar)," *Minotaure* 2.
1934 "Le culte des Zars à Gondar (Ethiopie Septentrionale)," *Aethiopica* 2.
1935 "Un rite médico-magique Etiopien: le Jet du Danqara," *Aethiopica* 3.
1938 "Le croyance aux génies 'Zar' en Etiopie du Nord," *Journal de Psychologie normale et pathologique* 1–2.
Leslau, W.
1949 "An Ethiopian argot of a people possessed by a spirit," *Africa* 19.
Lévi-Strauss, C.
1949a "Le sorcier et sa magie," *Les temps modernes* 41; reprinted as "The sorcerer and his magic" in: Lévi-Strauss, C. *Structural Anthropology,* New York 1963.
1949b "The effectiveness of symbols" ("L'Efficacité symbolique"), *Revue de l'histoire des religions* 135 (1); reprinted as Chapter X of *Structural Anthropology.* New York 1963.
1950 "Introduction à l'oeuvre de Marcel Mauss," in: Mauss, M., *Sociologie et anthropologie.* Paris.
1955 *Tristes tropiques.* Paris.
Lewis, O.
1951 *Life in a Mexican Village.* Urbana.
1958 *Village Life in Northern India.* Urbana.
Lienhardt, G.
1961 *Divinity and Experience.* Oxford.
Lifschitz, D.
1940 "Quelques noms de maladie en Etiopie," *Communication au GLECS, Séance du 21 Fevrier 1940, Paris, Sorbonne.*

Lindblom, G.
1920 *The Akamba*. Upsala.
Linton, R.
1936 *The Study of Man*. New York.
1952 "Cultural and personality factors affecting economic growth," in: Hoselitz, B. G. (editor), *The Progress of Underdeveloped Areas*. Chicago.
Littmann, E.
1915 "A song about the Demon Waddegenni," *Publications of the Princeton Expedition to Abyssinia* 2.
Lowie, R. H.
1935 *The Crow Indians*. New York.
1952 *Primitive Religion*. New York.
Lyall, A. C.
1899 *Asiatic Studies (first series)*. London.
Majumdar, D. N.
1958 *Caste and Communication in an Indian Village*. Bombay.
Malinowski, B.
1922 *Argonauts of the Western Pacific*. London.
1925 "Magic, science and religion," in: Needham, J. (editor), *Science, Religion and Reality*. London. Reprinted in Malinowski, B., *Magic, Science and Religion and other essays*. Glencoe 1948.
1926a *Myth in Primitive Psychology*. London. Reprinted in Malinowski, B., *Magic, Science and Religion and other essays*. Glencoe 1948.
1926b *Crime and Custom in Savage Society*. London.
1929 *The Sexual Life of Savages*. London.
Marwick, M. G.
1952 "The social context of Ceŵa witch beliefs," *Africa* 22.
Mauss, M.
1906 "Essai sur les variations saisonnières des sociétés Eskimos," *L'Année Sociologique* 9.
1960 "Esquisse d'une Théorie Générale de la magie (1902)," in: *Sociologie et Anthropologie*. Paris.
Mendelson, E. M.
1957 *Religion and World-View in Santiago Atitlan*. (Microfilm collection of manuscripts on American Indian Cultural Anthropology 52, University of Chicago).
Messing, S. D.
1957 *The Highland-Plateau Amhara of Ethiopia*. Doctoral dissertation, University of Pennsylvania.
Middleton, J.
1954 "Some social aspects of Lugbara myth," *Africa* 24 (3).
Mitchell, J. C.
1956 *The Yao Village*. Manchester.
Moore, O. K.
1957 "Divination—a new perspective," *American Anthropologist* 59.
Nadel, S. F.
1935 "Witchcraft and anti-witchcraft in Nupe society," *Africa* 8.
1946 "Shamanism in the Nuba Mountains," *Journal of the Royal Anthropological Institute* 76.

Nash, M.
   1958   *Machine-Age Maya* (Memoirs of the American Anthropological Association 87).
   1960   "Witchcraft as social process in a Tzeltal community," *America Indigena* 20.
Newcomb, T. M.
   1959   "Autistic hostility and social reality," in: Kuenzli, A. (editor), *The Phenomenological Problem.* New York.
Oakes, M.
   1951   *The Two Crosses of Todos Santos: survivals of Mayan religious ritual* (Bollingen series 27). New York.
Ogunbiyi, T. A. J.
   1940   *Yoruba Oracles and their Modes of Divination.* Lagos.
O'Malley, L. S. S.
   1935   *Popular Hinduism.* Cambridge.
Opler, M. E.
   1958   "Spirit possession in a rural area of Northern India," in: Lessa, W., and E. Vogt (editors), *Reader in Comparative Religion.* Evanston.
Parker, E. S.
   n.d.   MS on medicine men and Indian dances, in Parker Collection, 1802–46, in Henry E. Huntington Library.
Parker, S.
   1962   "Eskimo psychopathology in the context of Eskimo personality and culture," *American Anthropologist* 64.
Parsons, E. C.
   1936   *Mitla: the town of souls.* Chicago.
Parsons, T.
   1952   *The Social System.* Glencoe.
Peristiany, J. G.
   1951   "The age-set system of the pastoral Pokot," *Africa* 21 (3).
Plas, V. H. Van den, and C. R. Lagae.
   1921   *Zande Grammar.*
Radcliffe-Brown, A. R.
   1952   *Structure and Function in Primitive Society.* London.
Radin, P.
   1915–16   *The Winnebago Tribe* (Thirty-seventh Annual Report of the Bureau of American Ethnology). Washington.
   1927   *Primitive Man as Philosopher.* New York.
   1953   *The World of Primitive Man.* New York.
Rapp, E. L. (tr.)
   1935   "The African explains witchcraft. XVII Akan (Dialect of Okwawu)," *Africa* 8.
Rasmussen, K.
   1929   "Intellectual Culture of the Iglulik Eskimos," *Report of the Fifth Thule Expedition* Vol. 7. Copenhagen.
   1931   "The Netsilik Eskimos," *Report of the Fifth Thule Expedition* Vol. 8. Copenhagen.
Rattray, R. S.
   1916   *Ashanti Proverbs.* Oxford.
   1927   *Religion and Art in Ashanti.* Oxford.

Reed, E.
  1949   "Sources of Upper Rio Grande culture and population," *El Palacio*
    61 (6).
Roscoe, J.
  1911   *The Baganda.* London.
  1923   *The Bakitara.* Cambridge.
Rose, H. J.
  1911   "Divination (Introductory)," in: *Encyclopaedia of Religion and
    Ethics* Hastings (editor), Vol. 4. Edinburgh.
Ross, A. D.
  1956   "Epileptiform attacks provoked by music," *British Journal of De-
    linquency* 7 (1).
Rouch, J.
  1954   *Les Songhay.* Paris.
Saler, B.
  1960   *The Road from El Palmar: change, continuity, and conservatism
    in a Quiché community.* Ph.D. dissertation, University of Pennsylvania.
  1962a "Unsuccessful practitioners in a bicultural Guatemalan commu-
    nity," *Psychoanalysis and the Psychoanalytic Review* 49.
  1962b "Migration and ceremonial ties among the Maya," *Southwest-
    ern Journal of Anthropology* 18.
Seligman, C. G.
  1910   *The Melanesians of New Guinea.* London.
Siegel, M.
  1941   "Religion in Western Guatemala; a product of acculturation,"
    American Anthropologist 43.
Silvert, K. H.
  1954   "A study in government: Guatemala," *Middle American Re-
    search Series* 21.
Simmons, L. W.
  1942   *Sun Chief: the autobiography of a Hopi Indian.* New Haven.
Skinner, D.
  n.d.   Seneca notes. MS, Pennsylvania Historical and Museum Commis-
    sion. Harrisburg.
Smith, S.
  1958   "The practice of kingship in early Semitic kingdoms," in:
    Hooke, S. H. (editor), *Myth, Ritual and Kingship.* Oxford.
South Africa, Union of.
  1913–44 *Office of Census and Statistics, Report on divorces, 1913–1944.*
Speck, F. G.
  1935   *Naskapi.* Norman, Oklahoma.
  1949   *Midwinter Rites of the Cayuga Longhouse.* Philadelphia.
Steenhoven, G. van der.
  1959   *Legal Concepts among the Netsilik Eskimos of Pelly Bay, N. W. T.*
    Ottawa.
Stevenson, M. C.
  1905   *The Zuni Indians* (Twenty-third Annual Report of the Bureau of
    American Ethnology). Washington.
Steward, J.
  1937   "Ecological aspects of southwestern society," *Anthropos* 32.
Stewart, K.
  1954   *Pygmies and Dream Giants.* New York.

Tait, D.
1952 "The role of the diviner in Konkomba society," *Man* 52.
1953 "The political system of Konkomba," *Africa* 23.

Tax, S.
1941 "World view and social relations in Guatemala," *American Anthropologist* 43.
1947 *Miscellaneous Notes on Guatemala* (Microfilm collection of manuscripts on Middle American Cultural Anthropology 18; University of Chicago).

Temple, R. C.
1884–86 *Panjab Notes and Queries,* Vols. 2–3. London.

Thurston, E.
1906 *Ethnographic Notes on Southern India.* London.

Tucker, L. S.
1940 "Divining baskets of the Ovimbundu," *Journal of the Royal Anthropological Institute* 70.

Van de Velde, F.
1956 "Les Règles du Partage des Phoques Pris par la Chasse aux Aglus," *Anthropologica* 3.

Villa Rojas, A.
1947 "Kinship and nagualism in a Tzeltal community," *American Anthropologist* 49.

Wagley, C.
1949 *The Social and Religious Life of a Guatemalan Village* (Memoirs of the American Anthropological Association 71).

Warren, H. C.
1934 *Dictionary of Psychology.* Boston.

Weeks, J. H.
1914 *Among the Primitive Bakongo.* London.

Westermann, D., and M. A. Bryan.
1952 *The Languages of West Africa.* London.

White, L. A.
1928 "A comparative study of Keresan medicine societies," *Proceedings of the Twenty-third International Congress of Americanists.*

Whiting, J. W. M.
1959a *Resource Mediation and Learning by Identification.* MS, Laboratory of Human Development, Harvard University.
1959b "Sorcery, sin and the super-ego: a cross-cultural study of some mechanisms of social control," in: Jones, M. R. (editor), *Nebraska Symposium on Motivation, 1959.* Lincoln.

—— and I. L. Child.
1953 *Child Training and Personality.* New Haven.

——, C. Kluckhohn, and A. S. Anthony.
1958 "The function of male initiation ceremonies at puberty," in: Maccoby, Newcomb, and Hartley (editors), *Readings in Social Psychology.* New York.

Wilson, G., and M. Wilson.
1945 *The Analysis of Social Change.* Cambridge.

Wisdom, C.
1952 "The supernatural world and curing," in: Tax, S. (editor), *Heritage of Conquest.* Glencoe.

Wisdom, J. O.
   1952   *Foundations of Inference in Natural Science.* London.
Wittfogel, K., and E. S. Goldfrank.
   1943   "Some aspects of Pueblo mythology and society," *Journal of American Folklore* 61.
Wolf, E. R.
   1955   "Types of Latin American peasantry: a preliminary discussion," *American Anthropologist* 57.
   1957   "Closed corporate peasant communities in Mesoamerica and Central Java," *Southwestern Journal of Anthropology* 13.
Yap, P. M.
   1951   "Mental disease peculiar to certain cultures: a survey of comparative psychiatry," *Journal of Mental Science* 97.
   1960   "The possession syndrome: a comparison of Hong Kong and French findings," *Journal of Mental Science* 106.